Dancing
Without
Music

Dancing Without Music
Deafness in America
Beryl Lieff Benderly

Gallaudet University Press
Washington, D.C.

Gallaudet University Press, Washington, DC 20002

Paperback edition published 1990 by Gallaudet University Press. Published by arrangement with Doubleday, a division of Bantam, Doubleday, Dell Publishing Group, Inc. Second printing, 1995

Printed in the United States of America

Library of Congress Cataloging-in-Publication Data

Benderly, Beryl Lieff.
    Dancing without music : deafness in America / Beryl Lieff Benderly.
        p.   cm.
    Reprint, with new pref. Originally published: Garden City, N.Y. : Anchor Press/Doubleday, 1980.
    Includes bibliographical references and index.
    ISBN 0-930323-59-9 : $12.95
    1. Deaf—United States.   I. Title.
HV2545.B39   1990
362.4'2'0973—dc20

90-41334
CIP

CONTENTS

PREFACE

The decade since *Dancing Without Music* first appeared has
been among the most momentous in the Deaf community's history. In those years, signing emerged from the shadows of social
disapproval into wide acceptance as a legitimate language, an
ordinary part of the curriculum in schools across the country.
Linda Bove's appearances on "Sesame Street" made sign language as familiar as Big Bird to a generation of young Americans. The major television networks featured deaf actors in roles
that dramatized issues of deafness for millions of adult viewers.
Sign interpreters became a routine feature of public occasions.
Children of a Lesser God filled the world's screens and stages
with vivid signing. And Marlee Matlin entered the American
pantheon as the first deaf person to win an Academy Award.

And if an Oscar were not enough, the Deaf community also
experienced important advances in communication technology.
Captioned TV brought the dubious benefits of network programming, commercials, and soap operas, as well as the very
real one of much fuller participation in American cultural and
political life. TTY equipment became more affordable and portable, making every phone potentially accessible. Businesses,
utilities, and service agencies woke up to the existence of deaf
customers and many installed TTYs. Personal computers

brought computer bulletin boards and electronic mail within the reach of many. Telephone relay services broke the closed circle of TTY and computer owners. Falling prices for fax machines promise to do the same in the near future.

And for one entire, thrilling week, the struggle for Deaf dignity held center stage in the world's consciousness, banishing old assumptions for deaf and hearing people alike. Observers everywhere marvelled at the Gallaudet University student protestors' discipline, courage, maturity, and resolve and then cheered their peaceful triumph. Deaf persons of all ages felt a new surge of pride and hope when Dr. I. King Jordan, Jr., the long-awaited first deaf president of Gallaudet, became the living embodiment of that spirit, tirelessly spreading, through precept and example, a message of high aspiration and boundless possibility.

So why reprint a book written before all that happened? Why read conclusions drawn in another time? Because, sad as it is for us Americans to accept, Alphonse Karr (a pessimistic Frenchman) was right when he said, "the more things change, the more they remain the same." In judging the dramatic events of the last ten years, we need to temper our vaulting American optimism with more than a pinch of Old World skepticism. We must ask ourselves how much these highly visible changes have actually affected the objective conditions of deaf people's daily lives.

In certain superficial aspects dear to the American media—technology and imagery—the situation of deaf Americans has indeed improved. They are now far less isolated from the general culture. Many feel far more confidence and self-respect. The general population seems friendlier, more accepting and tolerant. But in other, more concrete respects, things have not gotten better and may even have gotten worse. The 1980s, which began with the promise of the Decade of Disabled Persons, have nonetheless seen substantial declines in government spending on social services, including those used by deaf clients. During eight years in the White House, a hearing-impaired president ignored the opportunity seized by Franklin Roosevelt and Betty Ford to identify publicly with a medical condition (polio and breast cancer, respectively) and use the office's immense prestige to raise the status and circumstances of those affected by it.

American Sign Language, furthermore, though now accepted

in theory by the hearing community, remains radically foreign to the vast majority of Americans, with fluency still limited to the small circle of hearing persons in close contact with the Deaf community. Neither total communication, cued speech, nor mainstreaming, each introduced with high hopes and good intentions over the past generation, has delivered on early promises to substantially improve the average deaf student's effective command of English. Most deaf people, therefore, must still depend heavily on interpreters for precise communication with their fellow citizens who hear. And though interpreting services are more widely available than a decade ago, they are no cheaper.

Paying for interpreting—and all the rest of life's goods and services—remains as great a problem as ever. Indeed, the computer revolution that helped liberate some has hurt others by destroying jobs in one of the traditional mainstays of deaf employment—the printing industry. Some employers, of course, do desire to make their workplaces more accessible to deaf employees, and some have even acted on that desire. To date, though, they remain a tiny minority. Federal legislation does promise wider opportunities for deaf workers. But if the history of other equal opportunity laws is any guide, reality will fall short of expectation. And the new laws will bring decades of costly and divisive litigation.

None of these reservations is in any way intended to diminish the tremendous and hard-won victories that deaf people achieved during these years. A true spiritual awakening, such as they experienced, must underlie any successful movement for significant social change. But as this nation's long struggle toward social equality confirms, spirit alone rarely suffices to overcome entrenched cultural, technological, or economic opposition.

Sadly, many old obstacles still bar the way to the Deaf community's social advancement. Many old disputes and animosities still cleave the deaf population into warring factions. Many old prejudices and misconceptions endure within the larger hearing society, now complicated by the new misconception that all it will take to integrate deaf persons into the wider community is good will and the ability to sign "I love you." But, after nearly two generations of trying, American society has yet to integrate fully its citizens of African descent—a group separated from the rest of us "only" by an accumulation of custom and belief, not by any physical impediment to communication. How much greater, then, will be the effort needed to fully include our deaf fellow citizens! And how much likelier is it to be made?

Despite our dearest hopes, therefore, despite our deepest convictions, things don't change simply because we want them to. Old divisions don't mend, old hurts don't heal, old prejudices don't vanish, old facts don't alter simply because it would be better if they did. Ten years later, the oral-manual controversy is no closer to resolution, although the balance of power has shifted. Ten years later, parents of deaf children face the same excruciating choices, the same cacophony of conflicting expert advice. Ten years later, more deaf children must search for ways of joining the Deaf community, having spent their young years as mainstreamed loners in hearing schools. Ten years later, the old debate over the merits of residential schools is heating up again, as enthusiasm for mainstreaming wanes in some quarters. Ten years later, the rubella babies, the deaf world's own "boomer" generation, have moved into the working world as young adults, there to encounter the slings and arrows of a fortune no less outrageous than that facing any human being bearing youthful dreams toward middle age.

Ten years later, therefore, the main conclusions of the original *Dancing Without Music* still stand. On the one hand, I regret that this is so; I had hoped for more progress. On the other, though, I rejoice that this book, this arduous offspring of my mind and heart, still lives in the minds and hearts of readers. An author cannot hope for more.

B.L.B.
Washington, D.C.
May 1990

PREFACE TO HARDCOVER EDITION

This book is about a holy war. Its seemingly innocuous subject has been rent by passionate disagreement for more than two hundred years. For all those generations and in a score of countries, well-meaning men and women have debated violently and relentlessly, struggling for their opposite views with the combined fervor of intellectual conviction, moral certainty, and emotional need. Anyone who would claim to report on the battle in a spirit of impartiality, therefore, and in the interest of its victims, must candidly consider her own biases.

There is a difference between bias and prejudice, Daniel Ling has observed. The latter consists of prejudging an issue, of deciding beforehand what the evidence will prove. Bias, however, is the reasonable product of an honest investigation; it consists of drawing conclusions from available evidence and then using them as a basis for further thought. Bias can become prejudice if it stands unyieldingly against convincing contrary arguments. But if it is no more in evidence at the end of an investigation than it was at the beginning, it has degenerated into mindlessness.

I cannot claim to have drawn no conclusions from my perambulations among the hearing-handicapped and their institutions. Nor can I claim that all these conclusions are based strictly on intellect. And least of all can I claim that they do not color the resulting book. But I can claim—indeed, I insist—that they arise from as honest, as disinterested, as open-minded and open-hearted a study as I am capable of doing.

The great truth of this debate came to me slowly, as I listened to many people tell me about their lives, and when it finally did emerge from the welter of anecdote and incident laid before me, I was stunned by both its simplicity and my obtuseness. It is simply this: there is no single truth. Many people frankly told me their own hard-won truths, and none of these could I doubt or question. Yet equally sincere and equally afflicted men and women passionately disagreed; they were all right about the truths their personal pain had taught them, and in this sense, all their truths must be equally valid for them.

But I, fortunately, have the luxury of viewing the fray, in Giraudoux's words, from a terrace. I am a noncombatant, a war correspondent, as it were, and so I can view it all more broadly (and necessarily more shallowly). I hope that readers, regardless of their loyalties, will accept this work in the spirit in which it is offered, that their biases and not their prejudices will guide them as they consider it.

This book results, possibly even more than most, from the kindness and interest of many people. They made their technical knowledge, their documentary possessions, and their life histories available to me unstintingly. I cannot thank them all here, but I trust that those whose names do not appear will understand that the reason is lack of space, not failure of gratitude.

First and foremost, I want to acknowledge my incalculable debt to Donna Chitwood. She was my first guide onto foreign terrain, and she has been this project's stalwart, devoted, and untiringly resourceful friend from its very inception. It is no exaggeration to say that without her there would be no book at all.

In the very next breath, I must thank Dr. Edward Merrill and the faculty, staff, library, and students of Gallaudet College. Their response to my many requests for help and information often brought to mind the biblical injunction "Ask and it shall be given you." The Alexander Graham Bell Association for the Deaf also graciously provided time, information, and advice.

Barbara Chertok and Mardie Youngloff took an enthusiastic personal interest in my progress; I am deeply grateful to them for introductions, guidance, and especially for keenly intelligent discussion. Rex Lowman and Don Peterson were patient and understanding teachers and encouraging advisers. Many other busy people gave substantial chunks of time to an inquisitive novice: Daniel Ling, David Denton, Latham Breunig, Kathryn Meadow, Nanette Fabray MacDougall, Orin Cornett, William Stokoe, Kenneth Lane, Harry Markowicz, Bernard Mottez, Frances Parsons, James Woodward, Anne Spragins, Raymond Trybus, Betsy Parker, and Bernard Bragg, to name but a few. My thanks to all of them, and to all the other individuals and institutions that provided my material. Mary Evans and Angela Cox encouraged me constantly, and Jordan and Daniel Benderly cheerfully tolerated bad temper, odd hours, and a generally distracted wife and mother. All these friends and helpers are largely responsible for whatever merit this book may contain. I am responsible for its shortcomings.

B.L.B.

Washington, D.C.
March 1980

CHAPTER 1

Two Different Worlds

When you turn north off Florida Avenue at 7th Street NE in Washington, D.C., you enter a foreign country. Not the embassy of a foreign country, although these abound in the city, but the capital, the intellectual and spiritual heartland.

There is no customs post to warn you, no threatening sign or barbed-wire barrier. There's just a gate in an iron fence and a path that winds a bit as it takes you up a little hill. Ahead stands a cluster of Victorian structures such as grace a thousand college catalogues: umber stone confections shaded by arching trees.

Indeed, you could come into this place without suspecting a thing, move among the buildings and across the lawns as if this were just any grassy college campus. It's not until you watch the people that you begin to notice. They're mainly young, of course, as lithe and elaborately disheveled as their counterparts anywhere. Boys and girls pass in bright, puffy vests, in determinedly ragged army jackets, in college sweat shirts and athletic gear. They're quick, active, attractive, and sociable, and somehow the whole scene seems extraordinarily, almost eerily, alive. And after a while, it hits you. It's also very, very quiet.

No one shouts to a friend across the quad; a knot of young male loungers emits no whistles as a stunning blonde goes by; a little group sits in expectant silence before a soundless raconteur, then erupts in sudden laughter. Indeed, with your eyes closed you'd think that not much was going on, but your eyes open take in a place alive with all the things that people do on any campus.

This is Gallaudet College, and most of these people going about their daily business—nearly all the students and many of the teachers—are deaf. Their deafness is why they are here; it is also why the college exists. Over a thousand people who find themselves unable to profit from other colleges because of hearing loss come here to study and to teach. They and their predecessors and successors are probably among the most able, and surely among the most successful, people of their kind in America.

They come to Gallaudet because there they can succeed. The scene may be quiet, but it is hardly devoid of talk. The preternatural liveliness, the uncanny vivacity of all the people around you results from all that talk, all that visual, manual talk. They're talking with their hands, their faces, their bodies. They're gesticulating and grimacing, rocking and swaying. Fingers and features move constantly, telegraphing messages across the silent air. That's really why the people have come. On this campus, and only on this campus, one can study for a liberal arts degree entirely in sign language.

It's early evening, and the knot of cars parked along the suburban street leaves no doubt about which of the neat split-level houses is hosting the meeting. Inside, people gather in a comfortable living room, chatting and greeting friends. Every so often a call to a newcomer across the room punctuates the steady buzz of talk. Through an arch one can see coffee cups and cake plates laid out and waiting on the dining table, but the fruitwood dining chairs ring the living room, along with an assortment of straight chairs obviously gathered from every room in the house. Gradually people find places for the evening on the white sofa against the wall, in the pair of armchairs angled toward the center, or on the array of miscellaneous seating placed in a careful circle around the room's perimeter. "Can you see?" people ask one another. "Am I in your way?" "You're sure I'm not blocking your view?"

A fair-haired young man in his twenties stands up from the

presiding officer's seat, a kitchen stool at one end of the room. He calls the meeting to order and asks, "Can everyone see me okay?" The voice is blurred, as if over a bad telephone connection, but each word comes through. All around the circle people gaze intently as he stands with his hands on his hips, announcing the evening's main order of business, appointment of committees to work on the group's planned weekend outing.

A slim young fellow sitting next to him, a committee chairman, asks a question about procedure. It emerges as a series of hoarse gasps. Some in the audience shift in their seats and concentrate harder. One or two whisper to their neighbors. A handsome woman in her forties raises her hand, is recognized, and says, "I understood we would cover that later." Her voice is strangely deep for so feminine an appearance, and though strong and animated, it is toneless. Now other people tap their neighbors for clarification. The woman turns away from the chairman and repeats her comment to those at the back of the room. Heads nod. The chairman says, "Right. Let's proceed."

The meeting inches down its prepared agenda. Names are proposed, each to a flurry of taps and whispered clarifications; points are raised, doggedly discussed, and disposed of. People talk generally to the chairman but often repeat their comments for the benefit of those without a clear line of sight to the speaker. Listeners concentrate steadily, sometimes to follow the discussion, sometimes to catch the words themselves. At last the committees take shape and the meeting breaks for dessert.

Most of these people chatting over teacups are hearing-impaired; this is a local chapter meeting of the Oral Deaf Adults Section of the Alexander Graham Bell Association for the Deaf. Those in the room who hear normally are friends of the chapter, mainly parents of young people with defective hearing. Conversation during the social hour, as in the meeting itself, proceeds almost entirely by speech. Those with normal hearing enunciate clearly, but perhaps a beat more slowly than usual. Those without it produce sounds ranging from clear and almost normal English to noises that rate as speech only through courtesy. Sometimes the normally hearing have the advantage in understanding, when the voice carries the message easily. But sometimes the advantage goes the other way, when the voice is so dis-

torted that ignoring the sound and watching the lips grasps the
message better.

There is a difference between this group and the people at
Gallaudet, but it does not have to do with the ability to hear.
Some of those signing in near silence on the college green hear
better, in a strictly physical sense, than most of the members of
the ODAS chapter. But the people at Gallaudet, and the others
belonging to the nationwide culture they represent, view themselves as deaf. Those at ODAS have chosen instead to be hearing-impaired.

Scientists understand many things about hearing loss, but to
understand others, it's more useful to be an experienced fanatic.
Veterans of Trotskyite-Stalinist propaganda wars or combatants
bloodied over the difference between "goals" and "quotas" will
feel more at home than scientists do in the ideological maelstrom
swirling around the apparently simple question of what it means
to be deaf.

It might seem, at first innocent glance, that a person is deaf
who cannot hear. If one can hear imperfectly, but well enough
for many purposes, then he's probably hard-of-hearing. And
probably anyone with hearing defective to any degree is hearing-impaired. But logic rarely helps when dealing with belief,
and the field of hearing impairment has been rent for centuries
by a conflict as fierce as any that ever sundered a party cell or
shattered a religious denomination.

The plain truth is that "deaf" and "hearing-impaired," when
used by people in the field, usually do not describe physiological
conditions but signal loyalties in a continuing war over communication and, ultimately, over the place of the hearing-
handicapped in society. Those who favor manual communication
tend to describe people with serious hearing losses as "deaf";
those who oppose it tend to call them "hearing-impaired." A
statement by Edgar L. Lowell, director of the world-famous
John Tracy Clinic in Los Angeles, gives the flavor of the dispute.
"Asking me to speak on the 'place of manual communication in
the education of deaf children' is like asking the Angel Gabriel
to speak on the place of sin in the life of Christians, or the shep-
herd on the place of the wolf in his flock,"[1] the good doctor

writes. But he has the grace to add, "I have some obvious prejudices."

The controversy arises from an empirical observation: many people with impaired hearing, even those with quite profound losses, retain some ability to hear. The usefulness of this so-called residual hearing is the core of the issue. Does it, if augmented by a hearing aid and enhanced by skills such as speechreading, offer a reasonable foundation for a communication system based exclusively or primarily on speech? Or is this hope the basis of a delusion leading to frustration, failure, and distress? Does use of speech, speechreading, and amplification (the so-called oral methods) truly provide the individual a wider range of life chances than the use of sign language; or does discouraging sign language merely mask a denial of individual dignity and freedom of choice? Should hearing-impaired people strive to integrate themselves into the general hearing society or should deaf people be free to establish cultural enclaves based on their own form of communication? Is it better, in short, to be like the people at Gallaudet or the people in ODAS?

To answer these profound and difficult questions, science offers little help. The measurement of hearing loss is far from exact; and beyond that, even knowing the level of a person's hearing does not always predict its potential usefulness. Hearing with understanding is a learned skill. Small infants register acoustical sensations, but do not intellectually grasp what they hear; only time and experience transform apparently random noise into meaningful sound. But how much understanding is possible in cases of serious loss, by whom, and in what circumstances?

In 1943 an English investigator reported on two adults with apparently identical, very grave losses. In the first, a woman had gradually lost her hearing after she knew speech, but she could still hear and understand a voice close to her ear without a hearing aid. A man born deaf, on the other hand, could hear a few sounds but understand nothing spoken near his ear or anywhere else. Part of the difference obviously lay in the woman's tremendous advantage in possessing a workable model of speech to guide her perception of it. But how much of the man's inability lay in the failure to train his hearing and how much in the sim ple lack of ability to hear enough of the speech code to learn to decipher it? The man showed some improvement after training, according to reports, but how much and at what cost? Was he a deaf man who could not hear, or a hearing-impaired man with a chance for substantial improvement?

There is no objective answer to this question, so ideology and emotion have traditionally filled the gap. Indeed, there are not even any universally accepted criteria on which to base such a judgment. Should one consider results from tests using pure tones or English words? Amplified or unamplified hearing? Audiological measures or a person's functional ability? In 1962 the British government decided to divide deaf from partially hearing (hard-of-hearing) children on the basis of educational needs rather than hearing loss. A child of impaired hearing who lacks speech counts as deaf; one whose speech appears to be developing, even if slowly, counts as partially hearing, regardless of actual degree of loss. The U.S. government in Public Law 94-142 defines a deaf child as one with a loss "so severe that the child's hearing is nonfunctional for the purposes of educational performance." A hard-of-hearing child, on the other hand, has a hearing impairment "either permanent or fluctuating, which adversely affects a child's educational performance, but which is not included under the definition of deaf." But when is speech development so slow as to be abnormal? How little speech is no speech at all? How bad must hearing be before it becomes nonfunctional? Who is to decide? And by what means?

The British definitions at least have the virtue of considering a crucial but often overlooked fact. The central problem is not that a person cannot hear, or perhaps cannot speak, but that he has trouble communicating in the normal way. And this, ultimately, proves to be the great divide in a chartless territory. Mary Switzer and Boyce Williams, two American governmental experts, put it succinctly. "The hard of hearing population differs only in degree from the general population, while deaf people stand apart psychologically and socially."[2] The hard-of-hearing may not hear well enough to escape all the awkwardness, embarrassment, or anxiety arising from ambiguous communication, but they can hear well enough to communicate as the vast preponderance of humanity does, through the ears.

When hearing becomes bad enough, however, people have no choice but to get most of their information through the eyes. Whether they read lips or sign language does not change this reality. The shreds of sounds they catch serve mainly to supplement visual perceptions. For the normally hearing and the hard-of-hearing the reverse is true; visual cues from expression, gesture, or stance enrich the information gained from sound. A reasonable distinction between the deaf and the hard-of-hearing considers communication style rather than test results; it considers the degree of understanding possible, not merely the level of physical audition.

But for deciding whether those with little or no useful hearing should be considered deaf or hearing-impaired, no basis exists apart from taste or emotion. It all comes down, those who favor oral methods insist, to whether one considers the glass half full or half empty; to whether one emphasizes the positive, that residual hearing does exist, or the negative, that it is imperfect. It all comes down, those who favor manual communication insist, to whether one accepts reality or chases illusion; to whether one accepts that shreds of hearing do not permit adequate oral communication.

This basic point, debated for centuries by people holding their opposing views with nearly religious fervor, is why residents of the same city afflicted with the same disability form two communities so distinct that they sometimes seem to come from different countries. When members of the two camps meet, they may have more trouble communicating with one another than either does with the hearing. A joint meeting may require two interpreters, one to render sign language for the manualists, the other to mouth the words close by for those who depend on lipreading.

So bizarre a situation did not arise by accident. The contentious and passionate history of attempts to help those who hear imperfectly stretches back more than five hundred years. The dispute smoldered in Jacobean England and Revolutionary France, it raged between three-named, bearded worthies in the America of Grant and Garfield, and it continues without letup in the space age.

America offers no simple answer to the hard-of-hearing and

the deaf (the term used here, and generally throughout this book, to mean those who must depend upon their eyes). To live their lives they must decide on some adaptation to their handicap. That is to say, they must choose what sort of people they will be. If one is hard-of-hearing and goes among the normally hearing as a slightly deficient specimen of their own kind, how does he deal with the constant anxiety and frustration or changing background noise, acoustical conditions, and voice qualities? How does he survive the trial of a college lecture or the purgatory of a dinner party?

And if one has hardly any hearing at all, how does he escape from the prison of isolation that can enclose those cut off from normal communication? Should he strive to live among the hearing, beating them at their own game, speaking in a voice he can never hear, "listening" with the eyes to words that flicker, half invisible, on the lips? Or should he spend his social life in the community of his own kind, in an insular society that uses a language hardly anyone else knows? There is no single answer. But that is partly because there is no single question either.

CHAPTER 2

Who Are the Deaf?

Hearing impairment has been called an invisible condition, but if so it is hiding everywhere. At least 14 million Americans—one person in fifteen—have hearing defective to some measurable degree, and 2 million meet the demographer's definition of deafness; they can neither hear nor understand speech with or without a hearing aid. True deafness is not common, but there are more than half as many deaf people in this country as Episcopalians, and almost three times as many deaf as blind. So why have most Americans never known a profoundly deaf person? Why do we meet so few hard-of-hearing? Who, in short, are the hearing-impaired that we know so little about them?

The simple answer is that they are ourselves, or people very much like us. For those with mild to moderate losses, this is literally true. Poor hearing leaves no mark on the body, and many people continue their lives, even wear hearing aids, without anyone noticing. "If you really looked, you could see my hearing aid on television," says entertainer Nanette Fabray, who wore one during all the tightly timed comedy skits on the celebrated "Caesar's Hour" programs, "but people didn't ever look. People don't look at your ears when they talk to you. They look at your mouth and your eyes and your face. Because they could talk to me, nobody looked at my ears."

Beyond that, many people who should wear hearing aids don't. At least 6 to 10 percent of the population has hearing bad enough to make the attempt worthwhile, but only about 1 percent use them. Even the industry considers their potential market no larger than an additional 2 or 3 percent. The ethos of that business in part explains why, and explains a good deal else about the plight of many hearing-impaired. In the popular mind and in the industry's promotions, the only good hearing aid is a small one, and the best hearing aid is nearly invisible. People who lose their hearing gradually or late in life may never admit to themselves that they have a problem; never even seek out one of those well-nigh invisible aids; and certainly never identify themselves as one of the class of the disabled.

Even profoundly deaf people are very much like ourselves, or at least were to start with. From a sociological standpoint, deafness strikes very close to randomly; the deaf come from all races, regions, classes, and religions. In social origin they form a fairly representative microcosm of the population at large. But if they start out as a roughly proportional sample of the rest of us, they do not end up that way. By adulthood those deaf from an early age have become demographically quite distinct.

In demographic terms, there are deaf people and deaf people. Of the 2 million Americans who can't hear speech, about a quarter lost that ability before the age of nineteen, and roughly one in eight either was born without it or lost it before the age of three. Possibly half of the deaf are elderly, and many more are approaching old age. But deafness has social as well as physical consequences, and when it strikes early and hard it has educational ones as well. Hearing loss attacks the aged and aging with no regard to social standing, but an adult who lost his hearing at an early age is very probably an alumnus of a special education program, and the earlier the onset and the profounder the loss, the better his chances of having gone to a residential school for the deaf. The better his chances, in short, of having lived a childhood and youth markedly different from that of the rest of us.

For the first time in decades, an accurate picture exists of Americans deaf from their early years. In 1974 Jerome Schein and Marcus Delk published the results[1] of a massive search for people they call prevocationally deaf—those who suffered a profound loss before the age of nineteen. Any census of the handicapped presents special methodological hurdles, and a census of the deaf is trickier still. The deaf have been unreachable by most ordinary means of mass communication. They don't listen to the radio or watch much TV and may ignore newspapers. Any attempt to find a substantial portion of them requires a rather special approach. Standard survey techniques—going from door to door, or even to a random sample of doors—will not reliably turn up the right two people in every thousand. Demographers have found it more fruitful to exploit social networks where the two in a thousand may be known—in other words, to ask those in a position to know the whereabouts of deaf people. Schein and Delk and their associates combed lists provided by thousands of organizations and individuals to build a master file of prevocationally deaf people. Then to check their accuracy they sought the same people in representative samples of the general population, and finally they extrapolated from these findings an estimate of the deaf population at large. Even so, they probably underestimate certain minorities within the deaf minority as well as social isolates outside the usual deaf networks.

But the resulting estimate is the best available since the U.S. Census gave up in despair in 1930. Up to that point, the Bureau had struggled through census after census, trying to figure out whom it should count as deaf. Until 1870 it enumerated the "deaf and dumb," those who could neither hear nor speak. Between then and 1890 it sought people who had suffered hearing loss and concomitant loss of speech before age sixteen. In 1890, it was back to "deaf and dumb." The 1900 criterion, however, deemphasized speech and counted all those who failed to understand loud shouts. Many objected, however, especially those who had lost their hearing but kept their speech; these people resented being put in a then very stigmatized category. So between 1910 and 1930, it was back to "deaf and dumb," along with totally deaf children under eight, adults totally deaf from childhood, and those who couldn't understand shouts even with a hearing aid. At this point the Bureau abandoned the effort as pointless. With no accepted criteria and no standard method of applying them (census takers would literally shout loudly at doubtful cases), the decennial census was not producing figures of any comparative or predictive value anyway. And for all its effort it was missing some of the most important things about deaf people.

"Of all physical disabilities," the psychologist Hans Furth has written, "deafness is the only one that makes its members part of a natural community."[2] Furth argues this partly deductively, reasoning that distinctive communication problems and distinctive experience ought to produce a particular shared identity; partly from the observation that many people deaf from an early age (and some of those who lost their hearing later) appear to cluster together for friendship and support; and partly from what deaf people believe about themselves. Schein and Delk's results give the idea a firmer empirical basis. Americans who lose their hearing early in life do form a distinctive social and cultural group, a society both strongly cohesive and highly endogamous. This is especially true for sign language users, but even among staunch oralists deaf from youth four out of five marry a deaf spouse rather than a hearing one. And most prevocationally deaf spend nearly all their leisure time and find their basic personal identity in the company of others like themselves. Unlike other disabled people, those who identify themselves as deaf form a true society, a genuine cultural group.

How does this happen if the deaf start out as a representative sample of the whole population? All other cultural minorities start out very unrepresentative indeed. Irish-Americans and Navaho Indians, Bayou Cajuns and birthright Quakers come from clusters of families severely skewed for country of origin, or place of residence, or racial background, or socioeconomic status, or all of the above. That is because other cultural minorities recruit their rising generation primarily from the children of their own members. Parents teach and children learn how to be minority people right at home.

But over 90 percent of the prevocationally deaf have two hearing parents. Put another way, only one in ten has at least one parent who is hearing-impaired, and only about five in a hundred have two parents definitely known to be deaf. Probably fewer than one prevocationally deaf person in eight has any blood relative who is deaf. Only a very small proportion of deaf people, therefore, can learn how to be culturally deaf in their parental homes; they must learn to be the adults they become from others, in other places, and often without their parents' knowledge or approval. This strange and melancholy circumstance reverberates through the entire life and history of deaf people all over the world.

Nor can most deaf people pass on their cultural membership to their own descendants. Almost nine out of every ten children born to deaf parents hear normally. They might be honorary members of the deaf community while children, and a high percentage of the professionals in the field of deafness seem to come from their ranks, but ultimately their fate lies in the general society of the hearing, not in the small, special one of their parents. The deaf culture, therefore, in all but rare cases recruits its new members in a very unusual way. Young people learn basic cultural identity and most social skills from contemporaries rather than elders. The school—the informal life of the dormitories—takes on some of the functions of family. Thus the immense cultural importance of age of onset and attendance at a school for the deaf. They alone largely determine who will be culturally "deaf." No one not educated as a deaf child ever becomes a "native" of the deaf culture. "I am not a real member of the deaf community," says I. King Jordan, a Gallaudet graduate and faculty member who lost his hearing in a motorcycle accident at the age of twenty-one. "I am a deafened hearing person."[3]

Not only age of onset but degree of impairment is culturally crucial. Most children with impaired hearing have losses in the mild range—between 26 and 40 decibels—and an additional third fall into the moderate group, between 40 and 55. Nearly all of the first group and a good number of the second can attend regular schools, if not wholly successfully, then at least not disastrously unsuccessfully. Only one hearing-impaired child in 200 has a severe loss (greater than 70 decibels), and one in 400, a profound one (greater than 90). From these two categories, and especially from the last, come most of the recruits for the deaf community. It is not uncommon to meet culturally deaf people of middle age or older who suffer hearing losses that today would qualify them for regular schools rather than for special education, but they were young before the development of portable, high-powered hearing aids and are now beyond the age when they can easily adjust to amplification or, indeed, have any desire to rearrange their lives.

Deaf children come from all sorts of homes, but they are more likely to be boys than girls. There are more deaf women than deaf men in our population only because there are more women than men, period. But there are more prevocationally deaf males than females in all age groups. The type of loss that Schein and Delk call "significant bilateral impairment" (any significant loss in both ears) occurs more than half again as often among men as among women. Why this should be is not altogether clear; maybe males suffer more diseases than females, or boys have more accidents than girls, or both.

A deaf child has a better chance of being white than black. No one knows for sure what causes this odd discrepancy, but socio-economics appears to combine with genetics to keep more white deaf children alive than black. Some scientists hypothesize that natural selective pressure may have relaxed somewhat among whites but not among blacks, Schein and Delk report; this idea, however, remains only a hypothesis. But whites, on the average, are better fed, housed, and doctored than blacks, and therefore probably survive serious illness better. At any rate, they more often live to be deaf. A striking set of statistics underlines the white deaf baby's apparently superior propensity for survival. Nearly three out of four white prevocational deaf lost their hearing before three, as against only two out of three nonwhites. Twenty percent of the nonwhite males lost their hearing after six and before eighteen, as opposed to 12 percent of the general prevocationally deaf population.

Children with hearing losses come from families at all income levels, but the wealthier the parents, the greater the chances that the child was born with the loss. In 1974 almost nine in ten of those from families earning over $20,000 were impaired from birth, but almost half of those from families earning under $5,000 became deaf sometime later. Does this mean that poor children succumb more often to serious illness, or does it mean that well-to-do, more sophisticated parents simply discover their children's hearing losses earlier? The statistics provide no answer.

Nor is it possible to interpret at face value the fact that parents of the hearing-impaired tend to have more children than the average. A 1974 survey of children in special schools and classes showed that their families averaged more than three children each; all other families with children under eighteen that year averaged slightly over two children each. Almost 60 percent of mothers in the general population had one or two children; only 30 percent of mothers of the hearing-impaired had so few. Does this mean that parents of handicapped children prefer to "hedge their bets" by producing additional offspring, despite the enormous burden that a deaf child imposes on time, finances, and energy?

A child deaf before the age of five traditionally has had a better than even chance of getting all his education at a residential school for the deaf. One deafened between twelve and eighteen has had a better than even chance of getting all his education at schools for the normally hearing. Between these extremes, deaf children attend several types of institutions: special day schools for the deaf, day classes for the deaf in regular schools, and many combinations of all these options. But again, age of onset and degree of loss appear to be controlling factors; the greater the impairment and the earlier it begins, the likelier the child is to receive all or most of his schooling among the deaf.

What type of adult does a deaf childhood produce?

Victor Galloway, a prominent deaf educator, describes the "typical deaf person"—that is, the typical self-aware, white male member of the deaf community—as a stable, productive, relatively well adjusted, and quite provincial member of the lower middle or working class. He supports his deaf wife and hearing children with a steady manual job, often skilled work that requires little communication with co-workers. He owns his own home in an average or slightly better neighborhood. He attended a state residential school and finished with a fifth-grade reading level. As a young man he participated in athletics at his local deaf club, and as he grew older he moved into club leadership. The club, or perhaps a deaf church, is his main social connection.

Schein and Delk's statistics support Galloway's impressions. Culturally deaf adults marry somewhat less than the hearing, but overwhelmingly they marry each other. More than 80 percent of their unions involve two deaf spouses. Only one deaf person in eight had a normally hearing spouse in 1972; and even fewer were married to hard-of-hearing. Once again, age of onset is influential; those deaf before age three were markedly less likely to have non-deaf spouses, and men born deaf were only half as likely as men with acquired losses to take wives. Deaf-born only sons are the least likely to marry of all. Nearly three quarters of them remain bachelors. Are they unpracticed in relationships or merely very self-sufficient? Does poor communication keep them single or a rich inner life make them prefer their own company?

Many more deaf people marry now than did at the turn of the century, but fewer become parents than hearing people—almost 10 percent fewer, according to 1960 statistics—and when they do they have fewer children—almost 20 percent fewer. Nearly all these offspring hear normally. Two congenitally deaf parents run the greatest risk of producing a child with impaired hearing—nearly one chance in five. A couple in which one partner hears and the other has an adventitious loss have less than one chance in twelve of producing a child with a hearing problem.

Like the rest of us, the prevocationally deaf generally hold jobs that reflect their education. But they face other problems in the workplace as well, and these seriously affect many careers. In the early 1970s only six in a hundred had bachelor's degrees. Twice that many had finished at least a year of college. About a third had ended their formal education with a high school diploma, but more than half had not finished high school and over a quarter had never even reached ninth grade.

So they overwhelmingly find employment in manual trades—four fifths of deaf people as opposed to under half of the hearing. Probably half of employed deaf people work for manufacturing concerns, compared to a quarter of the hearing. But these figures are falsely cheerful; nearly all of these deaf employees are operatives or menials, while many hearing have managerial jobs. More than half of working Americans wear white collars on the job; fewer than one deaf person in five is so lucky. And the deaf, like others of the deprived, suffer more unemployment than their hearing counterparts.

It's no surprise, then, that the prevocationally deaf earn much less than the hearing. Their family income is only 85 percent of the national average, and even that figure is overoptimistic because in many households more than one person works. Deaf individuals in fact average a bit over 70 percent of the earnings of the non-deaf. For the black deaf, the situation is worse still; male heads of households earn only about three quarters as much as all nonwhite male heads of households.

The system fails deaf workers not once but twice. They get less education than the hearing, and they don't get jobs that fully exploit the schooling they have. Nearly half of those with a year or more of college work as clericals, operatives, laborers, or domestic and service workers. To this day Gallaudet offers a few courses in printing, the traditional occupational last resort of the educated deaf. Part of the problem is pure prejudice, but communication can also present very genuine obstacles to advancement. Supervisory and executive positions, as well as many professional and technical posts, require constant conversation and frequent meetings. Although a skilled speechreader can hold his own in discussion with one hearing person, groups of hearing people present an almost insuperable challenge to even the hard-of-hearing. E. Latham Breunig, for example, suffered a profound loss at age seven, but went on to earn a Ph.D. from Johns Hopkins and pursue a successful career as a scientist and statistician with the Eli Lilley Company. He retains an easily understandable voice even in his late sixties. But even this dedicated oralist, who served as president of the Alexander Graham Bell Association, the nation's chief proponent of the oral point of view, and who belonged to hearing chapters of the Toastmasters International, readily admits that throughout his career he found that "committee meetings are impossible, unless you're the chairman and can control the agenda."

For the person without either Breunig's early opportunity to learn proper speech or his fierce drive, however, or whose voice has deteriorated over many years of not hearing it, or who finds speechreading difficult, Breunig's virtuoso performance is beyond hope. Not accidentally, therefore, deaf workers tend to cluster in industries such as the manufacture of non-durable goods, and in trades such as printing and sewing, where they can get by with stereotyped, and thus reasonably predictable, oral communication. Only the rare employer truly accommodates the deaf worker.

The importance of communication on the job probably accounts for the depressingly direct correlation between average personal income and age of onset. The congenitally deaf, who have the least exposure to spoken language and the greatest difficulty learning it, have the lowest incomes, and those deaf after age eleven, the highest. But no single factor, helpful as it might be in predicting group results, accounts for all the variation in individual behavior. Schein and Delk uncovered a surprising fact: pre-lingually deaf people (who lost hearing before age three) appear to hold a disproportionate share of the more desirable jobs. Whether this represents pure sampling error or hints at some more profound difference, the demographers cannot even surmise.

Survey after survey of professionally eminent deaf people, however, turn up the same constellation of factors: privileged family background, good education, talent, drive. These outstanding deaf people may not—as the old Borscht Belt joke goes —count as admirals among real admirals; their attainments would hardly rate Who's Who among the hearing. But the difference between them and the mass of deaf adults is no smaller than that separating the careers of hearing people considered prominent from those of the ordinary hearing person in the street. These deaf are successful, upper-middle-class people, by and large, working in business and the professions. Few, understandably, sought careers in law, medicine, the military, or politics, common routes to eminence among the non-handicapped. And surprisingly, the congenitally deaf among the leaders do not appear particularly handicapped by the early onset of their losses. In one study, 30 percent of the eminent had congenital losses, as opposed to an estimated 37 percent of all deaf men. In another, the split was close to even among pre- and post-lingually deaf.

Like the eminent hearing, the successful deaf came from prosperous families that prized, and could provide, good education. Not only Latham Breunig but his three hearing brothers did well in school. The fathers of the respondents tended to be professionals and executives. The children overwhelmingly attended schools for the deaf, a disproportionate number of them private. Those educated in hearing schools nearly always had extra tutoring or other help. Nearly all in the samples had gone to college, and the vast majority had at least one degree. In one study of eighty-seven such people, seventeen had master's degrees and five had doctorates.

A striking feature of these eminent people is their ability to mediate between the two cultures. Nine out of ten use oral communication at work, and eight out of ten use sign language among friends; not surprisingly, the best speech correlated strongly with late onset. Like their less successful confreres, fewer of these eminent deaf men married than the American norm; but unlike other deaf, they had a close to even chance of marrying a hearing or hard-of-hearing woman.

A small group of prosperous exceptions, unfortunately, does not deny the terrible obstacles that deafness poses to ambition. A survey of young deaf adults in the New England states showed that they earn 22 percent less than their hearing siblings, whom we can assume they match in socioeconomic background and genetic endowment. And not all the fault can possibly lie with the deaf employee; much of it comes from plain exploitation and discrimination. Oscar Cohen, a leading educator of the deaf and the hearing son of a deaf man, recalls his father's frustrating working years—always getting the hardest and dirtiest work and the fewest benefits, always up against the boss's certainty that he couldn't argue and wouldn't complain.

And sadly, the bosses were not far wrong. Repeated surveys show that the deaf make good workers—steady, patient, dependable, with low absenteeism and high loyalty to employers who often don't deserve it. They tend to stay longer in the same jobs than hearing workers, and to get promoted less. They might even help train those who eventually rise above them. Experienced deaf skilled workers often find themselves stuck among co-workers at the same level of pay and advancement but inferior in experience, ability, seniority, and skill, and way ahead in advancement potential.

And shaky though their economic foothold may be, it has been steadily eroding for the better part of a century. A hundred or even eighty years ago, deaf Americans came very close to matching the educational and occupational status of the hearing. In 1886 the American School for the Deaf in Hartford, Connecticut, the oldest such school in the country, polled its graduates. Over half the employed men worked in seven trades: farming, shoe repair, mechanics, carpentry, teaching, shoe assembly, and mill work, and over half the employed females worked in mills. But the graduates included ministers, an artist, a lawyer, and the owner and founder of an insurance company. And significantly, the graduates earned, on the average, as much as the general work force of New England. A 1926 survey still showed the deaf concentrated in the same few trades—printing, carpentry, farming, shoe repair, and sewing. More than half worked at the trade they had learned at school.

Anyone with even a passing acquaintance with the American economy in the past fifty years will recognize that list of occupations for what it has become, a roll call of the jobs we have lost to foreign competition or to mechanization or to changing habits, a compendium of dying crafts in shrinking industries. And still, in 1959, a study of 10,000 deaf adults showed the main occupational categories to be printing, shoe repair, and tailoring and the main vocational training received to be printing, carpentry, baking, cabinet work, and shoe repair. Even in the 1970s, the typical deaf person worked as an operative in a manufacturing plant, perhaps assembling clothes, doing printing, or fabricating other non-durables; competing, in short, with both the cheap labor of Asia and the advance of automation, trapped in the most stagnant reaches of American industry.

Nor does the future appear especially bright. Thousands of old job types have passed from existence in recent decades, and thousands of new ones have taken their place. The future belongs to the worker broadly trained and flexible enough to learn new skills throughout life; to the highly educated; and to those active in the service sector. Fewer jobs than ever exist for the illiterate and the marginally literate, and competition for them increases steadily. The American School for the Deaf graduates of a century ago may not have read any better than their present-day successors, but they competed in a wholly different job market, one offering so much work for the energetic but unschooled that the country eagerly admitted boatloads of the poor from many lands to man the mills, mines, farms, and railroads.

And in 1900, proportionately as many deaf students as hearing went to college. Collegians then accounted for under 2 percent of all those enrolled in school. In 1960, deaf college students still numbered under 2 percent of all deaf students, but the hearing college population had grown year by year; one hearing student in ten was by then in college. Until 1960, only one college in the world made special provisions for the deaf, Gallaudet. Since then, a number of other institutions have developed special centers or curricula for deaf students, and by the early 1970s the percentage of all deaf students in college had tripled, to nearly 6 percent, and continued to rise, but the comparable percentage of the hearing was nearly three times as high. It is no longer true that deaf students capable of college work lack for institutions to enroll in, but the crippling effects of inadequate early education still probably keep many with adequate native intellect from acquiring the necessary skills and qualifications.

The shocking lack of educational opportunity is in part to blame for the dismal vocational prospects now facing many older deaf Americans. As the labor force shifted away from production and toward management, services, and high technology, the deaf, until very recently, had few chances to get the requisite advanced training, even though a number of expanding fields fall well within their ability to communicate. The booming health care sector, for example, includes a number of technical specialties that require little oral communication but offer good pay and excellent growth and security. Laboratories, pharmacies, and X-ray services already employ some. Deaf people have successfully colonized the computer field, which also makes low oral demands, and could probably do the same in accounting and other specialized business fields. What has been lacking is not ability or willingness to work, but rather knowledge that such career areas exist and training to prepare for entering them. And most glaringly of all, the willingness of the hearing to give ability a chance.

Even despite a rapid, federally funded expansion of higher education for the deaf in the 1960s and 1970s, some observers worry that existing facilities—which now include the National Technical Institute for the Deaf at Rochester, New York; programs at California State University at Northridge; and regional junior college centers at New Orleans, St. Paul, and Seattle; as well as scores of smaller programs—will not be able to accommodate the huge bulge of "rubella babies" (born deaf during the epidemic of 1963–65) as they move into early adulthood.

Nor is it clear that improvements in educational possibilities will substantially improve the lot of probably the most deprived segments of the deaf population, the nonwhite. In racial distinctions, as in other features, the deaf community mirrors American society. Like the rest of us, deaf Americans divide along racial lines socially, economically, and to some extent culturally. In southern and border states sign language traditionally appeared in both white and black dialects—a division fostered and maintained by racially segregated state schools. The black deaf carry the dual burden of deafness and blackness and suffer the predictable economic consequences—more unemployment, poorer education, lower pay, less security, less skilled work than the white deaf. Carolyn McCaskill, a Gallaudet graduate who was among the first black children to integrate the white campus of the Alabama School for the Deaf, recalls, "At the black school for the deaf they never expected us to learn anything. I noticed that the black deaf who left school always ended up getting a job in a factory, working with machines, or as a maid," while the white school offered academic preparation. "I knew that some of the black students had the ability to do better than that, but they went along, saying that blacks are dumb, that they can't learn. I decided I was going to have to work harder than anyone else."

Despite the many problems they face throughout their lives, Americans deaf from an early age appear to enjoy reasonably good health. The National Fraternal Society of the Deaf, an insurance company established by deaf people denied coverage by ordinary insurers, enjoys a better experience on its life policies than an average of twenty-five companies serving the general population, Schein and Delk report. Whether this represents a shrewder selection of risks or a truly lower mortality rate is not clear, nor is it known how representative the "Frat's" 12,000 policyholders are of the deaf population at large. But these figures certainly indicate no propensity to premature death. Deaf drivers, incidentally, rack up automobile accidents at only half the rate of the hearing drivers with whom they share the roads. Why should they do so much better than the rest of us, "normal" and at least as well endowed? Perhaps they approach driving as many approach life in hearing society generally: with patience, with caution, with alertness and attention to detail. And with the knowledge that the road, like much of the rest of life among us, is inhospitable and even perilous.

CHAPTER 3

What Is Hearing Loss?

People may to some extent choose how and with whom they communicate, and even, arguably, how well they use what hearing they have. But no one chooses how well his body handles sound waves. This depends on the functioning of a system of tiny, highly specialized, and incompletely understood organs. Different parts of the system control different parts of the process. Different sorts of malfunctions thus produce different sorts of problems. And different kinds of hearing losses have different ramifications for man as a communicating being.

No one thinks about hearing until something goes wrong with it. We don't wonder that we should hear any more than we marvel that the sun will rise tomorrow. Only when ears go awry do we notice that they work as elegantly and as mysteriously as the heavenly bodies.

Nor do we often question the effects of hearing on our lives, any more than we ponder those of gravity. Hearing, however, binds us into our human orbits as surely as gravity holds the planets in theirs. It is absolutely basic to normal human consciousness, and all human cultures are built on that fact. In a world without sound, what's missing is not only birdsong, traffic noise, thunder, radio. What's missing is the knack that makes most human communication possible: the ability to process speech sounds and to learn spoken language. Other animals may hear more acutely or in a wider range than we do, but no other creature has mastered this secret; no other animal, therefore, has anything like the elaborate cultural baggage we have accumulated over our career as a species.

Hearing, quite simply, ties the individual listener or speaker into the web of human communication. A mishap to one or two tiny bones, therefore, or a malfunction in a microscopic fiber, or a malformation of an infinitesimal membrane can spell calamity not only for the organism as a processor of auditory signals but also for the person as a social and cultural being. "Communication" and "community" arise from the same Latin word. Few things so easily remove a person from the normal life of society as a loss of hearing. The person who cannot hear is a permanent foreigner in the country of speech.

Essentially, the ear is a mechanism for transforming energy in the form of oscillating air waves into energy in the form of electrical impulses that can be processed by the nervous system. The mechanisms accomplishing this occupy a couple of inches on either side of the head. They represent a perfection of engineering that has defied the best abilities of science to understand, let alone to duplicate. We need to understand them in some detail if we are to understand the human effects of hearing loss.

The ear consists of three basic parts, known, not surprisingly, as the outer ear, the middle ear, and the inner ear. The outer ear is both the most obvious and the least important, consisting of the parts we can see, the protuberance used to support eyeglasses and earrings, and the canal that leads from it into the head. The external part (the auricle or pinna) has very little to do with hearing, or, indeed, with anything else. In some other species it serves useful functions: pivoting like a radar bowl to gather sound, pinpointing the exact direction of a sound by scanning to find where the signal seems strongest, snapping shut to protect the organs inside. But if our ancestors ever had those capacities, they lost them long ago. Our auricle serves merely as a shallow funnel directing sound inside.

The ear canal is an empty oval passage leading to the real working parts of the middle ear, which begins at the eardrum. Stretched across the opening of a cavity filled with air, the so-called tympanic membrane is concave, rather than flat, and points toward the center of the head. Behind it, in the bone-girded chamber of the middle ear, are three tiny bones (ossicles), the hammer (malleus), anvil (incus), and stirrup (stapes), each whimsically named for its shape. They fit one into the other to form a well-articulated but flexible chain of independently moving parts.

The base of the stirrup fits into the oval window in the side of a membrane that encloses the organs of the inner ear. Unlike the middle ear, this innermost portion is filled with fluid. It is cradled within an elaborate construction of passages and cavities carved from the temporal bone. These canals, the bony labyrinth, guard a most extraordinarily delicate mechanism known as the membranous labyrinth. A sealed container of fluids and sense organs, it fits loosely inside the bony passages. Its central portion, called the vestibule, gives access to two adjacent areas, the snail-shaped cochlea and the cluster of three semicircular canals set at right angles to one another. Within these tiny organs sit the sensors for several of our important space senses. The cochlea detects sound; the semicircular canals, body orientation; and the vestibule, gravity and change of motion. Because the sources of such seemingly different senses lie so close together, a problem attacking one might attack others as well. Hearing losses often go along with problems of balance or orientation. Even a cold or earache can cause dizziness, and a major hearing loss often means a complete deadening of the sense of balance. Deaf people who lost both hearing and balance to meningitis, for example, have served as subjects in centrifuge studies of weightlessness because they can tolerate motion unbearable to those with inner ears intact. Within the cochlea, the perception of hearing depends on the organ of Corti, which lines the snail shell and supports a carpet of tiny hairlike sensor cells. These connect to nerve fibers that carry the impulses to the brain via the VIIIth cranial nerve.

Sound comes to us as air waves caused by the vibration of some sound-producing body. This circular definition means to indicate that the vibrations we hear differ from other similar ones (such as ultrasonic) merely in the fact that they lie in the range that the human hearing apparatus can perceive. Our hearing, rather than their own nature, defines them as sound.

Most solids, when set abruptly in motion, will vibrate and disturb the surrounding air. The molecules of the vibrating body strike those of the nearby air and they too jostle around and bump into the molecules next to them, and so on across a considerable space. We might picture a large, tightly packed crowd, say New Year's Eve at Times Square, and imagine that some people at one end of the crowd abruptly push those standing nearby. This is how the air molecules act. Each person lurches or tumbles into his neighbors, knocking them, in turn, into others farther along. No person (or molecule) moves very far, but the original "push" can travel a long way.

In short, a vibrating object emits a sound wave. When the waves reach the ear they pass down the canal to the drum, which begins to vibrate as well, and thus passes the vibration along the three bones, to the oval window. The ossicles narrow the wave's width somewhat, but their lever action increases its force. At the oval window the foot of the stapes transfers the vibration to the fluid of the inner ear, which also begins to vibrate in sympathy. The energy that began as waves in the air is now waves in fluid; very shortly the inner ear will be able to perceive it. The wave sweeps through the cochlea, and the tiny hair cells, jostling and bending as it passes, like bathers in the surf, fire signals that travel along the auditory nerve to the brain. There, by some process as mysterious as hearing itself, electrical impulses become the sensation of sound.

The sensor cells can also pick up vibrations transmitted by the bones of the head. This is why your own voice always sounds strange to you in a recording; the recorder "hears" only sound waves in the air, but you are used to hearing, in addition, the vibration of your own skull. This peculiarity, in fact, permits an excellent test for the location of hearing loss. If you hear bone vibrations no better than air vibrations, then both types are getting through and the fault lies in the perceptive mechanism. But if you hear bone vibrations markedly better than those in the air, then the cochlea and nerves are intact and the problem is in the middle ear.

We hear as we do because the ear is designed to preserve,

transmit, and perceive two features of sound waves, intensity and frequency. Intensity is the energy driving the waves, the pressure with which they strike and pass into the ear. This we perceive as degree of loudness. Frequency has to do with the shape of the waves, how often they come, and thus whether they are large or small, jagged or smooth, simple or complex. We perceive this as pitch and as related qualities such as timbre.

Experts thus talk in terms of two basic measures of waves, one of their strength and one of their height. The bel, a unit of pressure or intensity, quantifies the force of the vibrating air molecules as they move back and forth, or, in other words, the amount of energy carried by the wave. That is to say, are the people in the crowd lightly bumping or wildly shoving? The hertz, or number of cycles per second, is a unit of frequency; it measures how long the wave takes to complete a single vibration. Does a member of the crowd strike his neighbor once a second or once a minute? The hertz is a straightforward arithmetic measure. Each time the wave completes a cycle, or each time the vibrating molecules return to their starting place, we count one. We total the number of cycles occurring in a typical second and translate that directly into number of hertz, and thus can describe the wave in terms of its rate of motion.

The bel, however, because of the magnitudes involved, is rather more complicated. To construct it (named, incidentally, after Alexander Graham Bell), we can begin with a more familiar unit of pressure, the watt, which measures the power of a vibrating sound wave in much the same way as we measure the power of an alternating electric current. Thus, the very faintest 1,000 Hz sound that a person with normal hearing is likely to hear probably strikes the ear with a power of about 0.000,000,000,000,000,000,1 watt.[1]

This number may be very exact, but it is scarcely very useful, and the range of values that a measure of loudness must cover is huge. The loudest sound that a normal ear can tolerate without discomfort packs about 1,000,000,000,000 times the power of the softest one it can perceive. Clearly, something must be done about the zeros.

Instead of struggling with an arithmetic scale, therefore, acoustic specialists use a logarithmic scale to base 10. This means they count not individual units but powers of 10 (in other words, they count the zeros). If we know, for example, that a whisper is 1,000 times as powerful as that preposterous number representing the normal threshold of hearing (the quietest sound we can hear), we can count the zeros and say that it is 10^3 times as powerful. In the system of measurement used worldwide to describe loudness, that whisper is 3 bels louder than threshold. To make the scale more flexible scientists divide the bel itself into ten smaller parts, known as decibels (or dB). One decibel, incidentally, represents approximately the smallest difference of loudness the human ear can perceive in the speech range.

The decibel gives us a simple means of handling measures of loudness. Normal threshold of hearing is called 0 dB. Our whisper, 1,000 times louder, registers at 30. A normal conversational tone, 1,000,000 or 10^6 times louder at a distance of three feet, can easily be recorded at 60 dB; a loud shout, 1,000,000,000 times louder, becomes 90 dB; and the point where sound starts to be uncomfortable to the normal ear, 1,000,000,000,000 times louder, is none other than 120 dB.

Now we can make a picture of what the normally hearing hear and what those with impaired hearing do not. As we have seen, the range of the normal ear extends in loudness from 0 dB (at this point a normal young adult will be able to hear a sound 50 percent of the time) to 130 dB, where sound actually becomes painful, and beyond. This spread of useful loudness (called the dynamic range), extends from the threshold of hearing to the threshold of discomfort. Hearing threshold, by the way, does not correspond to the same physical pressure at all frequencies, and tends to be higher, in physical terms, outside the zone of frequencies involved in speech. In other words, evolution has made our ears most sensitive to the frequencies of the human voice.

But we still hear a wide range of frequencies. The lowest piano note is about 30 Hz, and human hearing extends down to about 20 Hz, where true audition gives way to the perception of vibration. The piano hits its highest key at 4,096 Hz, but human hearing extends on and on into the range of 20,000 Hz, where we can perceive a faint hissing before sound passes into ultrasonics.

But all the segments of that enormous range are not equally important. To do its major work, which is hearing the human voice, the ear ought to register sounds from a bit below 200 Hz to a bit above 4,000. (This, by the way, is the range of the telephone.) And it must be able to perceive those frequencies when they are not much louder than 60 dB. To understand conversation normally, not even the whole range is absolutely necessary, and hearing that is somewhat less acute will do. Human beings have, in fact, vastly more hearing than they need for ordinary purposes.

If you could hear nothing softer than 40 dB, you could still catch a lot of speech, but at three feet it would sound like a loud whisper. If you heard nothing less than 70 dB, on the other hand, you would miss nearly all conversation but could still be able to get a certain amount of normal shouting and most of the speaking done very close to your ear (both of these would sound very faint). But if your threshold stood at 90 dB, which is to say that a sound must be 90 dB loud before you could even faintly perceive it, you would miss everything the human voice is likely to produce, as well as almost every other sound that has meaning in human culture. These examples, of course, provide only a very rough guide to the possibilities of understanding. The loudness of speech varies over a range of 30 to 40 dB, in part because the various sounds composing speech have their own characteristic loudnesses. Shouting merely increases the size of the range because the soft sounds stay soft and only the loud ones get louder.

The jargon of the hearing business describes hearing loss in terms of the difference between an individual's hearing threshold and that taken as normal. A person who begins to hear faintly at 40 dB, for example, is said to have a 40 dB loss. But most people with impaired hearing, and even most who hear normally, do not hear identically at all frequencies. The sensory cells lining the cochlea are "tuned" to different frequencies. The lowest sounds register at the apex, or the innermost point of the coil, and those at the base, or mouth of the shell, pick up the highest. All along the coil's length, different cells register sounds of their own characteristic frequencies. A condition that damages some cells may not damage all, so people with defective hearing can often hear better at some frequencies than at others.

In constructing a picture of a person's hearing ability, therefore, an audiologist tests each ear separately for threshold of hearing using pure tones of several customary frequencies. The audiologist would have you listen to a number of tones, varying their loudness to find the faintest you could hear at 125; 250; 500; 1,000; 2,000; 4,000; and 8,000 Hz. Then she would plot these values on a chart (or audiogram) whose horizontal axis is frequency in Hz and whose vertical is loudness in dB. Connecting the points produces a line that defines the person's threshold. Averaging the values in the speech range produces a convenient shorthand. Thus, if your right ear shows an average threshold of 60 dB and your left shows 75, you are said to have a 60 dB loss in the better ear.

The average, of course, is as misleading as it is handy. It tells nothing of the contours it represents. That 60 dB loss, for example, might mean that the threshold is exactly 60 at every frequency tested or that it varies from 20 to 90 or below. (Charts generally end at 110 or 120 dB.) The same average may hide the fact that one person hears fairly well in the higher frequencies while another has all hearing concentrated near the bottom of the range. For even greater convenience (but even less precision), custom groups hearing losses into five classes that theoretically indicate the functional level of the hearing that remains. In the frequency range of 500 to 2,000 Hz, thresholds of hearing from 0 to 20 or 25 dB represent normal hearing. Thresholds between 25 and 40 dB show mild loss; ordinary conversation may present annoying, but not serious, problems. Between 40 and 55 dB, hearing loss is considered moderate, and problems increase but generally are not disabling. The moderately severe category extends from about 55 to 70 or 75, and unaided reception of ordinary speech is now problematic. By the time a hearing loss enters the severe range, between 75 and 90, understanding speech, or even loud shouting, has become a very considerable difficulty. And the person with a profound hearing loss, with a threshold at 90 or 95, has difficulty hearing nearly all the sounds of the ordinary human environment.

Impaired hearing, however, can involve more than mere loudness. The ear's parts have highly specialized functions; different malfunctions, therefore, have different effects. The two great classes of problems parallel the two main functional parts of the ear. A malfunction in the outer or middle ear hampers the transmission of sound, and causes a conductive hearing loss. Sometimes no more than an obstruction of the outer ear, such as an accumulation of wax, is at fault; or it may be something more serious, like a defect in the middle ear caused by fluid from infections or the loss of free movement of the ossicles. The latter commonly results from the disease called otosclerosis, which affected Nanette Fabray.

Conductive problems formerly posed very serious threats, but most now either respond to treatment or simply do not occur. Antibiotics prevent the continuous, damaging infections of the inner ear and the dreaded involvement of the nearby mastoid bones, conditions that blighted childhood only decades ago. People born as late as the early 1940s lost their entire middle ear when the infected bones were surgically removed. The alternative was allowing the infection to reach the brain. New techniques now also permit surgeons to free or reconstruct the moving parts of the otosclerotic middle ear, with nearly complete restoration of hearing in nearly all cases. A riskier and less successful operation called fenestration, which opens a new window in the cochlea, was the rule until the surgeon Samuel Rosen accidentally rediscovered in 1952 a technique used in the nineteenth century and then forgotten. His patient had already received local anesthesia and was waiting for Rosen to finish final preparations for a fenestration. But suddenly, startlingly, he heard, loud and clear. The astounded physician had inadvertently knocked the stapes loose, restoring function to the middle ear. There was now no need to open a new window to let sound detour around the embedded bone. Gradually other surgeons began doing on purpose what Rosen had done by accident, and they have further refined the technique to include inserting artificial ossicles where necessary. Nanette Fabray says she owes her new excellent hearing to "a head full of wires."

Conductive losses involve mechanical failure to transmit sound. We perceive them essentially as a decrease in loudness. Simple amplification often does the trick in these cases. Little of the disabling hearing loss in this country, therefore, is purely conductive.

The same cannot be said, unfortunately, for the results of malfunctions further down the line. Problems in the organs of perception, the cochlea and the auditory nerve, produce perceptive or sensory-neural losses, both more complex and far less tractable. Science as yet knows no way to repair nerve tissue, so damage to the delicate sensor cells or to the nerve itself remains beyond human help. Attempts to make an artificial cochlea have so far produced only rudimentary substitutes that sometimes restore a crude awareness of sound, but nothing like the awesome subtlety and precision of genuine hearing.

Beyond this, amplification generally can correct sensory-neural losses only partially, if at all. Very often damage to the cochlea is uneven; some parts end up hearing better than others. The perceived signal is thus not only too soft; it is also distorted. Amplifying a badly distorted signal that lacks some important components is probably better than nothing, but still far from satisfactory. The hard-of-hearing author Richard Rosenthal likens a conductive loss to a radio with the volume turned down; making it louder solves the problem. But a sensory-neural loss, he writes, is like listening to a station poorly tuned in. The signal comes through garbled and muffled and hard to understand; raising the volume only delivers a louder garbled signal.

In any case, hearing aids, unlike eyeglasses, rarely offer anything like total correction and even the best of them may introduce some distortion of their own. Many damaged ears, furthermore, can't take full advantage of the amplification now available. The dynamic range of the normal ear, the spread of loudness it can handle, extends over more than 100 decibels. Especially in sensory-neural loss, however, the dynamic range may shrink drastically. Profound losses often require amplification to 90 dB or more just to bring sounds to the barest glimmer of consciousness, but the damaged ear may be too sensitive to pain to tolerate anything so loud. To make matters worse, people with sensory-neural losses may suffer from an abnormal increase in the sensation of loudness, the loudness recruitment phenomenon; this makes a small rise in intensity seem unduly large. And if a person hears markedly better at some frequencies than at others, the sounds at the strong frequencies may mask those at the weak unless the aid can be adjusted to account for this. Some sounds come through clearly while others vanish. Speech becomes a shifting code with half the letters missing. Sadly, fitting hearing aids is more high-level guesswork than exact science.

Nor do available testing methods give all the help one might wish. The standard audiogram involves listening for selected pure tones, but tells nothing about the ability to hear frequencies not tested or to perceive other types of tones; most importantly, it tells nothing about the potential for processing speech. Tests for speech comprehension and discrimination do exist, but they generally presuppose an *understanding* of speech, and so are not suitable for small children and many of the profoundly deaf. Other, more sophisticated electronic tests exist, but they are expensive, complicated, and not universally available.

It all comes down to the distressing fact that many people do not know exactly what or how bad their problem is or what can best be done about it. They and their families must make do with best guesses. Many, many people now profit from hearing aids, and probably a good many more could if they obtained even the tests readily available. Modern technology includes sophisticated electronic techniques to help mold the amplification to the wearer's known needs. Peaks of loudness can be "clipped" at appropriate frequencies; FM systems can amplify selected voices over the background noise; masking of weak frequencies by strong ones can sometimes be overcome. Nonetheless, the hearing aid often presents only a partial solution.

But still, we probably ought to marvel that so few rather than so many people have trouble hearing. We live surrounded by dangers. Countless different things go wrong with the hearing because many different causes are at work. Damage can occur at any stage of life from conception to old age, with a staggering array of microbes and mishaps to blame. A good deal of very serious hearing loss is congenital, arising perhaps from one of sixty different known types of dominant or recessive hereditary deafness. Non-hereditary causes of congenital loss include maternal infections during pregnancy, especially viral diseases. The German measles (rubella) epidemic of 1963–65 more than doubled the number of profoundly deaf children born during those years. Mothers who suffer from certain nutritional deficiencies, such as diabetes and beriberi, or who take certain drugs such as streptomycin or quinine, also risk having their babies born deaf. Toxemia of pregnancy can have the same result.

Birth itself presents many perils. Certain kinds of perinatal injuries, as well as Rh incompatibility and prematurity, are also associated with high incidence of hearing problems. Then after a child is safely born, he can fall victim throughout life to perhaps unsuspected hereditary problems, which might appear in childhood, adolescence, or adulthood; otosclerosis, for example, causes a gradual deterioration leading to notable losses in early adulthood. Bacterial and viral diseases lie in wait: mumps and measles in rare cases cause hearing loss; meningitis not infrequently attacks the lining of the auditory nerve, with resulting near-total deafness. Even the common herpes virus—the cold-sore germ—can attack the inner ear. The garden variety earache, if recurrent and unchecked, may ultimately destroy the hearing by damaging the middle ear or destroying the inner ear. Antibiotics have almost eliminated this threat, but they themselves present a new and terrible peril. The so-called ototoxic drugs—streptomycin, neomycin, and kanamycin—have caused sudden and profound sensory-neural deafness in a significant number of cases by destroying the cochlea's hair cells. All sorts of accidents can also damage the ear; where unruly horses once cracked skulls, crashing cars now do the job. The lower skull fracture common to crash victims without head restraints has damaged many middle and inner ears beyond repair.

To make matters worse, other abnormalities accompany many cases of early deafness. The rubella virus that crosses the placental boundary and attacks the developing cochlea can and often does kill the growing cells of eyes and brains too. Deaf-born children are four times likelier than the normally hearing to have been premature; why this should be is not clearly understood, but possibilities include nervous system damage, perhaps from lack of oxygen or cerebral hemorrhage. These also obviously pose a threat to the vision, heart, and central nervous system. Meningitis, an inflammation of the membranes surrounding the brain and spinal cord, can cause blindness, mental retardation, and paralysis in addition to hearing loss.

Genetic causes, on the other hand, usually mean a "cleaner" case, a person who is deaf but otherwise completely normal.

Sometimes, however, genetic deafness appears as part of a flashy syndrome. Waardenburg's, for example, frequently combines perceptive deafness with abnormalities of coloring: a white forelock, eyes of different colors, dappled skin. The body's pigment and the cochlea's neural components arise from the same portion of the embryo, possibly because hearing and coloration served the same protective function in our ancient evolutionary past. At any rate, damage to both apparently occurs quite early in the embryonic career. The terrible hereditary Usher's syndrome also involves pigment, which deposits abnormally in the eye, stealing sight from a person already profoundly deaf from birth. The deformities accompanying the Klippel-Feil syndrome concentrate in the neck, which may be very short or altogether absent, lack mobility, and be covered with hair. The Treacher-Collins syndrome involves malformations of the lower face, the lower eyelids, and the ears.

Despite the vast profusion of known causes of hearing impairment, however, diagnosing particular cases remains maddeningly haphazard. Through more than a hundred years, up to very recent decades, the single most common cause cited by Americans with hearing loss was "unknown." Even now as many as 25 to 30 percent say they don't know the cause of their loss.

Science—or its rapid advance—is partly to blame. Maternal rubella's connection with deafness was established only in 1944; Waardenburg's syndrome was first reported only in 1951. Year by year, new causes come to light, but this gives little help in pinning a particular cause to a particular case. If the cause arose during pregnancy, for example, the mother's symptoms may be extremely subtle; rubella and other infections can pass totally unnoticed. An estimated half of early deafness is genetic, and of that, perhaps 90 percent is recessive. These genes are widely dispersed; possibly one person in ten carries one or more. But because so many different kinds exist, and because recessive traits generally show only when both parents transmit the same gene, many generations can pass without a case of deafness in an affected family. Completely unaware we might carry a gene for deafness, we naturally fail to identify its result as hereditary.

But the trauma of discovering a child's deafness often means an equally traumatic hunt for a culprit. Parents often can't pin down any likely incident during pregnancy and childbirth, but their guilt—their need not to have even inadvertently hurt their child—may suggest factors over which they have no control: diseases, accidents, fevers, falls. Experts, when stymied, may take the easy way out and pronounce a case genetic. This sounds scientific and means no one is to blame. Exact time of onset gives important clues to the cause, but is often impossible to know exactly. A bitter and frustrating search for a reason ends in a best guess as often as in firm knowledge.

Nevertheless, some definite trends are obvious, and these are the ironic fallout from medical progress. A hundred years ago well over half of the hearing-impaired children in this country lost their hearing after birth; in technical language, they were adventitiously deaf. Childhood diseases long since conquered, along with ear infections, took this sorry toll. Among adults, otosclerosis, blamed for half of all conductive deafness, responded consistently to no effective and safe treatment until the development of the stapedectomy operation in the 1950s.

It is a bitter irony that science now permits, or even produces, a population with very different and more difficult problems than those common fifty or even thirty years ago. Today, antibiotics save meningitis victims who would formerly have died. The drugs can generally halt the infection, but often not until it does serious damage. Many of today's meningitics are two or younger. One Maryland mother remembers November 22 not as the day President Kennedy died, but as the day she knew that meningitis had left her one-year-old deaf. Neonatal pediatrics now saves unbelievably premature and highly defective infants who only a few years ago would have perished. Many survive to be severely handicapped. Thus, an ever rising percentage of young hearing-impaired people suffer from other serious handicaps as well. Vastly more have lost their hearing before the critical age of three or four, when true mastery of speech begins; in technical terms, they are pre-lingually rather than post-lingually deaf.

And the future promises more of the same: fewer but more seriously handicapped young deaf people, a smaller but harder to educate deaf population. The rate of genetic hearing loss should remain constant and the rate of non-genetic early loss should continue to fall. But the percentage of such people suffering multiple handicaps will grimly and inexorably rise.

For as long as Americans have collected them, statistics on the causes of hearing loss have been notoriously unreliable. One in three of Schein and Delk's informants reported illness as the cause (almost 10 percent mentioned meningitis). Congenital and hereditary causes accounted for almost 40 percent (maternal rubella alone for 10 percent). Nearly one in ten blamed accidents. But nearly a quarter of those responding fell into the category "other" or "unknown." In other words, almost one in four could give no reason for their affliction. They had suffered for years without knowing why.

If Schein and Delk had asked children instead of adults, they would have found a gigantic bulge of rubella cases—the infants of 1963–65, then in late childhood, now in their middle teens. Since the mid-1960s facilities for handicapped children have strained to serve this tragic baby boom, victims of what could well be the last great rubella epidemic in this country. The German measles vaccine that became available shortly afterward should, if widely used among small children, spare thousands of women a few days of rash and mild fever and their unborn babies a lifetime of irreparable disability.

The very large numbers of people whose hearing fails in adulthood are victims of yet another array of factors. Noise looms as a growing cause of damage, much of it involving permanent impairment of the cochlea. Industrial racket and rock music take many unsuspecting victims every year. "My hearing's not that good anymore," a young race driver said cheerfully. "I didn't wear earplugs the first couple of years." Writer Richard Rosenthal, among others, lost his hearing one afternoon on an Army rifle range. And medicine has found nothing to combat the deterioration accompanying aging or the onset of many genetic conditions.

All this might be as exotic as the epidemiology of pancreas disease were we not to a large extent what we hear. Our own voices mimic what we've listened to since infancy. Our lives are meant to echo to the voices of others. The way the ear functions, and especially the ways it malfunctions, set the psychic boundaries for countless lives. Hearing loss, at bottom, is a social disease.

CHAPTER 4

Growing Up Deaf

The distraught father struggled vainly to gain some control of his feelings. Never in his prosperous, successful life had he experienced anything like the waves of panic and despair, bitterness and impotence, that now broke over him. He stared, speechless, at the woman who had just pronounced a death sentence on the baby daughter of his dreams. For her part, the woman regarded him calmly, armored against emotion by her professional composure, her detached, impersonal compassion. "Yes," she repeated, as if they had not heard, although her words still thundered in the man's mind and had instantly turned his wife, seated next to him with the child in her lap, to stone.

"I'm afraid there's no doubt. She is profoundly deaf," the woman said. She idly tapped the folder on the desk before her, as if summoning the prestige of her famous clinic's name.

Still the parents found no words, and the woman, a prominent audiologist, continued with the gentle briskness of the experienced imparter of calamity. "As soon as we can, we ought to see about hearing aids, and then about some plans for her education."

"But—but—" At last the father had found his voice, and now the turmoil of his mind and heart forced itself into words. "But where will she ever find a nice Jewish boy to marry her!" he exclaimed.

Tolstoy was wrong about unhappy families, at least about those whose problems stem from the deafness of a child. Many, perhaps most, of them are unhappy in the same way. The father may have spoken a line out of vaudeville, but he meant to express his darkest anguish for the future of his beloved baby. He asked the question that haunts the minds of many parents of deaf children: "How will she or he become a reasonable adult, a member of the grownup world? How will she get along when I can no longer take care of her? Does she have any chance for happiness?"

Demography gives part of the reason for their fear and distress. In nine cases out of ten, a deaf child is born to two hearing parents, that is to say, to people who know nothing about deafness or deaf people. They might think perhaps of some sour old relation muttering and complaining, or of some obsequious vendor of little oddments they once saw on the street. The phrase "deaf and dumb" probably pounds in their brains. But rarely have they any knowledge, experience, or acquaintances to tell them what the child's impairment might really mean.

"The crisis of the deaf child occurs within the family rather than within the child itself," writes social worker Gill Rimmer.[1] "The greatest burden of the small deaf child is the emotional disturbance of his parents," concurs psychologist Edna Levine.[2] And truly, the discovery and confirmation that a young child is deaf lives in the memory of many parents as a time of emotional devastation.

This country has no general or routine screening of infants' hearing, not even of those babies at high risk because of known conditions. Knowledgeable parents of such children may be alert for hidden defects, but the average person with a new baby in the house has no thought of hearing loss in his mind. Sometimes an observant mother or father feels a vague uneasiness, a dim awareness that something is wrong. She or he might try homemade tests, which may or may not allay the fears, but even a response (possibly by perceiving vibrations) to slamming doors or loud footsteps or clanging pots says nothing about the ability to perceive and process the sounds the baby most needs to hear, those of speech. Often a particular incident crystallizes months of suspicions: "He didn't hear me when I came into the room and called his name." "The fireworks were booming but he didn't seem to hear." "We were stuck in a traffic jam and the cars all around us were honking, but she slept right through it." And often, the child simply fails to develop speech when he should.

So one parent or the other gingerly, painfully, raises the issue, only to discover that both had suspected separately for some time but had kept silent to spare the other's feelings or to preserve the illusion that it might be only imagination.

Then it is off to the baby's doctor, a worthy but overworked individual who usually has far too much experience with overanxious parents and far too little with deaf babies. Congenital deafness occurs once in a thousand births; even quite experienced pediatricians may never have seen a case. The first counsel is likely to be for patience, that the baby will grow out of it, that late talking is nothing to worry about, and that one shouldn't take comparisons with friends' children too seriously. The message comes through that Baby is fine but Mother may be neurotic and overprotective rather than observant and justifiably worried. So the parents go home confused and intimidated by advice that violates their instincts. Their frustration is far from rare. One study found that half the parents of children at the California School for the Deaf had been told by doctors not to worry, that everything was all right.

But the truth doesn't go away. Soon or late, parents press to find an answer. Mixed and painful emotions spur them on: hope that someone will convincingly prove that it isn't so, desire for the relief of knowing the worst at last, longing to find a cure for the child's differentness. And, tragically, those consulted may not agree. Mary, mother of a deaf son now in young manhood, describes nightmarish years while experts of various disciplines debated whether the boy was deaf or retarded or aphasic or autistic. "Was I supposed to be happy that he was maybe autistic but not deaf?" she asks. "Or maybe deaf but not autistic?" And she believes that the strain of this time opened fissures between herself and her husband that led to their divorce some years later.

"We didn't grieve together," she recalls. "We each reacted in a way that tended to shut the other out."

Ironically, the time of uncertainty may be especially trying for families of children with milder losses. The signs are subtler and seem to point in more directions. The child may develop some speech, albeit defectively. He may attend to some things said to him but not to others. More often the experts call him slow, ornery, inattentive, disobedient, when his real problem is that he cannot hear reliably.

Finally, however, a child's hearing loss is determined beyond doubt, and the real heartache begins. Here the centuries-old communications war begins to take its most grievous toll. It is now generally accepted practice that children known to have seriously defective hearing receive hearing aids as early as possible, usually a powerful, body-worn instrument for each ear. Beyond that, however, the experts split into different theoretical camps, each armed with doctorates, learned tomes, dire warnings, technical vocabularies, and ready answers. Just as the adult world of the defectively hearing consists of oralist and manualist groups, so the child's world of deaf education is split between the philosophy of oralism and that of "total communication." Both promise success and warn against their rival.

Before the parents can absorb intellectual arguments, however, they must recover from their state of shock. Authorities on early deafness may be at daggers drawn about a great deal, but they all agree on one thing: that the parents' reaction to the discovery and their ways of coping with it are absolutely crucial for their child's future. And the parents have only their feelings to guide them through the crisis. Powerful emotions assault them— guilt, anger, frustration, disbelief, impotence, sorrow—and people stand, bend, crumble, or crack along the secret fault lines of their characters. Some—the healthiest, psychologists believe— plunge into mourning for the child of their dreams that cannot be. This is a terrible, excruciating process for many, because the child embodies the unspoken but profound hopes of his parents; he is, in the apparently limitless potential of his unformed life, an extension of themselves into the future. "The lovely, healthy hearing boy has died," writes Hans Furth, "and in their acceptance [of this fact] the parents must give birth to a lovely, healthy deaf boy."[3] The parents must, write Eugene D. Mindel and McCay Vernon, "give up the hope of having a perfect and normal child."[4] It is a grief as fierce as that after a real death; the mourner passes through the same wasteland of anger and denial before coming on the understanding that the loved one is truly deaf. But ultimately, he should arrive at a place where the loss is a simple, if painful, fact, and not an open wound.

Not all parents, however, achieve this result. Many, too many, keep a ghost child alive in their hearts. They persist in the hope that their child will cease to be deaf, or if he must be deaf, then at least that he can appear and behave normally. Consider the mother of a boy we'll call Freddy Howard, a shy but cheery eight-year-old with profound sensory-neural deafness and very little speech. Mrs. Howard is a compact and energetic woman, under five feet tall even in the high wedge shoes she habitually wears. She has the slight belligerence and abruptness of manner that very short people often have, and an underlying edginess that her small size does not contain. The boy's obvious lack of success after years of oral training has not affected her outlook. She is determined to make him speak. "He will succeed," she says. "I will make him succeed." And with the relentlessness of the mothers of child film stars and pre-teen Olympic hopefuls, she doggedly brings him to his speech lessons and doggedly arranges her household around his presumed future success. She speaks of a new hearing aid that will, she has it on good authority, shortly "revolutionize" the field, using miniaturized circuits to permit Freddy to separate voice from background noise. "And when Freddy is twenty-five," she adds, "we may have implants." This, she is sure, will repair the damage done to her boy by the scarlet fever she suffered while pregnant. And until then, she intends to follow the advice of the first audiologist she spoke to years ago: "Keep this child oral. He can make it."

Adhering to the oral philosophy does not necessarily imply rejecting the reality of a child's loss, of course, but maintaining goals contrary to experience and reason does. Teachers have told her that he needs something besides oral training, but she always manages to find another who agrees with her. Not all holdouts go to this extreme, of course, but they continue to hope, rather than merely to wish, that some miracle will commute the sentence.

Deafness is first and foremost a disability of communication; the main arena of conflict is the child's developing language. For many parents at first discovery, and some even many years after, the question is whether he will learn to talk; the more serious the loss, of course, the less the likelihood that speech will develop normally, if at all. The normal child learns to speak through an intricate process of imitation, experiment, insight, and feedback; the deaf child needs special help over a period of years to achieve even a low level of performance. He needs skilled, painstaking instruction and enormous amounts of practice. And according to the oral point of view, he needs an oral environment.

And here the battle for the soul of the deaf child truly centers, in the decision about what kind of communication best meets his lifetime needs. Oralists have maintained at least since the time of the French Revolution that a deaf child permitted to sign early in life will not make the arduous effort to speak. For nearly all of the past century, this was the dominant philosophy of early education both here and abroad. In the mid-1960s, however, t 3 rival philosophy of manualism emerged from a long dormancy in the murky back halls of the state residential schools and found a bracing new slogan, passionate new advocates, and surprising new respectability in the guise of "total communication."

This movement claims that the best environment for the child is one where he can develop natural communication with his family by all the means at his command, and that he should not have to depend on his very weakest channel, the ears. In practice this translates to encouraging parents to use sign language along with speech.

Since the late 1960s a slightly heretical branch of oralism has offered a third possibility, a manual extension of oral English called cued speech. This method promises the best of both worlds: a visual precision at least matching that of sign language plus a natural introduction to correct English. And it is supposed to be easier to learn and to teach than either traditional sign language or traditional oral methods.

So the parents, in their time of greatest vulnerability and distress, with aching hearts and swimming heads, must make a pressing and difficult decision of the utmost gravity. And they must make it quickly. Among the few things the various camps agree on is the extreme urgency of starting systematic steps to develop language. By the time the hearing-impaired child gets a definite diagnosis, he has already fallen months or years behind the normally hearing child, who starts learning language almost on the delivery table. And perhaps graver still, increasingly persuasive evidence indicates that every child has only a definite, quite brief period of maximum propensity to learn a first language. By the time a normal child has provisional mastery of syntax, about age four, his power to learn a native tongue has already begun to decline. The felt urgency thus stems as much from the inexorability of neurological development as from the enthusiasms of ideology, and this makes it all the more difficult to think clearly rather than feel acutely.

And perhaps most difficult of all, the choice often appears exclusive and final, although it need not be. Many people feel it is signs or speech, now and forever. Thus, the adviser who first gains the parents' confidence has enormous influence. A philosophy, once accepted, becomes a prism for refracting the claims of competitors. But coming to the subject as confused novices, few parents realize that the history and logistics of this conflict have permitted very few unbiased practitioners. No advice is safe and disinterested, none devoid of ideological leanings. Everyone has trained at a school or under teachers identified with one philosophy or another, and despite the efforts of a new generation of workers to strike a fairer balance, such influences prove pervasive and long-lasting. "The oral-manual controversy," says sociologist Kathryn Meadow, "is about the emotional experience of having a deaf child." It is about parents' hopes for their children and about their image of themselves.

Up to the present generation, the only people who used sign language when very small were the children of the manual deaf. They are also the only ones whose impairment did not throw the household into turmoil and their parents into anxiety and despair. Perhaps this is the reason that deaf parents seem to do better by their deaf children than hearing parents. Several factors may be at work. It's not clear why these children appear to grow up with less stress and with greater academic and social success, but it is clear that they do. The only area where deaf children of deaf parents fall measurably behind those of hearing parents is speech.

A deaf parent can experience and accept his deaf child in a natural way denied to many hearing parents, as a possibly more hopeful but nonetheless recognizable replica of himself. Because the deaf parent has achieved a certain success in his own life, at least in his own estimation, and has coped with problems and found a *modus vivendi,* he has little difficulty imagining that his child can do the same. Deafness per se holds neither mystery nor terror. Thus the parent can more easily and completely love and accept the child as an individual and as a whole and valuable person.

In addition, deaf parents communicate with their children, whatever their hearing status, in their own habitual language, most probably the language of signs. Most hearing children of deaf parents early become bilingual (or, more accurately, bimodal) for sign language and the speech current in their surrounding community. Such children can act as intermediaries for their parents at very early ages, as for example the five-year-old Nebraska farm girl who accurately placed her father's bids at livestock auctions. And for the deaf child of deaf parents, communication is no issue. He spends his infancy in the midst of language, just as in a hearing home, and thus avoids the intellectual deprivation often suffered by the deaf child of hearing parents, who may receive no understandable symbolic communication for years on end. Deaf babies raised in natively signing homes appear to develop language (sign language, that is) on the same timetable that guides the normally hearing child's progress toward speech. The signing baby attempts phrases and sentences at about the normal ages, makes the normal kind of mistakes in his "baby sign." One ten-month-old asked for "milk" —correctly squeezing his closed fist. Another signed "light"— shooting fingers out from a closed hand—when the overhead fixture came on. They may "talk" earlier because the hand's musculature comes under conscious control somewhat earlier than that of the mouth, throat, chest, and tongue.

And communication forms no emotional barrier between child and parents. Nor, indeed, does his deafness. Being the same kind of person as his chief role models, he has no early sense that his lack of hearing sets him apart from those important to him. In a strange inversion of the usual situation, a boy who had always signed and never spoken was found, upon entering a school for the deaf at age six, to hear perfectly. But he had learned his home language from his deaf parents and two congenitally deaf siblings, and had never considered that he might differ from them. He immediately entered regular school, spoke normally, and made good progress.

But in a hearing home, raising a deaf baby or toddler involves special strains. Unless child and parents communicate early, problems tend to build on themselves. The deaf baby doesn't behave as his parents had imagined he would, doesn't provide all the pleasure his mother expects in return for her efforts, doesn't respond to her as joyfully as she would like. She might feel subtly rejected and begin to reject him in turn; the important early months might not produce a growing, loving relationship.

As the child gets older, discipline and control grow into real problems. Unable to learn through hearing, deaf children often become demon explorers. The child's first attempts at speech normally coincides with his first successes at walking. The hearing parents of a hearing child (or, for that matter, the deaf parents of a deaf child), can use language as a leash to help keep the energetic toddler in check. They can answer, explain, warn, punish, correct, and command; they can both keep the child from danger and mischief and teach him what they can't allow him to learn at first hand. But for parents who have no effective communication with their young child, the toddler years mean mounting frustration and anxiety.

In its various forms, the oral philosophy recommends that children be exposed only to oral communication. Depending on the particular variety, this might mean attention to the auditory cues from hearing aids, or to speechreading, or to both. But unless the child has sufficient residual hearing and sufficiently expert training to make quick progress, communication might remain stunted and inexact for quite a long period. Susan Gregory found, in a study of English hearing-impaired children raised in hearing oral homes, that a quarter of the two- to three-and-a-half-year-olds understood no one and only half the five-year-olds understood "almost anyone." Admittedly, the majority of these children were not receiving instruction embodying the highest modern standards of skill and knowledge, but their training was probably no worse than the average available in this country. And the English children received hearing aids free from the government by right.

As the normal child approaches three or four, language takes on a new function as an expressive tool. He begins to explore his world in words as well as in action, asking questions, trying out ideas, building society's symbols into his own developing thought. And in this regard as well, Gregory's findings offer no encouragement. Fewer than half the five-year-olds used the spoken word as their main mode of communication; a third used homemade gestures (not systematic signs) and the rest a combination of gestures and speech. Over 60 percent of those between three and a half and five, when the normally hearing child speaks fluent English, used gestures to communicate. Not only do these children get by with a makeshift argot understandable, if at all, to only a small circle of family and close friends; their communication, and that of their parents, lacks what Gregory calls "subtlety and qualification." And this, she believes, is the root of many problems. The child sees "no" rather than "no, because . . ." The parent might spank rather than explain.

Deaf children receive speech messages that are incomplete, ambiguous, or both. They have to speechread or understand truncated sounds in a language they barely know (impressive accomplishments even for those fluent in the language), so they miss much of the emotional overtone and even of the factual content. Roslyn Rosen, herself deaf from childhood, has observed, "Deafness is the handicap that allows a child to see the hustle-bustle of life without permitting him access to its meaning." Gregory tells of a profoundly deaf girl who enthusiastically joined her hearing sisters in preparations for Christmas. The children happily spent days making cards, hanging decorations, wrapping packages, baking cookies, and their efforts culminated in a joyful celebration. The next day, however, and for days afterward, the deaf girl wanted to continue the fun of making cards and tying ribbons on gifts. She did not grasp, nor could she be made to understand, that the event had climaxed and was finished. She had missed its meaning.

Bad communication raises many everyday problems as well. Parents find discipline more difficult, and necessarily more physical, when rules, expectations, and exceptions cannot be explained. The deaf child may not catch that Mother says, "No, I'll do it in a few minutes," instead of just "No." In cases of danger— the child on the bicycle is the classic example—no one can shout a warning. Many parents try to keep a child from harm by keeping him from activities and explorations—from things other children his age or even younger do with no problem. And it is close to impossible to include the child in family discussions, if those discussions occur solely in speech. Even the most skilled lipreaders find hearing groups almost impossible. "My family never discussed anything important at dinner," one man bitterly recalls. "Whenever they would laugh at the table I would ask them what had happened, and they would say, 'Oh, it's not important.'"

Beyond the obvious strain of extraordinarily difficult child-rearing, a deaf child places new, unfamiliar, and very specific responsibilities on the parents, especially on the mother. Experts tend to view, or at least to present, the child's problem as essentially educational, as a matter of special teaching. And because it must start so early and run so continuously, the distraught and inexperienced mother usually finds herself cast as major teacher. In the most common oral methods, she bears the brunt of maintaining a "talking environment," and providing the needed "language experiences." She's damned if she does and damned if she doesn't. She strongly needs success to justify her enormous efforts, and must take much of the blame for any failure.

But how real is her chance of success? Is it fair to burden her with the notion that she *can* succeed? And will she know progress when she sees it? If she expects her child eventually to appear "normal," she may dismiss results that fall short of her dream but far surpass the average. Or in her desperation she may, like Mrs. Howard, cling to illusion, taking every slight, even trivial improvement as a harbinger of imminent triumph. Only if she has a highly skilled and intellectually honest teacher-therapist to guide her will she begin to develop realistic criteria for her lonely task.

A booklet distributed by the John Tracy Clinic, a world-famous Los Angeles institution providing correspondence courses for the parents of preschool hearing-impaired children who have no access to professional teaching, offers an extreme, but not atypical example of the kind of "encouragement" parents often receive. *My Child: A Picture Story about Deaf Children* states, amid inviting photos of happy tots: "His biggest difficulty is that it will be hard for him to learn to talk. It will take time, but he *will* learn to *talk*. *You can help*. Most children learn to talk by *listening*. My child will learn to talk by *lipreading*. *He will have to do his listening through his eyes*. He won't learn to talk if we rely on gestures to talk to him. *No one is totally deaf. My child will learn to talk*."

Though comforting, a number of these statements are, to put the matter politely, plain untrue. The child's biggest problem is not that he cannot talk; it is that he cannot hear. Speech has been called, only partially in jest, "a symptom of hearing"; it arises as a normal consequence of hearing. Even the most respected oral teachers, such as Daniel Ling of McGill University in Montreal, believe that a child's chance of learning to speak relates closely to his ability to hear. This is not to say that it correlates with the pure-tone audiogram; most good results involve teaching children with severe and even profound losses to hear every particle of language they are capable of and to squeeze all the information possible from everything they hear. Speaking understandably doesn't require normal or even close to normal hearing; but the worse the loss, the harder the process and the more skilled the teaching must be. And even Ling, as highly regarded as any teacher in the world, claims only about 60 percent success with his carefully selected profound-loss cases. Like others of his persuasion, Ling habitually refers to his young students as "hearing-impaired"; but some children, he admits, are plain deaf. They hear nothing, or next to nothing; nothing, at any rate, that they can use in learning to speak.

So an inexperienced parent, shouldering the weight of training a deaf child with insufficiently skilled help, and expecting that "my child *will* learn to *talk*," courts disappointment, heartbreak, recrimination, possibly lifelong guilt. The worse the child's loss, the less he responds to amplification, the less skilled his teachers, the poorer are his chances of talking understandably.

Becoming the child's teacher in addition to being his parent loads a new burden on an already strained relationship. The parents now must assure that the child advances in the curriculum, that he misses no lessons or study halls. Speech might even become a test of their love for him or his love for them. And just as normally hearing children test their powers in routine matters like toilet training and bedtime, speaking makes a dandy arena for struggles over defiance and control. Even in the most mundane terms, oral training at home makes unnatural demands; to get the most from lipreading, the child must closely study the speaker's face. So, as Mindel and Vernon say, the mother must "impose herself upon his natural play-learning patterns, often against his will."[5] She has to pull him from his play to make him watch her lips.

And even if the family opts for one of the manual communication techniques—either sign language or cued speech—laborious and unfamiliar exertions await them. First, the parents must choose a method; they must evaluate the competing claims of a number of sign languages or the system of cues; these are generally couched in a new vocabulary and dispute points of fact and interpretation quite foreign even to most highly educated Americans. Then they must learn the system and use it consistently. Claims for the amount of effort involved vary, but in no case is it negligible. Fluency in signs, like mastery of any language, requires serious application over an extended period. Extensive contact with relevant "foreigners"—fluent adult users—doesn't hurt either. Learning the essentials of cuing can take as little as two or three workdays, according to its proponents; but learning the essentials and mastering the very rapid phonetic analysis required may not be the same thing. Real fluency takes months.

The biggest hurdle facing the family that chooses signs or cues, however, is not technique but emotion. The choice means accepting the disability so completely that the family feels comfortable making an invisible condition visible; they must feel comfortable making it obvious to neighbors, strangers, casual passersby in restaurants, on beaches, in the supermarket, that something about them is not normal. And this, many believe, lies at the bottom of much anti-manual fanaticism. Hilde Schlesinger and Kathryn Meadow, a psychiatrist and a sociologist who have written extensively on early deafness, acknowledge the very practical and valid reasons for wishing a child to speak and lipread. "But the unwillingness of hearing parents and teachers to accept a second, different communicative mode is often so strong as to reflect feelings of stigma regarding differences."[6] Oralists have long argued that they proscribe manual communication for a very practical reason: that it interferes with learning oral skills. The empirical evidence on this point, Ling says, is "at best equivocal."[7] But the passion on both sides approaches that found in religious wars rather than scientific debates. Freddy Howard's mother justifies her years of struggle by stating, "I want him to have the chance to be normal." Admittedly, she is an extreme case. Freddy's older sister, a teacher of the deaf, knows signs, but the mother forbids them in the house. The strength of a religion is revealed by the obstinacy of its martyrs.

But no one can deny that signing families avoid certain kinds of troubles: the frustration and confusion of inadequate or nonexistent communication. A hearing acquaintance once remarked to the actor Bernard Bragg, a deaf-born son of deaf parents, that because his mother and father signed he probably had no problems communicating with them. "No," Bragg answered, "only the same ones you had."

For the family to take a concerted approach, the parents must agree. And here, as Mary warns, lies another minefield. The parents must agree both on their estimation of the objective situation and on their hopes for the child's future. They must master their feelings of loss and guilt and not transfer their anger either to the child or, as sometimes happens, to his hearing aid, which he then "accidentally" loses, damages, or forgets to wear. And they must not transfer it to each other.

The expectation that parents take an active and informed role in their deaf children's education is relatively recent, and it arises from good, practical reasons, but it is psychologically very onerous. Even the well-informed and well-to-do sometimes stagger under its weight. How much worse is the plight of the family without the time, money, or education to understand and master the skills expected of them. Teachers and counselors, unconscious of their own biases, may dismiss as "uninterested" those parents who fail to replicate the official image of a "committed" home. "A lot of our parents just aren't interested," said the head of a large day school serving a poor inner-city. "Do you mean they don't care about their kids," he was asked, "or that they don't have the time or money to get very involved?" He thought for a moment, obviously disturbed. "Of course they care. . . . It's just that they can't do what the children need. Maybe we ask too much." A middle-class child's deafness ranks among the greatest crises his family will ever face, but in a poorer home it must take its place among many continuing crises. Next to no money, no space, no job, or no food, no hearing seems less than immediate. Giving a young deaf child the attention he needs constitutes, in one expert's words, "a full-time career for at least four years." Many parents have too many careers already.

Dr. Robert Davila, now a nationally recognized educator, attended the California School for the Deaf in the days when the parents' responsibilities stopped at the door of the state school. "I'm glad my parents weren't expected to have anything to do with my education," he says. "If they had been, they wouldn't have been able to do it and would only have felt guilty." Mexican-American migrant farm workers, the senior Davilas struggled to provide bare necessities for their children. They had much love but no concrete resources to help the boy deafened at eight by meningitis.

Ironically though, deafness was Robert's passport out of the narrow world of his childhood. "If I hadn't been deaf, I'd probably be a farm worker today," he says. The residential school gave him his first chance to stay put long enough to discover his very considerable academic talent. Before he finished school he was serving as his parents' intermediary with the English-speaking world. This poor but gifted boy made the deaf education system work spectacularly for him. But for many others the middle-class bias of the professionals and their programs creates just one more insuperable barrier to "success."

A deaf child is not like other children in some important ways and neither, in equally important ways, is his mother like other mothers. In studies of preschool deaf children and their mothers, Schlesinger and Meadow found that many mothers were more didactic, that they intruded more in the children's play, that they were likelier to overprotect. They tried to safeguard their children by manipulating their environment more, and generally kept a closer watch. The research has also shown, however, that mothers who established good communication with their kids (in this study that meant sign language) showed more flexibility and humor, tended to butt in and boss around less and to permit more. Another study found that mothers of children who communicated poorly tended to communicate with and respond to their children less than other mothers. They had less eye contact, a measure the investigators took as a good indication of the quality of an emotional relationship.

By the time their study children reached four, Meadow and Schlesinger could discern differences related to level of communication. Those with good communication appeared happier, prouder, more creative, and more obedient, and had more fun with their mothers than those who couldn't communicate well. And by the age of three language has normally become a two-way street. This means not only that the child can understand the parent, but that the parent can understand the child in some detail.

Deaf children and their mothers are special. Their relationship is often special too. In many cases (sometimes even after the child is grown), the mother may be the *only* person who understands him. If the child signs, there may not be many other people around who do. And if he speaks, he may use a private argot. Only a very small circle may understand anything he says at all. The child perforce is tied to his mother in a way that children normally are not; her values, her ideas, her outlook can loom larger than they do for a child with access to other adults, his own friends and older children, radio and TV. "I'm a pushy mother," Freddy Howard's said. "I admit it." "Behind every oral success is an enthusiastic parent," an interviewer suggested. "No." Mrs. Howard shook her head. "I'm a pushy mother."

This often becomes severe overprotection. Quite apart from the real dangers that can befall deaf children, a hearing parent has never experienced soundlessness. She may forget that the child is otherwise unimpaired. She has no rational picture of what he may safely attempt or even what level of known risk is acceptable for fostering independence. So anything posing the least danger—and for small children that is almost everything—becomes off limits. Psychiatrist Kenneth Altshuler has observed parents who easily transform hearing loss into "almost total helplessness."[8] One mother, for example, dressed an otherwise normal deaf four-year-old every morning, while letting his two-and-a-half-year-old hearing brother dress himself.

So the family spends a deaf child's early years coming to grips with the problem and devising a way to cope. Unspoken, even unconscious values may guide the choices, pervading the parents' approach to many aspects of the child's life. One study shows, for example, that by the time their children are four, oral and manual parents diverge on something as basic as the goals of schooling. The former, writes psychologist Donald Moores, thought formal education was to "develop speech and speechreading skills." For the latter its main purpose is providing "appropriate instruction in academic skills such as reading, language, and writing."[9]

Diagnosis and beginning school are two times of crisis. Families of hearing children share the next one, the onset of adolescence. At this stormy time all the unresolved problems of early childhood, buried during the relatively placid intervening years, suddenly reappear, now sometimes grown into serious estrangement.

As with all else in the deaf child's life, these problems outwardly appear to concern communication, but they are really about identity and the child's now undeniably (and perhaps painfully) obvious future as a hearing-impaired adult. Hope for drastic improvement in basic communication skills must, if it has any rational basis, be abandoned in late childhood. The capacity for learning language (and especially a first language) declines markedly at puberty. The child without a usable communication system at eleven or twelve may never have one. But many children who still lack understandable speech (and many who have it) have learned sign language, with or without their parents' approval. Even Freddy Howard rides a school bus to his oral day classes; that he has not been "contaminated" by the signs of his companions, some of whom attend total communication classes, is inconceivable.

Like Freddy, most children with serious hearing losses go to school with others like themselves. Even most of those headed for "mainstream" programs in regular schools start in special classes learning the communication skills they will need. And it is a truth observed throughout the world, at least since biblical times, that when deaf people are together, they sign. "If you cut off our arms," a deaf man observed, "we will sign with our shoulders." If they cannot learn formal signs, they develop their own argot. The adventitiously deaf poet and author David Wright, a convinced oralist and graduate of Britain's most prominent oral school, vividly describes the "freemasonry" of his schoolmates at supper, unsupervised by hearing teachers. "A maelstrom of energy pulsat[ed] round the table," with boys "apparently engaging every limb and feature in the service of communication."[10] These boys couldn't use the standard sign language of the British deaf community, having been purposely cut off from it; but over the years this isolated country campus had developed its own body of commonly understood signs, without guidance and in secret. And each new boy was "initiated into their freemasonry."

For those who attended the traditional American state residential school, this initiation represented one of the most important steps in the development of identity. The schools have traditionally cradled deaf identity and nurtured each new generation of the deaf community. Like Wright's classmates, the established students quickly begin the new arrival's induction into sign language. Mary's adolescent son learned his first standard signs in the entrance lobby of the Lexington School in New York. The first student he met when he set foot inside began teaching him. Behind the backs and under the noses of school authorities, the children handed on their precious but forbidden "tongue."

Under the rather haphazard system general in this country until the late 1960s, the early school years were oral. Sign language emerged in the classroom only when the "slow learners" of eleven or twelve were permitted to study vocational subjects using manual communication. Until then, however, it had been the children's vernacular and, for many, their only true language. Not until the late 1960s did more than a very few parents of deaf children have any opportunity or encouragement to learn it; some schools threatened to exclude children from signing homes. Many children arrived at school without any usable communication beyond a few makeshift "home signs," usually gestures of the child's own invention. The children of deaf parents, already fluent signers, played a crucial role in this linguistic underground because they and not teachers or houseparents taught the younger children to sign. The adults either couldn't or wouldn't. School authorities saw sign not as a language but as a distasteful, illiterate patois. It took on, writes novelist Joanne Greenberg, "a part of the places where it was learned. It seemed to smell of standing water, bathroom, shame, hiddenness, and lye cleaner."[11] And for an older generation of deaf people, sign language remained something to hide from all outsiders, like poverty or madness in the family.

So the child came abruptly from his starkly uncommunicative home as young as four or five. He usually understood neither the reasons for the move nor the plans for his future; no one had the means of explaining concepts so elaborate. Deposited among strangers, kept from his family for months on end, he came to see the school as his real home and the slightly older children, rather than the hearing adults nominally in charge, as his real parents.

By the time a child reaches his teens, therefore, sign language may be a major element of his identity. And no matter where he goes to school, the relations of his agemates are becoming more subtle. Attention shifts from active play to flirtations, team sports, social status, and the telephone. As a teen-ager, he needs a peer group to identify with, a clique or gang or crowd to belong to, a model of selfhood to use in prying himself apart from his parents.

Now the difference between himself and the hearing becomes an inescapable, perhaps a dominant fact of life. And because a secure adolescent needs to be an acceptable peer to some peer group, the deaf child keenly observes how members of his "minority" fare in his particular social universe.

Schlesinger and Meadow frankly worry about the deaf child in a hearing school environment. Basing their views on studies of racial and religious minorities, they conclude that being the only or almost the only person of one's kind is bad for the developing self-image. They're not concerned with "minorities" in the word's current debased meaning, but with anyone who differs perceptibly from the mass of those around him in some socially significant way; the only white child in an otherwise all-black school or the only Christian in one predominantly Jewish suffers the same stigma of differentness. Only when a child has enough people of his own kind on hand to build a complete and "normal" social life among them will he escape minority status in this sense.

So even the oral "success" may surprise his parents when he discovers that he is, socially at least, deaf. Now the parents' original acceptance or denial of the child's deafness again arises as a crucial issue. Drawing on his experience as educational director of the Lexington School, which takes a moderate position in the oralist camp, Oscar Cohen writes: "Adolescence is a time when children are asking 'Which world?' As the child reaches out toward his adult identity, he may follow a typical teenage pattern of exploring relationships with people unlike his parents, perhaps disapproved by them."[12] For the deaf child, this may mean friendships with people markedly more "deaf" than have been welcome in his parents' home, both young people who depend mainly or exclusively on sign language and possibly adult members of the deaf community. The parents' reaction to these friendships casts the die of future relationship with the grown child.

"It is essential," Cohen writes, "that hearing parents make every effort to feel comfortable with deaf persons. Otherwise, the adolescent risks having to choose between the deaf community and the hearing world of his parents. . . . This need not be an either/or choice."[13] But only if, and it is often a very big if, the parents can reach out to the deaf community in some substantial way and show the child that the friends who embody that part of himself are acceptable and even welcome in his parents' home.

Making manual deaf people comfortable and welcome involves some basic, concrete steps. The first and most practical is learning sign language—if not enough to converse fluently (an undertaking that requires months or even years of effort), then at least enough to make social pleasantries. A second very crucial requirement, Cohen believes, is a teletypewriter (TTY) for the home so that the teen-ager can call friends without his parents' help. Then he can spend hours in gossip and speculation, like all his hearing contemporaries, and also make easy contact with a wide range of deaf families and special services. At least in this area of the deaf culture the hearing find themselves at no disadvantage; using the TTY requires only standard typing.

Cohen emphasizes that parents of adolescents can take these steps without changing the communication patterns in the family or lessening their commitment to the oral philosophy. A child's hard-won oral skills become no less valuable among hearing people because he has deaf friends in addition.

But, Cohen observes, "we see very little of this reaching out by parents, perhaps because it is an extremely uncomfortable and painful thing to do."[14] Why the pain and discomfort? Because admitting the deaf community to one's home and consciousness may mean admitting the defeat of years of hope, work, and illusion. If the parents had hoped to make the child "normal" in the hearing world, able (and, by implication, preferring) to live and function as a hearing person, then anything less, even so prodigious an accomplishment as achieving understandable speech in the face of pre-lingual profound deafness, represents at best failure and at worst ingratitude for the parents' years of struggle and effort. But experience and statistics overwhelmingly agree: it is unlikely that pre-lingually deaf children will grow into anything other than adult members of the deaf community.

And if parents understood what finding themselves as deaf people can mean to some hearing-impaired adolescents, they would think twice about condemning the impulse. One young man we'll call Steve, academically successful at a hearing high school, entered Gallaudet College and learned to his amazement that he was a deaf person. (He also learned that he could attract women and be a leader among men.) Until then, he had viewed himself as "someone with a hearing problem" but not a member of a class made distinct by their impairment. Above all, he says,

Gallaudet taught him to "accept his deafness," to ease up on himself, to assimilate hearing loss as a legitimate part of himself instead of the source of all his troubles, "as a human difference instead of a handicap to overcome." This is a crucial distinction, and the source of a growing movement for deaf pride that claims that deaf people have the right not only to be visibly deaf but to be proud of it too. But before coming to Gallaudet, Steve had known no deaf people well. But now he saw, he says, marveling at his own naïveté, "that they weren't deaf and dumb." He winces a bit as he makes this pun, so odious is the stereotype behind it. But he learned, in short, that the hated stigma he had long denied applied no more to his bright, attractive new friends, or to his teachers or the college's administrators, than it did to himself.

This confusion of identity, this misapprehension of the meaning of one's loss, worries many sensitive observers of deaf youth. Mindel and Vernon tell, for example, of asking a "profoundly deaf 10-year-old boy if he knew sign language." No, the child answered. "'That's for deaf mutes.' It is as if he regarded himself as a hearing person 'temporarily out of order' who with proper concentration on speech and speechreading would become like everyone else, like his parents' and teachers' fantasies would have him become."[15] Small deaf children who see few deaf adults often believe that they will hear when they, too, grow up.

Adolescence may bring other problems as well: struggles about competence and independence. David Wright, in his eloquent and fascinating autobiography, describes a lengthy and, for his mother, painful period as he established his right to move freely about the neighborhood and city, first on foot and then by bicycle. His technique had the directness and offhand cruelty of youth: he simply stayed away from home for longer and longer periods, leaving his mother alone to imagine the many calamities that might, but somehow never did, befall him. At last she accepted the empirical evidence of his expeditions; he always returned safely, and so he probably would in the future. In any case, she could not stop him.

But the problem of misplaced supervision can afflict deaf adolescents wherever they live. Residential schools have routinely restricted their young charges' freedom, to the great detriment of maturity and independence. Acting *in loco parentis* to students as old as twenty or twenty-one, the schools responded to youthful sexuality with regulations preposterously strict for a convent high school. Young people therefore often emerged from the schools with little or no experience in self-discipline or personal responsibility. The Model Secondary School for the Deaf in Washington, D.C., among other institutions, recognizes this problem and has developed rules and policies that administrators hope will foster self-reliance and sound judgment.

The great tasks of early adulthood, are, to paraphrase Freud, finding love and finding work—for most people, finding a mate and finding a trade. For many deaf young people, these tasks are achieved in the context of a third, finding an identity as a deaf adult. Although they marry later, on the average, than the hearing, deaf people who are going to establish their own households commonly do so in their twenties. Often this step—marrying another deaf person—solidifies their identities as deaf adults. Religious intermarriage appears somewhat more common among the deaf; the realities of deafness override what may be merely the family's preference for a particular church. Parents who rejected deaf friends usually accept a deaf son- or daughter-in-law no more easily. By marrying a person he views as his "own kind," the deaf young adult may make estrangement from his family permanent and complete. And estrangement by now can be very deep. "One of the saddest things you can see," said one knowledgeable observer, "is parents who need interpreters to talk to their own kids at their graduation from Gallaudet."

Finding work may broaden the abyss, especially if the young person falls short of his parents' vocational aspirations. Highly educated, professional parents probably suffer the greatest risk of disappointment, because their children have the least chance of maintaining the class position of their birth.

The deaf child of deaf parents, however, probably escapes this problem, just as he has probably escaped most of the problems that bedeviled the majority of his schoolmates. On many measures of achievement and adjustment, and at every age level, the deaf children of deaf parents uniformly score higher than deaf children from hearing or hard-of-hearing homes. On essentially every dimension except speech (but not speechreading) deaf children born of deaf parents and attending residential schools appear to do best.

Authorities can't agree on why this should be so, but it does appear to involve a more positive self-image than a deaf child develops in a hearing home. A deaf home presents a more emotionally natural environment to a deaf child, perhaps. One is like one's parents and can realistically aspire to grow up to be like them. Visits, parties, picnics, celebrations, the whole social life of the family involves deaf people, and thus reinforces the child's opinion that he is like the worthy people of his world in the most important ways. At home communication is "normal," in effect, if not in form—it binds the child to his family rather than cutting him off from it. The stages and transitions of his life probably don't mean severe crises for his parents. Perhaps they wished for a hearing child, but deafness is no stranger to them; the diagnosis may disappoint, but it doesn't shock. Some studies suggest, in fact, that although deaf parents may say they prefer to have a hearing child, they often feel more comfortable raising a deaf one.

They avoid the hearing parents' struggle for a *modus vivendi;* the child simply copes in the same way the parents have done. Deaf parents may want their children educated somewhat differently from themselves—more effective auditory and speech training, for example—but they can make their choices intellectually rather than emotionally.

Deaf parents sending a child to residential school do not see themselves as "institutionalizing" him, any more than an upper-class father entering a son at Choate or Andover sees himself in that light. The deaf parent is simply sending a second generation to the affectionately remembered school where he, his friends, and probably his spouse passed their young years. For the child's part, he arrives not in a strange new world but in an extension of the culture of his home, and already fluent in sign, he enjoys considerable instant prestige.

What sort of person is a deaf childhood likely to produce? Is there, as some have suggested, a "deaf personality"? Or perhaps more accurately, are there traits of personality and character that deaf people exhibit more often than hearing? If so, what are their causes and their effects?

After communication, this is perhaps the most hotly debated and emotionally charged issue in the field of hearing impairment. The whole idea of a "psychology of deafness" offends some people; studies should emphasize deaf people's normality rather than their oddness, they argue. Or attributing a "psychology" to a handicap smacks of something akin to racism, they believe; allowing any single characteristic, whether deafness or blackness or left-handedness, to override all others degrades the individuality and humanity of people who happen to have it, along with many other characteristics. But, writes McCay Vernon, "the environment is a major factor in the psychological development of all of us. . . . When environment is systematically altered in a significantly consistent way for any given group of people, these individuals will tend to be different in some shared ways from those whose environment has not been altered in this systematic manner."[16] We are, to a large extent, what our environment makes us.

Responsible modern scholars argue that a "deaf personality" arises from the specific distortions that the handicap imposes on the surroundings, not, as some earlier writers appeared to imply, as inevitable concomitants of deafness itself. This is a distinction less subtle than it seems. It is the difference between arguing, for example, that black people, should they exhibit any distinctive personality traits, do so because of the conditions of their upbringing and later lives, rather than because of any characteristics genetically associated with skin color.

What might be called the fallacy of sticky correlatives has also clouded these discussions. Even if two phenomena invariably occur together, they still may not be causally related. Thunderstorms tend to correlate closely with ice-cream sales; obviously neither causes the other but both depend on a third cause, the temperature. Thus, the observation that deaf people tend to be "immature" gives no grounds for assuming that deafness is the cause. Both features may relate to some third factor, in this case the residential school. Most deaf adults attended these schools, which have traditionally allowed little practice in independence and responsibility. So the observation could more accurately be couched: people who attend very restrictive boarding schools tend to be immature; most deaf adults attended such schools; Q.E.D.

Two basic approaches have dominated psychological studies of deafness. Some observers view personality as adaptation: how does it permit people to achieve a satisfactory adjustment to a highly unsatisfactory life situation? Others have emphasized deviation from the hearing norm: how do deaf people differ from "normals"? Deviance, writes Donald Moores, "comes to be used interchangeably with *deficiency*."[17]

From years of psychological probing emerges a mosaic of fascinating paradoxes. The deaf are said to be rigid and immature, impulsive and egocentric, cautious but lacking good internal controls, naïve about the motives of others and short on empathy. Possibly most tantalizing of all, they appear much less susceptible to obsessive and depressive ailments. In short, a childhood full of confusion, ambiguity, and isolation generally produces not a psychotic but a particular sort of eccentric.

It is an eccentricity playing variations on a single theme: bad communication. Immaturity we have already discussed. Rigidity, egocentricity, and insensitivity seem all of a piece, along with naïveté. They are the traits of a hermit, a person who lives and finds his own way all alone—whether through the wilderness of uninhabited land or of a silent childhood. They are the traits of a person unused to shading his thought for the convenience or acceptance of others, of one who has spent long and formative times in no company but his own. Internal controls also come from practice in living with others, as the child learns to sublimate his primitive rage into angry speech acceptable to those around him. Many deaf children lack expressive communication supple enough to contain even their curiosity, let alone their anger. So the latter may remain violent, physical, and unchecked, and the former may wither into immobilizing caution.

But why should such a person suffer less from depression? Some theoreticians believe that depression is at bottom also learned by living with others. It is a disorder of the superego, the internalized image of others' opinion of oneself, the deeply buried voice of the scolding parent. Anger becomes depression when the superego turns it not outward against the world but inward against the self. Alone in his private silence, the deaf child lacking good communication is immune to many of the values of society. "It is possible," Vernon speculates, "that society is unable to force upon deaf people the superego (childhood irrational conscience) which in some hearing people leads to internalization of anger and finally depression and suicide."[18] The child's developing psyche, building alone along its own plan, may end up quite original in construction. "Rigid" may be another way of saying "strong-minded." "I would speculate," writes Hans Furth, "that deaf children derive a considerable amount of ego strength from the simple fact that they are the originators and masters of their symbolic life to a much greater degree than hearing children. This theory would explain why deaf children can overcome obstacles that would be practically insurmountable for comparable hearing children."[19]

In all the ponderous and opinionated literature on the psychology of the deaf, one astonishing fact stands out beyond dispute: deaf people, on the whole, pass through radically abnormal childhoods and emerge stunningly normal adults. Whatever particular features may distinguish them in general from the hearing, it is their sheer normality, the dazzling ordinariness of their adjustment, that amazes. They are undeniably and on the whole sound, cheerful, reasonably well-balanced people who live their lives and go about their business without much more visible distress than people blessed with the faculties denied them. This is not to deny, of course, that some deaf people suffer serious emotional disturbances; but their rate of real maladjustment is not excessive, considering the rigors of their youth and the frustrations of their daily lives. They suffer schizophrenia, for example, no more often than the hearing. In general, they work, they play, they raise families, gardens, and down payments. They support their own communal institutions and participate in social life. Many pass in and out of two worlds and maintain friendships and acquaintanceships in both. In short, they get by.

But they remain at bottom people with the same needs and desires as the non-handicapped, just with fewer means of making them come true. They live lives of constant minor irritations: stupid misunderstandings; dependence on others for such routine needs as telephone messages; small, perhaps unintended daily unkindnesses by the score. The bland cheeriness of a first meeting dissolves on second look into one of the many tactics of the subordinate—like shuffling, head-bobbing, forelock-tugging, grinning—to hold the powerful at bay. But the problems lying below are no less real for being hidden.

A hearing woman once told David Denton, a founder of total communication, that she wished she had more chance to practice her new sign language, but hesitated to strike up conversations with deaf people for fear of feeling awkward. Denton pointed out a deaf woman sitting nearby. "She goes through that every day of her life," he said. "Do you really think she has feelings less sensitive than yours?"

She merely has tougher calluses around the tender parts, perhaps. Her affliction may have made her weak where hearing people are strong, but daily life has made her strong where we are weak.

This is one of the amazing achievements Furth wrote of. There are others: living a normal life without hearing; functioning as an adult despite a grievous deficit; finding a reasonably satisfying way of life, even if it does not happen to include "a nice Jewish boy," or any other parental image of happiness.

CHAPTER 5

Learning to Think

"The most important day I remember in all my life," wrote Helen Keller, "is the one on which my teacher . . . came to me."[1] As all the world knows, Anne Mansfield Sullivan brought the deaf and blind girl, at six as wild and apparently untrainable as a little forest beast, into the circle of educated humankind, even made her a celebrated prodigy.

But on the morning of Annie's arrival, and for some time afterward, Helen remained, by her own description, "dumb." She embodied both aspects of the word deaf people hate most: she had no speech and also appeared stupid. But she yearned and hungered, her autobiography recalls, for something she could not name or even frame in consciousness, for some way out of the dark silence and into the light of the mind. And then, in the celebrated moment at the pump, she found it. "Suddenly I felt a misty consciousness of something forgotten—the thrill of returning thought; and somehow the mystery of language was revealed to me."[2] Helen learned, or more accurately, suddenly *knew* without learning, that the letters Annie was spelling into one hand stood for, in some inexplicable sense *were*, the cool, running sensation she was feeling in the other. W-A-T-E-R was water. Quite simply, everything had a name.

Scientists would give a great deal to know what happened in

the space of that semicolon, but the laconic Helen reveals no more than that at one moment she did not know and at the next she did. She claims to have perceived even then that something extraordinary had happened, that nothing would ever be the same again.

Exactly what happened to Helen and exactly what it meant are questions as profound as any that can be asked about deaf or blind people or about human beings in general. She learned, or relearned, to use words as symbols, and words obviously bear some very influential and intimate relationship to thought; but exactly what that relationship might be has eluded researchers, both scientific and speculative, for centuries. That, of course, has not prevented the luxuriant growth of theory and dogma about language as it relates to the thought of the deaf. Sound answers require arduous, exacting work by absolutely first-rate minds, and the study of deafness has not, for various reasons, attracted many of them.

The hearing-impaired, and especially the pre-lingually deaf, constitute one of nature's most enthralling experiments. Helen implies that intellect has trouble developing without symbolic communication. But then, how can we explain her apparent understanding that she lacked something? Can children who know no language think logically? Is it, indeed, possible to think at all without language? And what does "language" mean in this context? For many centuries philosophy assumed it to be the common spoken form general in society. But in the seventeenth century hearing people became aware of certain deaf people who showed undeniable signs of cogitation but no hint of talk. The idea dawned that perhaps speech and language were not necessarily the same thing. Daring thinkers suggested that perhaps any grammatically organized system of symbols could be a language and that speech was merely one of the possible forms. But the confusion between language and speech is so pervasive that in 1966 when Hans Furth, one of the area's boldest and most fertile thinkers, published an influential book on the intellectual development of children who use only manual signs, he called it *Thinking Without Language*. Furth meant, of course, thinking without *verbal* language, but the distinction disappears occasionally in his discussions and frequently in the discussions of others.

That such an impression should exist, of course, is hardly mysterious. Speech dominates the general culture and hearing people take verbal ability as the measure of intelligence. How else could Helen Keller have been "dumb"? This bias robbed her and other deaf people of the chance to show their ability. Most do not speak cleverly; many don't even speak intelligibly. Deaf people's writing often has a slightly "foreign" feel—many simply don't know English perfectly. Going to school with the hearing puts them at a disadvantage. Working beside us, they often remain silent. Many lack a real mastery of reading, and therefore do not read very much. As a consequence, they may be ill-informed about many things hearing people take for granted, not very skilled at most tasks involving numbers or words. Our language is the history of popular thought; "dumb" in both its senses is the culture's traditional view of the deaf.

And yet, we have already seen enough to know that this stereotype is false. The overwhelming majority of people deaf from birth lead reasonably successful adult lives, work at moderately skilled occupations, manage some of the complexities of insurance policies, real estate contracts, form 1040; they must possess adult intellect. They act in a rational way even though many of them lack the supposed medium of rationality, a mastery of verbal language. Something is wrong.

And yet, intuition insists that society's language relates very closely to abstract thought. Helen Keller's firsthand testimony tells us the same thing. Helen, however, is not a perfect experiment. She didn't experience the birth of thought, she tells us, but its return; or, more precisely, the return of language. Her hearing loss was pre-lingual but not congenital; a fever deafened and blinded her at eighteen months, but left her, apparently, with a memory of language. (She also had some memory of sight.) She later proved to be a brilliant woman; she was probably a bright baby as well. And by eighteen months, a bright baby may not speak very clearly, but she does speak, and she understands much more than she can say. The age when Helen relearned language is also significant; she was close to six, and that is close to the age at which a bright child can begin to think abstractly. At any rate, it is well beyond the age when a child learns language as a baby does.

Furth's studies of deaf children suggest an answer. The relationship of language to thought is not constant, he suggests, either for the hearing child or for the deaf. The child's intellect grows as a young insect does. It doesn't start out a miniature version of its adult self and simply get larger as it matures; instead, it passes through a series of discrete stages, rather as a butterfly starts as a larva, then becomes a chrysalis, and finally assumes its adult shape.

Furth is a follower of the Swiss psychologist Jean Piaget, who spent half a century exploring the growth of the human mind. Piaget wondered how children learn to think and what effect the process has on the way they deal with their surroundings. The wormlike larva uses and exploits the environment very differently from the winged adult. Likewise, the infant, the toddler, the preschool youngster, the schoolchild, the adolescent each live an intellectual life of a particular kind.

Like many others, Furth views early profound deafness as a natural experiment in cognition, and he used it to test Piaget's theories. This work represented a significant departure. Until then students of the intellectual effects of deafness had concentrated on comparing deaf people's measured intelligence with hearing people's; in other words, they used what the previous chapter called the "deviance model." And it was not hard to prove those deaf from an early age deviated a good deal, both quantitatively and qualitatively. Studies in the 1930s and 1940s found substantial differences in IQ and concluded that deaf people were considerably less bright than the hearing. In the 1950s the difference appeared basically qualitative. The deaf were not seen as necessarily less intelligent, but they seemed to have intelligence of a different kind. Their thinking was more concrete, it was said, less abstract. This concreteness supposedly derived from sign language, which, unlike highly developed verbal languages, was said to be "iconic" or pictorial. Some suggested that it mimics objects rather than presents concepts; it therefore supposedly did less well at expressing abstractions. These studies pretty much assumed that speech equals adult-level language.

But the early tests given in deaf people's own language showed no difference in reasoning.

These speculations may appear to be just that—mere academic theorizing of interest to no one but a few professors. But their real importance goes far beyond theory. The deaf are a small and relatively powerless minority. What hearing people think of them—the ideas that thoughtful and informed hearing people have of their abilities—importantly influences what society permits them to attempt and achieve. The speculations of professors can translate into greater or lesser civil, social, and human rights.

Furth was among those accepting the idea that deaf people might have normal intelligence. He wanted not to measure deaf intellect so much as to examine it; that is, he hoped to find out how it worked instead of only what it produced. He gave to prelingually deaf and hearing children of various ages "thinking tasks" that Piaget had invented. These logical puzzles depend on the mind's ability to manipulate concepts. He found that when understanding did not depend on some verbal nicety, deaf children did as well as the hearing and sometimes better. He somewhat regretfully concluded that deaf children appear less adept at discovering concepts than their hearing agemates. But the upbringing of the average deaf child hardly fosters intellectual curiosity. The congenitally deaf Bernard Bragg concluded after years of teaching at a leading school for the deaf that curiosity had been systematically wrung out of youngsters from hearing homes. Unable to question during the great preschool years of "what?" and "why?" they sought answers by experiments and on-the-spot investigations. These led so often to disasters of broken crockery and angry parents that the children simply lost the habit of questioning, or perhaps formed a new one of stifling the urge to know.

But Furth's basic hypothesis stands: language is the product, not the origin, of early thought, just as Piaget said it was. At least until the age when children have traditionally entered first grade, deaf children keep pace with the normally developing mind.

Piaget's thought has only recently begun to filter into the common discourse of American upper-middlebrows, their baby-care manuals and their college texts. Many find him a difficult thinker. First, he radically opposes the psychology taught in our colleges and practiced in our laboratories for most of this century; he wants to understand the content of thinking, not to quantify behavior. Secondly, he writes in a French technical jargon of almost obstinate opacity. Books by and about him have an unmistakably European intellectual texture that many Americans find very slippery. He uses some crucial words in unfamiliar, almost startling, ways. He is not easy, but he is worth understanding in some detail because of what he indirectly tells us about deafness.

For Piaget, the mind serves the child as a means of adapting to his universe. This is possibly his key concept, and the one most vital to understanding how a deaf child can think. Almost from birth the childish intellect acts dynamically, creatively, forcefully, actively inventing the framework of its knowledge. No *tabula rasa* passively recording sensation, no trained white rat mechanically responding to stimulus, the mind from the beginning steps in and organizes what it perceives. It builds the structure of thought out of the stuff of experience. This basic idea of Piaget's has great power. We will meet it again in other places and in different forms. Essentially he compares the learner to the growing body. An organism takes in food, the image goes, and extracts from it the elements of nourishment it needs to construct itself according to an innate plan specific to the species and unique to the individual. Thus, human beings, lions, and giraffes may ingest identical elements, but they arrange them rather differently. Black people, white people, men and women may all eat the same meal, but never forget to arrange the amino acids into the right kind of person. Indeed, husbands and wives, brothers and sisters eat identical food for years on end without themselves becoming identical.

So, just as the child knows how to digest his food and use it to mature physically at a roughly predictable rate, all the while inventing an original but recognizably human person, he also knows how to take the stuff of his experience and arrange it, according to a preordained but original plan, into his own distinctive yet predictably human mind. And the intellect, like the body, grows in logically unfolding stages.

Surprising though this idea is to people who learned about

learning by running rats through mazes, Piaget's concept of thinking is more surprising still. To him thinking is one of many ways of behaving, the activity a person undertakes to organize his experience; it is not very different from (and is closely related to) motor activity in the young child. And like his motor activity, it develops by quantum leaps that separate broad levels of integration. The child wriggles on his stomach, for example, until he rather abruptly gets on his knees and crawls. Then, as abruptly, he walks. And each of these attainments takes him into a new realm of learning and exploration, a new relationship with his environment. Thus, says Piaget, the child moves through discrete stages of intellectual development, each with its own characteristic habits and opportunities. The child's thought does not advance steadily but by great intuitive leaps that represent whole new organizations of his experience and that carry him onto whole new planes.

For the first year or so, the baby lives in the sensorimotor stage of awareness. His own self is the limit of the universe, his own experience the sole means of learning. Whatever he knows— about time, space, people, cause and effect—he learns from his own senses. By the age of about one and a half, Piaget says, he has mastered the idea of "object constancy"; he knows that things separate from himself exist permanently, even when out of his sight or hearing. It is no accident that this period normally coincides with the beginnings of speech. The child simply uses speech as one of several symbolic means to express what he already knows. He starts speaking by naming things, by expressing their separateness from himself.

Much early talk is not expressive communication in the adult sense, however. The child expresses himself all right, but often not for the conscious benefit of anyone else. He often may not talk *to* other people but merely in their presence. Much of the talking aloud that strikes adults as senseless chatter is the child's way of talking to himself. He won't have the silent inner voice adults use for another four years or so. At the present stage he uses speech as one of several symbolic systems for expressing the order he is making of the world; imitation is another important one.

By the time the child enters the pre-operational period at

about two, his language is well along. Words and thoughts are quite interrelated now, but experience is still the stuff of his thinking. He has sorted out the boundaries between himself and other objects, but the world still centers on him. He still cannot think abstractly, or relate two or more variables or change the direction of his thought. He knows what he perceives, but can't manipulate what he knows about it. A child is out of the pre-operational stage, and at least seven years old, for example, before he can understand that a wide container and a narrow one hold the same amount of liquid although (or, really, because) their water levels are different. He understands cause and effect only crudely at this stage; he asks "why" to elicit a sentiment or a time connection rather than a true relationship of cause and effect. But he bursts with questions and endlessly accumulates both information and practice in acquiring it.

Even without language, Furth says, the child's mind can grow satisfactorily through this stage. Make-believe, drawings, block constructions, and playacting by little deaf children up to the age of five or six match the hearing in sophistication and daring. But although the architecture of thought is keeping pace, the child without useful communication has already begun to fall seriously behind in furnishing his mind. His problem is not lack of intelligence but a large and relentlessly growing deficit of knowledge.

The balance begins to shift significantly as the child reaches six or seven and the concrete operational stage. To understand this one must understand first that by "operation" Piaget means thinking, the mind's activity. The child can now "operate"—act logically—both on objects and events he concretely experiences and on symbols of them. He can handle several variables at once, see a situation from different angles, reason from different ends of a train of thought. And the normally hearing child has already spent years perfecting his vocabulary and syntax, so he arrives at this stage, and at school, with a precise, flexible, expandable, perfectly adapted tool all ready to use. "How," "why," and "when" start to take on new meaning; the method of living in relation to language begins to shift.

And at the age of twelve, when the capacity to learn a first verbal language has dwindled almost to nothing and the capacity to learn any language perfectly is rapidly waning, the child enters the formal operational stage, when true abstract thought begins. Now he learns to manipulate the stuff of thinking itself, to work with hypothetical situations and wholly abstract or formal considerations. And here, at last, language becomes a major means of thinking. For Piaget, Furth says, language is "a principal and preferred medium of thinking of a developed mind, of an adult mind, but not an important tool for the developing mind."[3]

If this theory is true—and it does have very important intellectual backers and considerable substantiation from physiology —then it explains much that is right with deaf adults and much that is wrong with traditional deaf education. The young child can think, reason, and learn without understanding the language of those around him. He needs to communicate with them not for the sake of his reason but for the sake of his relationships. He needs language to grasp in a factual as much as a conceptual sense what is going on around him; to begin his lifetime stock of information; and perhaps most importantly, to tie him into the values of his culture.

Indeed, at this point the society needs the child to learn its language possibly more than the child needs to learn it. Society can use his developing linguistic competence to mold his growing mind to its own purposes. Left to his own devices the child will invent his own symbolic universe. Many hearing families who reject formal signs for their deaf children nonetheless come to use arbitrary gestures of the child's invention, "home signs," as deaf people call them. Helen Keller implies, for example, that she could get across simple and concrete ideas long before she learned language. These symbols may work as well as English words or standard signs for expressing the child's thought, but they suffer two fatal flaws as communication: hardly anyone understands them, and they lead on to no accepted grammar or vocabulary. By learning or devising them the child essentially wastes precious time. They add nothing to the communication skills he ought to be building for the future. But if his environment provides no ready-made vehicle of communication, a normally intelligent deaf child plunges ahead and tries to make up his own.

The future intellectual consequences go deeper still. "Linguistic competence is rooted in the beginnings of intellectual life as an acquired symbol medium and frame of social expression,"[4] Furth writes. Just as a river will run in any channels that lie in its path, a child's developing thought will flow along the lines of any symbolic system presented at the right time of his development. But if the child must dig his own channels it is possible, even likely, that they will not replicate those of his society. This, rather than the failure to develop understandable speech, may be the greatest danger of leaving a child to his own symbolic devices. Indeed, the two dangers may be related. A child's own symbolic system, if allowed to establish itself firmly, may well interfere with attempts to learn standard languages for the rest of his life. No one can teach him English as a second language because no one understands his first "language," the symbols of his own invention, well enough to use it as a medium of instruction. Indeed, he himself may not be able to express or articulate his inner mode of thought so that anyone else can come to understand it.

This is the obverse of the self-contained personality we met in the previous chapter. A deaf child who must invent much that hearing children are taught can develop an extreme independence of mind—that "stubbornness" and "rigidity" that people talk about. Einstein, it is said, did not talk until he was three, and he is supposed to have lived quite an interesting symbolic life during those first years. Did his extraordinary ability to see relationships hidden from others, his penchant for manipulating symbols in wholly unconventional ways, come, as some have suggested, from years spent in an entertaining and quite original universe of his own?

The fact is that we know very little about how deaf people think. Furth's experiments show that deaf children arrive at the same point as the hearing in resolving a logical problem, but, because he omitted Piaget's "clinical interview," which queries the subjects on their approach, we do not know whether they travel the same path to get there.

Scattered researchers have begun to look into this question, but we have only very spotty knowledge as yet. Some hope to find out whether using gestural rather than verbal language makes any neurological difference; new knowledge about the hemispheric specialization of the brain suggests that it does. Others are groping toward an answer to so basic a question as the nature of a pre-lingually deaf person's inner "voice." Piaget believes that thought itself occurs outside consciousness, that in listening to our inner voice we eavesdrop on a report or summary rather than on thinking itself. But the inner voice obviously bears some close relationship to the framing of questions, the positing of propositions, the cataloguing of knowledge. Hearing people converse with themselves using what amounts to a silent but audible soundtrack. But what can people use who can't even imagine what listening means? They have reported a variety of alternatives. One sign language user who lost her hearing at eighteen months and now speechreads well but speaks badly says that her inner voice is a silent film. She sees signs in her mind's eye when she talks to herself. A congenitally deaf man with very poor speech but an excellent command of English semantics and syntax talks to himself in silent spoken English. That is, he feels his own speech rather than hears it, he imagines the muscles moving to form the unsaid words. Some people seem to sense signs in the same kinesthetic way or make rudimentary gestures to themselves. A man educated mainly in finger spelling checks the spelling of words that look wrong on paper by repeating them on his hands, much as a hearing person might pronounce a doubtful case to jog his memory. And some oral deaf people may use a picture of English in some way based on lipreading.

But none of this really tells us how deaf people think. Tantalizing research by R. Conrad of Oxford opens the door to their minds the tiniest crack and reveals a whole unsuspected world behind. He tested orally educated, profoundly pre-lingually deaf adults to see how they handle and remember written English. To his amazement, just about half the subjects processed it as sound and the other half as sight. Specifically, Conrad had people memorize and then reproduce written lists of letters. The mistakes they made told the story. Those who process auditorily tended to confuse letters that *sound* alike, X with S or F, for example. The visualizers, on the other hand, confused X with Y and K; their mistakes hinged on how the letters *looked*. Styles of coding did not correlate with degree of hearing loss or intelligence or ability to memorize. Auditory recall did correlate with better speech (and perhaps, therefore, with better residual or amplified hearing). In the present state of knowledge, however, this merely suggests a chicken-and-egg question.

And Conrad found something like the linguistic interference that we speculated about earlier. Both groups extracted the same amount of information from prose paragraphs when reading silently, but when they had to read aloud, the visually oriented had great difficulty. For these people, Conrad believes, "articulation itself actively impairs learning."[5] When people can't use their preferred inner code they can't concentrate fully on the content as opposed to the form of written material. It's as if one had to read aloud in English from a book written in French. The effort needed for the words would leave little energy for remembering the story. "There is unquestionably a cost to some children in learning in oral verbal language," Conrad concludes.[6] He refers here to intellectual cost, but there are also social costs of not doing so.

We know so little about the structure of thought that Conrad can only speculate on the possible consequences of using a visual internal code. He wonders whether teaching can successfully "force a child out of a preferred mode easy for him into a more fashionable mode preferred by teachers."[7] This question, of course, is crucial to the educational strategy used with children exposed late to language. And he further muses: "Can a variety of concurrently used modes lead to enriched, or to confused and impoverished, thinking?"[8] Is it possible, at least conceptually, that people with multiple codes enjoy enhanced imaginative and abstractive possibilities, just as bilinguals have wider symbolic resources than monolinguals? But is it not also possible that a child may lack the flexibility and inventiveness to blend his two systems into a usable whole? And the system of his own invention probably lacks the richness and versatility of a language like English, which arises out of centuries of experience by millions of people.

Other examples of such interference have turned up elsewhere. When a University of Minnesota graduate student tried to teach signed English to a group of junior high children from a strictly oral program, she found that their own invented signs interfered with learning "real" signs. They had no training in systematic signs, but had developed their own conceptual gestures, and these proved very persistent. The interrogatives—why, where, who, what, how—were especially intractable. The children didn't have the normal array of precise and very useful questioning concepts, but only a single sign for any and all. This mimicked the hearing person's unconscious asking gesture: shoulders tense, elbows against the body, palms upward and separated. They had apparently learned this from their "oral-only teachers." "The irony is," psychologist Donald Moores comments, "that teachers who have slapped the hands of students for gesturing unconsciously provided the model of limiting, restrictive gestures."[9] And the tragedy is that the children were thus deprived of concepts that, in Mindel and Vernon's perceptive phrase, have "meanings reaching deep into the basic structure of language."[10]

Freddy Howard, for example, the bright but almost speechless eight-year-old son of the "pushy" oral mother, has much the same problem. He lacks neither curiosity nor ability to learn. His art work includes wickedly observant caricatures of his mother and he can tell complete and emotionally satisfying stories in a series of finely detailed drawings. But neither his mother nor his oral therapist nor both of them together could convey to him the sense of a visitor's question: "Why don't you make more picture books?" He knew that it was a question, and he tried to answer what he understood it to be, but the meaning of what began as a rhetorical aside continually eluded him.

We don't know the form of a deaf child's interior monologue, but we do know that acquiring a language is one of his central intellectual tasks, and often a long-term difficulty. This is a highly unusual situation. For the overwhelming majority of humankind, learning a first language is easy. At least it must be so because almost all hearing children of anything approaching normal intelligence, and many of markedly subnormal intelligence, have mastered the essentials of their native tongues by the age of three and a half. They continue to refine their pronunciation, syntax, and semantics for some time after that, but they speak the language fluently in all its essentials by the age of four. And they learn it without being taught. No one *teaches* a normal baby his mother tongue. People around him merely talk to him, at him, in his hearing, and he extracts the phonemic and grammatical structure of the language from this undifferentiated mass of verbiage, just as he constructs his image of reality from the undifferentiated mass of his sense data and experience.

Once American psychology fought free of strict behaviorism, it became obvious that children do not learn language by imitation and reinforcement. Very young children do not, strictly speaking, imitate the speech of adults. Probably most parents have had the frustrating and mystifying experience of trying to teach some particular linguistic point to an apparently obstinate small child. "These are baby's feet," you say. "Baby foots," comes the angelic reply. "These are baby's feet," you repeat. "Baby foots," says the child, nodding happily. "No, they're baby's *feet*," you say, hoping your mild irritation doesn't show. "Baby foots," he says again, beaming with triumph. At this point you give up, mystified as to why he won't simply imitate something so simple.

The reason is that he can't. His personal diagram of English grammar may include plurals, but it obviously has thus far slighted plurals of the stem-changing sort. Until he derives the principle for himself, he is unable to grasp its linguistic reality.

This is a very crucial point. A child appears to learn language not by accretion of many small facts but by a series of inductive leaps that carry him to ever higher, broader, and more exact approximations of adult language. This process should sound familiar; it is, in fact, extremely similar to Piaget's picture of the growing mind. Language develops as part of the development of cognition; as the child's intellect controls more of reality, he comes to control more language as a means of expressing what his intellect knows.

It may even be that "learn" is the wrong word to describe this process. Eric Lenneberg and other students of language acquisition believe that a small child no more "learns" to speak than an adolescent girl "learns" to menstruate. In both cases, onset marks a landmark of maturation, not a result of training. Lenneberg places the origin of the process deep in the physiological nature of the species. "Cognitive development," he writes, "is essentially the psychological correlate of brain development."[11] Each species, he believes, carries a genetic program for its own characteristic version of cognition. That human beings perceive and "cognize" in a certain way is no more surprising than that they breathe or excrete in a certain characteristic way. Language development correlates with normal cognitive development; it occurs on schedule as part of the total human plan whenever the neurologically normal child has access to a sufficiently large and clear sample of language to permit him to sort out its principles.

We can return to the nourishment metaphor, or try another that Lenneberg uses to make a related but slightly different point. The growing mind is a construction site where "the basic capacities and characteristic modes of cognizing develop without the aid of a mastermind. The environmental conditions are not the architects of an individual's cognition; the environment merely supplies the raw materials."[12] The essentially genetic nature of this process, Lenneberg argues, shows in the fact that children around the world use essentially the same "strategy" of language acquisition and pass the same landmarks in roughly the same order and at roughly the same age.

The child learns language by discerning the outlines of its patterns and structures. He does not begin by mastering discrete elements, apparently, but by making ever finer discriminations along the dimensions he perceives. In pronunciation, for example, he starts with a few large, crude sounds and gradually refines them into whole families of related phonemes. A phoneme is a class of sounds that a language treats as functionally identical. English recognizes a phoneme often represented by the letter K, for example. Most native English speakers hear all members of the class as phonetically and acoustically the same. But the K in "key" and that in "caught" are quite different sounds, both in their acoustic properties and in how they are formed. They differ sufficiently, in fact, for Arabic to recognize them as two different phonemes and for Arabs to "hear" them as two different sounds. Spanish speakers, on the other hand, hear no difference between the sounds symbolized as B and V or between those symbolized by Y and J. They perceive them merely as variations of the same sound, much as we hear the two kinds of K.

The child begins producing his first, imperfect sounds based on what he knows about phonemes, and testing his productions against what he hears, gradually refines them until they match the speech of adults. Many parents will remember this process. The child speaks of "keople," for example, until one day he suddenly says "people."

But speaking may not be the true core of knowing a language. Knowing precedes and underlies speaking; "it must," Lenneberg writes, "be prior and, in a sense, simpler."[13] He tells of a boy with normal hearing who did not speak, but who read and understood English perfectly. Speaking adds a layer of muscular ability on top of knowing the grammar and semantics.

Have these speculations brought us any closer to understanding what happened to Helen Keller? Or what might happen to any deaf child? We have seen that thought develops apart from language in the very young child and that language first functions as one of many forms of knowing. Later, we found, language comes to the fore as the vehicle of adult thought. We have seen that learning a language involves inventing a mental image of its rules. We know, too, that the mental images of language possessed by many profoundly deaf people remain a deep mystery to science.

But at bottom, we have seen the indomitability of the human mind, its almost palpable will to understand. Deaf people are not without intellect, as some have argued; they are not without means to make sense of their world, even if hearing society is too obtuse to give them credit for doing so. Making sense of the world is as inherent to the human animal as breathing, and almost as automatic. The normal child teaches himself his native language as simply one aspect of the larger process of making sense.

But what happens if the environment gives the child no native language to analyze or imitate? What if, in other words, the growing body receives no food or the construction site no shipments of building materials? Then obviously the normal process of development will not take place. This appears to be the situation of many deaf children. They do not perceive language at the proper time in their own development and consequently they do not learn it adequately. This is the heart of their linguistic problem.

Some deaf children do learn a language in the normal way,

however. Mainly the children of manual deaf parents, they generally learn sign language. They pass the same milestones in the same order as hearing children. They put their skills to the same practical use. They merely replace a systematic code of sounds with a systematic code of gestures. Does this substitution damage the development of their language (as opposed, of course, to speech)? Not necessarily, Lenneberg argues. "Sensory modalities are avenues over which the building supplies enter, raw materials that are needed during growth to build up cognitive functions," he writes. "If one avenue is obstructed, little harm will be done so long as the building supplies (specific sensory input) can be transformed (e.g. from visual to tactile) without losing their vital or specific importance in the process."[14] From the point of view of the structural understanding of language, therefore, there is no difference.

But he continues: "There are transformations in which precisely the most important objects get lost; in such cases the transformed input no longer has the power to enter into cognition-building processes."[15] And there's the rub. The essence of speech is sound, and that cannot be transmitted in signs. Cued speech, a relatively new manual code for English phonemes, does appear to transmit rather exact, if abstract, information about the sounds of conversation, but the system is neither old nor widely used enough to have had much impact on the present generation of deaf children. A small number of Americans and probably a somewhat larger number of Australians have learned it and they have developed remarkably good English. The forecast for cued speech may be less bright than these results suggest, however. Political and practical clouds hang on the horizon. We shall discuss them in detail later.

To return to the main point, most deaf children do not master English for the simplest of reasons: they don't get to hear enough of it at the right time of their lives. Amplification often can help a great deal, but it cannot help everyone, and those who benefit from it still miss important aspects of speech. And missing even small things can cause real grammatical problems. A very common type of hearing loss, for example, cuts out the high tones and thus devastates English syntax. The S phoneme, one of the very highest in English, carries three of our most im-

portant grammatical markers, the possessive, the plural, and con-
tracted forms of the verb "to be." "There's Pat's friend," for example, comes across to a person with a high-tone loss minus any
indication of tense, number, or relationship between the people
mentioned. "Whose friends?" also lacks information about number and relation. Miss the tiny, very hard-to-hear hiss and you
miss a large portion of the structure of English. Speechreading
doesn't help much either; the S flits by on the lips with hardly a
trace. Other types of losses wreak other types of havoc on the
sound of our language. Much of the helpful redundancy of
grammar disappears when reception is distorted, making clear
understanding and accurate replication very difficult.

So most deaf children have to base their guesses about English
on very faulty samples. With very skillful teaching some children
can learn to salvage enough information from what they hear to
produce a fairly accurate version of what they miss. For many
others, however, English remains an impenetrable mystery. And
no wonder; they have no way of finding the important clues.

The salience, the sheer noticeability of a morpheme (a unit of
grammatical meaning) seems to affect when, and whether, it's
learned. Children appear to master first those aspects of the language that leap out at them first. Those that never strike their attention they won't learn at all. It is hardly surprising, therefore,
that the less a child hears, the less sure is his grasp of the language. Lipreading does not appear to offer most people sufficient
information to learn a spoken language; indeed, it does not even
offer many already fluent speakers sufficient information to make
out what is being said. And until fairly recently, most deaf children were expected to learn English from reading the lips. Robert Davila, who is fluent in both English and Spanish, says he
finds the latter somewhat easier to see. It contains many more
sounds formed at the front of the mouth. A higher percentage of
them therefore appear on the lips.

Learning a language, of course, means more than knowing a
collection of sounds and words. True native mastery means a
faultless intuitive control of its structure, and this means more
than the ability to manipulate grammatical rules. Anyone who
has ever studied a language by the old conjugation-declension
method knows that a conscious control of syntax does not easily

translate into that subconscious fluency of the speaker as opposed to the student. And "subconscious" is the right word for it. Modern linguistics sees language structure as existing at two levels, the surface structure level of grammatically correct utterances and the deep structure level of relations and meanings. To make what they mean into what they say, fluent speakers use the language's transformational grammar to change deep structure into "well-formed" or syntactically and semantically correct utterances.

The difference between deep and surface structure comes clear in Noam Chomsky's famous pair of sentences. These differ profoundly on the deep level but not at all on the surface. "The boy is eager to please." "The boy is easy to please." The old-fashioned Latinate grammar you learned in high school probably doesn't even recognize that there is a difference. The two sentences would parse exactly alike. But any native speaker, Chomsky says, can feel that they are opposite in intent. One is active, almost bursting with enthusiasm, the other passive, in meaning if not in form. In the two sentences different people do the pleasing.

Deaf children miss out on both deep and surface levels. Many tests of their writing, reading, and speaking have shown that in general they have small and inaccurate English vocabularies, incomplete control of syntax, and hardly any grasp of deep structure at all. Henry Tobin, a prominent audiologist, tells of a boy who read that the young Columbus spent hours watching ships at a wharf. "What is a wharf?" Tobin asked. "A big fight," the boy replied. Psychologist Edna Levine writes about a personnel man at a clothing factory who became concerned when most graduates of a nearby state school for the deaf who filled out his company's employment application answered "yes" to the question "Have you ever had fits?" His inquiries revealed that the school's dressmaking course emphasized the importance of proper fitting of garments. And a group of Gallaudet students, when asked for the sign for "ordinary," puzzled for a few moments, then agreed on "strange."

At deep structure levels problems become even more hopeless. Consider, for example, the case of an eight-year-old given watercolors and paper and told to paint a picture. He studies the speaker quizzically, shrugs, and then goes and applies paint to a picture hanging on the wall.

Most deaf children write not only more poorly than the hearing, but qualitatively differently. In a classic paper handed in at Gallaudet, a student described his problems with four pet turtles. "My room is not pretty because of the turtles. Turtles make my room filthy. We spend our money to turtle's supplies instead of our entertaining. Another reason, our air is full of turtle like turtle's soup. Before the turtle, my air is fresh and health. My room is neat as shine. During the turtle time, my room is mixed-up." This young man surpassed many of his fellow students and, indeed, many hearing collegians in imaginative flair, but unfortunately, his grammar is not atypical. And sadly, his teachers report that as his mastery of grammar grew, his freshness seemed to wane.

Some, like Helen Keller, learn to write correctly, even compellingly, but most compose rigidly, choose grammatical units almost at random, fashion structure out of stereotypes, in general approach the task simplistically and mechanically. Good writers probably do little more than take dictation from their inner voices. Good writing may well presuppose an inner voice that speaks good English—and that means that many deaf youngsters are in real trouble.

But despite its apparent grammatical zaniness, most writing by deaf children does follow certain rules. One researcher concluded that three erroneous rules explained most mistakes. If you (1) ignored negation; (2) ignored passives and read them as actives; and (3) in sentences like "the man called the woman," where the noun elements could be reversed without creating a logical impossibility, you reversed the nouns at will; you would produce writing like that of most deaf children tested. In their ignorance of the deeper meanings of English, many deaf children read surface structure only and understand all sentences as stereotyped active, present, transitive statements. Thus, for example, "The boy was visited by the girl" is taken to mean that the boy paid the call. "We went to the movies after we had dinner" means that first we went to the theater and then to the restaurant. "Has" frequently becomes "is." In tests asking subjects to rephrase sentences while keeping the meaning, hearing children succeed with ease but the hearing-impaired generally violate both syntax and semantics. A single, dismal conclusion rises out of all of this: on the average, deaf children simply do not have a native grasp of English. Indeed, some researchers have compared them to bilingual children speaking their weaker language. But, write Alice Streng and Richard and Laura Kretschmer, "unlike the Spanish-dominant children, too many deaf children are not dominant in any language."[16] Indeed, a provocative essay by Aaron Cicourel and Robert Boese suggests that native mastery of a spoken language is impossible by definition for most deaf people. Knowing a language like a native, they say, requires the ability to monitor accurately one's output, and very few deaf people can ever achieve this in speech.

That deaf reading is a disaster should come as no surprise. The hearing six-year-old comes to school with a full and flexible command of the language he is about to read; he merely masters a new version of that already familiar tongue. Even Dick and Jane assume some clear idea of English, and a phonic approach to reading is worse than useless if one doesn't know how the language sounds. The more advanced the material, of course, the more one needs to know. Anyone who has studied a foreign language knows the special uneasiness of reading a not wholly familiar tongue. You're never sure you've gotten everything the sentence means, and you're certain you have no idea of everything it *could* mean. Undertones and overtones vanish as words lose all sense but the one or two in the glossary. Frequent trips to the dictionary derail the train of thought, but guessing words from context makes the context begin to disappear. The exercise yields little enjoyment and few people undertake it often enough to gain any real skill or much information from the passages laboriously deciphered.

Indeed, a person with an inexact image of English as his only reading language probably faces far worse obstacles than an average American student slogging through *Madame Bovary*. There are dictionaries giving English equivalents of the words in all major verbal languages; there is no really useful dictionary translating English into sign. And a rough idea of English will not guide a reader through a dictionary meant for a fluent speaker. As a hard-of-hearing middle-aged man tearfully told

Henry Tobin, he doesn't understand English suffixes and prefixes well enough to find anything in a dictionary, and he doesn't know how to learn what he doesn't know. Even knowing a lot of words is not the answer. Real understanding hinges on grammar. In one study of passages from popular magazines, a mere two dozen words comprised a third of all the words used, but they were crucial words and hard to define—pronouns, prepositions, auxiliaries, conjunctions, articles. A full 10 percent of the words were "the," "and," and "a." Can a dictionary help much in differentiating the two senses of "had," between "a" and "the"?

Most deaf people, children and adults, read poorly. Study after study, decade after decade, has documented this. If we take reading at grade 4.9 to equal literacy, then 1 percent of deaf eleven-year-olds were literate in the 1950s. Tests in the 1960s found more than 30 percent of deaf students older than sixteen functionally illiterate, 60 percent reading at grade 5.3 or below, and only 50 percent reading at the tenth-grade level and above. And most of these were adventitiously deaf. The 1970s brought results no more encouraging. "In the 10 year period from age 8 to age 18 the average hearing impaired student increases his vocabulary only as much as the average normal hearing student does between the beginning of kindergarten and the latter part of second grade,"[17] writes Carl Jensema in a report of the Office of Demographic Studies at Gallaudet. The reading ability of deaf students in special education increases very little between age thirteen and age twenty, and only one deaf young adult in ten can read easily at the level of the newspaper, which is the eighth grade. Some critics even argue that most standardized tests overestimate the ability of deaf young people. The tests are aimed at a particular range of grades and it is impossible to score below a certain year and month, no matter how badly one does. Multiple-choice tests can also artificially inflate results.

But deaf adults have much more success in their lives than deaf children do in school. Could it be, as Furth suggests, society simply overvalues reading ability? But the sad fact is that academic credentials become more important every year. College may be the single greatest social divide in this country. And if that is so, then reading skill—verbal ability generally—is very important indeed.

Over a period of many years, Gallaudet College has developed sophisticated measures of the academic potential of the hearing-impaired. The college considers them a special case of cultural deprivation (indeed, in Furth's study, deaf performance resembled that of poor rural youth). Like other culturally deprived, they do poorly on standard college admissions tests, so poorly, in fact, that their scores generally fall into the chance range on the College Board Scholastic Aptitude Test and so permit no useful discrimination among individual levels of ability. Gallaudet therefore developed its own battery of admissions tests and these now predict success in college very accurately. One of the most predictive of all ingeniously measures working knowledge of English. Each item presents three ideas, which the applicant must combine into a single sentence. The questions test concepts such as cause and effect, time sequence, and alteration, and the score quite reliably forecasts four-year grade-point average. Results on vocabulary tests also correlate well with college grades; the ability to learn a lot of words before reaching college seems to foretell success in understanding those encountered in college. "Apparently it is verbal intelligence which is called for in college," Gallaudet admissions director Bernard Greenberg ruefully concludes, "and no amount of non-verbal intellect can compensate for verbal inadequacies."[18] Bad English, in other words, can keep a person out of the white-collar middle class.

The shame of this is that deaf children with no other handicaps traditionally do better on mathematics tests than on verbal tests and score normally on non-verbal intelligence tests. Scores on mathematical computation, and to a lesser extent on mathematical reasoning, come much closer to the norm for hearing children of the same age. That math is their "strong" subject has become a dogma of special education. But some perceptive math teachers, among them Charles Dietz of the Model Secondary School for the Deaf, believe that this idea grows out of a simplistic conception of mathematics. Computation, Dietz says, is not math. "All that computation tests prove is that deaf children can learn by rote as well as hearing children. Real mathematics is the ability to know when to do which computation and why." And in this too, shaky language concepts create hazards. "If pipe A discharges 7 gallons an hour and pipe B 2½ quarts every 15

minutes . . ." "If George has 9 apples worth 8¢ each and Henry
has 14 pears worth $1.00 a dozen . . ." "If Mary can drive home
in 2 hours and walk home in 14 . . ." These and all the other
bugaboos of high school algebra must be conquered as strings of
words before they can be attacked as strings of numbers. Even
more abstractly logical concepts such as implication depend to a
large extent on concepts at bottom linguistic, in this case "if . . .
then."

Dietz's fears notwithstanding, educated deaf people have
found the computer field reasonably hospitable. They seem to
suffer relatively less disadvantage here than in some other professions and occupations that depend more heavily on prose
style; no one, after all, is a native speaker of Fortran. But their
success need not depend on any particular deaf knack for mathematics. "Computer work is a white-collar field that doesn't require much oral communication," Dietz says. Bright deaf people
learn it because they're bright, not because they're deaf; people
without excellent oral skills can do well at it because the work
requires them to communicate more with machines than with
people.

The intellectual damage caused by deafness may grow to be
extensive, but it starts out small. Deaf kids don't learn because
many of the things people try to teach them simply don't get
through. The surprising bright spot in this almost universally dismal academic landscape neatly proves the rule. In general, deaf
children spell at least as well and often better than their hearing
counterparts. Many of them have much more practice. Those in
programs that depend heavily on finger spelling may begin to receive and send messages letter by letter at kindergarten age.
When a deaf child makes a mistake, furthermore, it is rarely the
same one that a hearing child is likely to make. Usually the deaf
child omits one or more letters; only rarely does he make the
typical hearing child's error, inventing a wrong spelling that
gives the same pronunciation. No less an authority than Dr. Samuel Johnson, the dictionary maker, made this observation two
centuries ago. Marveling at the orthographic skill of deaf pupils
at Thomas Braidwood's school in Edinburgh, he remarked that
"letters to them are not symbols of names, but of things; where
they write they do not represent a sound but delineate a form."[19]

It may even be that deaf children have an advantage in spelling English, the most unphonetic of alphabetic languages. They're not misled by sound.

So the blame for deaf children's disastrous verbal performance cannot be laid to any innate intellectual disability; the way they are taught must be at fault. Until very recently in this country as throughout the world, formal instruction always presented language to young deaf children in its most difficult form, speech, with supplementary materials in writing. Sign language appeared in the school curriculum only when oral teaching had failed. We will discuss this remarkable phenomenon and the controversy surrounding it in a later chapter. For our present purpose we must consider the content of the teaching rather than the medium of its presentation.

There are only two basic ways of teaching any language to anyone. The natural or mother method immerses the learner in an environment of the language to be learned and knowledge is supposed to osmose into his consciousness as naturally as a child learns to speak at his mother's knee. The grammatical or analytic method presents a grammatical analysis of the language, and the child is supposed to learn its workings as a student does at school. Both systems have been tried on and off and in combination for generations and neither has worked very well except with children who have considerable residual hearing. The first influential teachers of the deaf in this country were disciples of the Abbé Sicard, a Frenchman. They imported the analytical methods used in his school in the early nineteenth century. Seventy years later the natural method was all the rage here, advocated by Alexander Graham Bell, one of the most important figures in the history of deaf education, and was practiced at the Lexington School and elsewhere. But as the twentieth century began, the pure natural method was banished from the forefront of educational innovation, to be replaced by the analytic method in inventive new guises. Now it took the form of Wing's Symbols, the Barry Five Slates, and the Fitzgerald Key, all of which allowed the child to construct sentences according to prearranged plans. These methods have considerable success in impressing the basic English sentence forms on schoolchildren; much of the rigidity and stereotyping that observers deplore in deaf children's writing seems to stem directly from them. So by mid-twentieth century, it was back to the natural method, this time incorporating any aspects of the older methods that proved useful. Educators call this the eclectic approach.

Both methods often fail; one presents too little too late and the other too much too soon. The natural method can work at home with very small children, but for those of school age, or even of four or five, several vital elements are missing. The emotional basis of learning from Mother, that closest of all emotional bonds, does not exist in the classroom and cannot be replicated. Extensive private tutoring apparently produced good results in the past, but only for very wealthy children. The Piagetians point out, furthermore, that by the time the child reaches school or even preschool, the optimal moment has passed forever. The analytical method, on the other hand, fails because it loads the child down with grammatical rules before he can think abstractly or has anything to apply them to. "The net result," the Lings write, "is often a young adult who can perform a wide range of grammatical operations, yet who is unable to construct reasonable sentences. Similar results are obtained with normal-hearing people exposed to a foreign language through the grammatical approach."[20]

Then what about teaching language to a child with little or no residual hearing through a medium he can readily perceive, namely manual gestures? How does this affect linguistic development? The communication controversy has swirled around this question for generations, crushing rational discussion in a vortex of passionate emotion. The deaf children of deaf parents appear to thrive intellectually, if compared to the mostly blighted deaf children of the hearing. Between 1914 and 1961, 90 percent of the children of deaf parents at the California School for the Deaf did better at school than the children of hearing parents; over a third of the former went to college, as opposed to 9 percent of the latter. Is the difference their early exposure to sign language and the intellectual stimulation it allows? Longitudinal studies of small samples suggest that children of hearing parents introduced early to both sign and speech (the so-called simultaneous method or total communication) progress simultaneously in both modes and use them appropriately. Oral advocates, on the other hand, argue that encouraging visual communication discourages the very hard work of learning to listen and learning to speak; that children become fixed early in a visual mode and so have even less chance of mastering proper English.

No one denies, however, that the training of deaf children has been generation after generation an almost unmitigated academic disaster. That the children manage to grow into reasonably rational and balanced adults argues persuasively for Furth's notion of the adaptive value of independence of mind and spirit. But we still don't know what happened to Helen, nor are we likely to any time soon. Beneath all our knowledge of the intellectual life of the deaf runs the same great vein of ignorance that underlies all serious discussions of all aspects of deafness. The most basic questions have yet to be answered. For the most part, they have yet even to be asked.

CHAPTER 6

Deafness Come Lately

Jean Mulrooney was unconscious when she crossed the border to deafness. She recalls the accident vividly, with the strangely heightened lucidity that often accompanies approaching but unavoidable disaster. She saw the other car coming toward hers, and when she knew that she could not evade it, time suddenly slowed, almost congealed. The onrushing car seemed to come slowly, slowly, ever more menacing for the slowness of its approach. She watched it coolly in the few endless seconds before the impact. Then it hit, with a hideous, grinding crash. That was the last sound she ever heard.

When she opened her eyes a day and a half later, her bearings came to her quickly. She is a nurse, and the hospital room neither frightened nor disoriented her. She knew what the machines were for, what the people were doing, and she knew almost immediately that she could not hear them, that she was deaf.

Jean Mulrooney is adventitiously deaf—deaf by outside causes and a long time after birth. As such, she represents close to three out of four Americans with significant bilateral hearing loss. She is not entirely typical, however, because her trauma was sudden and very severe. Many people lose their hearing gradually and endure a long period of less acute but nonetheless serious distress. But if it can be said that so terrible and unexpected a shock as Jean suffered has any advantages, at least it forced her to face the situation squarely and to seek what help she could find. She could not deny or dissemble, kid herself, gradually alienate friends and associates, and watch her social circle dwindle to nothing without admitting why.

When she did arrive in the country of the deaf, furthermore, she came with relatively great advantages. She had good language and good speech. She had already effortlessly achieved the goals that many who lose their hearing early must spend their youth struggling for, often in vain. Conserving usable speech, once established, is much simpler than developing it in the first place. Speechreading comes easiest to those already fluent in the language. Reading and writing are hardly affected at all. Her problem, in short, was mainly emotional rather than intellectual.

Realizing she was deaf began "a long journey through the paths leading to a new identity as a deafened individual," Jean Mulrooney has written. "It was not a single trip. It involved learning and relearning, unbelievable isolation, barely controlled rage, the depths of depression, personal devaluation, acute sustained anxiety, and continual feelings of conflict in interpersonal relations."[1] But at last she arrived at a point where she could live a life in a new way.

Her hearing loss has an almost symbolic shape; it mimics death and rebirth. Perhaps this is what makes the experience so vivid and, on a superficial level at least, not difficult to understand. But even if a loss of hearing has no dramatic form, no apparent beginning and no definite end, it can (and probably should) still mimic death and rebirth. Out of her own pain and introspection, Jean Mulrooney has extracted the psychic essence of going deaf: discarding the old identity as a "normal" person and taking on a new one as a "deafened individual."

She came to deafness, like all other such migrants, as an unwilling exile from the hearing country of her birth. And there's the rub. Taking on a new identity is work, even under the best of circumstances. There are new skills to learn and old habits to unlearn, people to meet, and explanations to make. Even those adopting new identities eagerly—new brides, for example, or new parents—often find the job harder than expected. What about a new identity that you never asked for, that you may despise or feel stigmatizes you, or that you don't even realize *is* a new identity?

Deafness is in many respects a social role masquerading as a physical condition. No one can deny the reality of the physical limitations it imposes, but like other disabilities, and perhaps more than most, its really basic consequences are social and psychological. In a shrewd and perceptive study of blindness in America, sociologist Robert Scott observes, "Many of the attitudes, behavior patterns, and qualities of character that have long been assumed to be given to blind people by their condition are, in fact, the result of ordinary processes of socialization."[2] People blinded as adults, Scott suggests, learn to be blind men. Likewise, losing hearing in adulthood involves learning to be deaf or hard-of-hearing.

This means learning many things. First perhaps, and most superficially, it means learning how to communicate; that is to say, remembering how to speak and relearning how to hear. People with adventitious losses generally can retain understandable speech without enormous difficulty. Frequent practice and sympathetic criticism for those who cannot monitor their own output usually allow voice quality to remain very good for many years. Young children who lose their hearing suddenly before speech is well established sometimes lose the habit altogether, but for older people deterioration occurs more gradually. Tone and intonation flatten. Articulation of some difficult consonants may blur. But such people ought to be able to retain the basic intelligibility of their voices because speech dimensions such as higher and lower, louder and softer, already have kinesthetic meaning.

Understanding other people is another thing again. The adventitiously deaf often derive relatively great benefit from hearing aids. They know the language well, so little clues have more meaning to them than to someone just learning it. Unless the loss is conductive, however, and most adventitious losses are not, no hearing aid can restore undistorted sound. Something will be missing and something may be added—often tinnitis, a continual ringing fairly common in damaged ears. Whatever the exact dimensions of a particular hearing loss, anything the person hears will sound different from what he heard before. The task is to learn again to interpret what sounds mean. This takes time and patience and some people are simply better at it than others.

It also means finding the right hearing aid, a not inconsiderable problem. Hearing aids are not eyeglasses. A patient cannot have his hearing loss examined and end up with a precise mathematical description of a device to compensate for it. There is no such thing as a prescription for a hearing aid, only a general description of the type of aid likely to help, and there is no expert with a degree in fitting the device, only salesmen representing different manufacturers with different degrees of integrity and skill. The patient is pretty much on his own. Richard Rosenthal, himself adventitiously hard-of-hearing, writes, "Finding the right aid is a matter of trial and error in which the patient must make his own decisions."[3] Even so the adventitiously impaired person has a better chance of finding a useful and appropriate aid than the pre-lingually deaf child, who knows nothing about how things ought to sound and whose diagnosis is probably quite inexact.

For all their efforts, Rosenthal believes, the hearing-impaired have less chance than they ought to find an aid that will deliver maximum benefits. It is an old economic law that one can't maximize more than one value, and in choosing between size and amplification the industry has opted for size. On the assumption that most adults would rather appear normal than hear well, aid designers have traditionally striven for as nearly invisible an aid as possible. As anyone knows who has ever compared the tone quality of a transistor radio with that of a good stereo set, miniaturization does not improve sound. "Hearing aids of the 1970s are far behind the capacities of their day, electronic absurdities at a time when man talks across outer space, eavesdrops on the mighty, and at a modest cost can fill a house with superb audio equipment," Rosenthal writes.[4] Why this should be is an interesting combination of social values and commercial imperatives. An industry composed of small companies and supplying a market composed mostly of elderly customers has neither the capital nor the imagination to develop a product embodying any other conception of hearing loss than a condition to be hidden. Hearing aids do not represent the best electronics our age can produce and are expensive besides. Rosenthal and other choosy consumers have gone so far as to have engineers design and build custom aids out of high-quality audio components. In his very useful *Hearing Loss Handbook* he tells how.

For some people trying to communicate, speechreading may be an important part of the answer. Betty, for example, lost her hearing mysteriously in a matter of days. She felt dizzy and off balance one day at work, and thought she was catching the flu. When resting on the ladies' lounge sofa made her feel no better, she left early and went home to bed. By the next morning she heard nothing in one ear and hardly anything in the other. Within a few days that little hearing was gone. Her family doctor continued treating her for a cold, until frustration drove her to a specialist who put her in the hospital for tests. Eventually he decided that the herpes virus—the same one that causes cold sores—had invaded her inner ear. Well before that Betty was lipreading; she began almost immediately and without training. Always visually observant, she became a virtuoso of silent speech. "You're from the New York area," she told a new acquaintance. But how did she know? "By your accent. You don't have much of an accent, but you have some." With her hearing essentially gone she depends on a hearing aid to provide her the prosody—the basic rhythm—of a person's speech and on speechreading to provide her the meaning.

But many people find the transition more difficult. Basic though it is to the adjustment of the deaf, speechreading is very little understood. As in other highly skilled performances, indefinable factors lumped under the general heading of talent appear to play an important role. Some part of the talent is obviously visual: the ability to perceive exactly and rapidly through the eyes. And some part is obviously neurological: the ability to process visual information instantly and in linguistic form. A capacity for close attention and an ability to pick up cues through peripheral vision also obviously help. A good speechreader must be a very fine guesser; he must rapidly synthesize reasonable sentences from incomplete data and he must immediately revise his guesses if further data prove him wrong. And he must know what to look for. Training helps to a certain extent, although no amount of lessons and practice will make the ordinary plodder a star.

It doesn't hurt to be very intelligent, of course, although that doesn't guarantee anything either. Speechreading ability does not appear to correlate very exactly with intelligence or, indeed, with anything else. Too much intelligence or a too intellectual approach may actually hurt. A good lipreader "goes with the flow," and over-analysis clogs the channels. Knowing the language intimately certainly gives a leg up. Conrad found that normally hearing teen-agers with no training lipread about as well as pre-lingually deaf youngsters of the same age who had taken ten years of lessons.

At first glance it seems surprising that relatively few adventitiously deaf adults learn manual communication. A second look tells, however, that sign language is not merely a means of conveying messages but the home language of a specific community, and one that has traditionally suffered a considerable stigma. Those who lose their hearing as adults may well be past an age when radical changes in social patterns or group identity come easily. They generally have established family, occupational, and social lives in the hearing world. They lack the lifetime of shared experience and interests that binds the deaf community together. "She's not really deaf," said a pre-lingually deaf man of Betty, and in his particular social sense he is not. Even if sign language represents too great a social wrench for many households, finger spelling serves some as a supplement to spoken English.

"If you ask someone if they've seen the latest Bergman film," says George, a mathematician who already had his doctorate from MIT before he lost his hearing, "you don't want to have to explain who Bergman is." Hertzberg has significant ties to the deaf community, but still feels most at home with hearing people of his own background; not because they hear, but because they share his interests. He had hoped that people with more experience at deafness could teach him some "tricks of the trade," little practical solutions to daily problems. After considerable association with the deaf culture, however, he concluded that he had already found most of them. Learning sign language relatively late in life has not had the effect on his identity that it often has with younger people, but he finds it easier and much less ambiguous

than his quite competent lipreading. Still, it serves only among
deaf people and he lives most of his professional and social life
among the hearing. Finger spelling, easily integrated into ordinary conversation, has served him and his hearing wife well for
many years.

Even if a deafened person does not join the deaf community,
his new condition means unexpected and often painful readjustments of role. Family relationships may begin to shift a bit, for
example. A man might no longer be able to deal with the insurance salesman, the accountant, or the bank without the help of
his wife. A woman might no longer be able to "run interference"
for her husband at social gatherings. The telephone becomes a
problem. Friendships and interests may have to change, as one
man found whose social life had previously revolved around a
serious interest in music. Other customary social events may also
become burdensome or impossible: card games, the theater, dinner parties.

In some ways the hard-of-hearing have it harder than the deaf.
For those who hear somewhat, social events can occasion endless
anxiety. One is at the mercy of ambient conditions; the level and
frequency of background noise drastically affects what he can
hear, and the level and kind of lighting determines what can be
lipread. There is no way of predicting performance in unfamiliar
situations. If the cocktail party is held in a room both dimly lit
and acoustically live, it will be a disaster, but if the lights are
good and there are carpets and drapes to take up the extraneous
racket, one might do very well. But because a person's performance differs from day to day for reasons one's normally hearing
associates do not notice, they tend not to understand when the
going gets rough.

Possibly the most drastic adjustment is the necessity many
deafened people face of finding a new occupation if the old one
depended on hearing. Jean Mulrooney, the former psychiatric
nurse, teaches psychology at Gallaudet. Betty gave up her advertising job with its heavy public contact.

Even beyond these obvious readjustments are numerous more
subtle effects. D. A. Ramsdell, a psychologist who worked in rehabilitation of deafened veterans, believed that much of the
deep depression many of the newly deafened suffer results from

losing the almost unnoticed noise that forms the background of consciousness. Deafness erases not only speech and music but also birdsong, footsteps, ticking clocks, sirens on distant streets, voices in the next room, traffic noise, thunder, rain on the rooftop, the refrigerator cycling on and off. All these sounds, in Ramsdell's view, form an unconscious tie to life. Without them, "everything moves with the unreality of pantomime,"[5] and, indeed, "nothing seems real" is the common observation of the newly deaf. The loss of what Ramsdell calls "this primitive level of hearing," this auditory background, can cause "an impairment more severe and more basic" than the loss of communication skills to the person who has unconsciously judged his connectedness to life around him by what he could unconsciously hear.

This loss is all the more insidious because people rarely realize they have suffered it. They only know that the world has suddenly gone dead, that they feel terribly alone and physically exposed, and that they do not know why. In Ramsdell's opinion, merely understanding the cause of the distress can relieve some of the depression. A hearing aid may also help; even if it doesn't produce a very accurate replica of speech, it might yield enough generalized background noise to restore the feeling that the world is alive.

Another cause for loss of confidence has a more pragmatic base. Losing his hearing, a person loses the auditory warnings he depends on for safety. The disappearance of car horns, sirens, warning shouts, a child's call means that new ways must be found to get the same information. This loss occurs at the conscious level, however; its emotional effects are less severe. People without hearing can move safely through the most congested cities; many do so every day. They can operate mechanical equipment, drive cars, even fly airplanes. Deaf drivers have an accident rate half that of the hearing. They have trained themselves to observe more acutely. They may not hear the siren of an approaching ambulance, but they can see the cars scattering to clear its path. Doorbells, fire alarms, and telephones can be wired to flash lights instead of ringing bells. A sensing device can turn on a light in the parents' room when a baby cries in his. Dogs have been trained to alert owners to particular sounds. The deafened person may never regain the full confidence he enjoyed when he could hear, but extreme fearfulness and timidity are totally unrealistic.

Loss of the symbolic aspect of sound can have another psychological effect, Ramsdell observed. Adventitious deafness seems to bring out paranoid tendencies. Possibly because of general depression, or possibly because of their unaccustomed isolation, people come to suspect deliberate exclusion and plots against them. Conversations they can see but not hear seem "behind their back." Trivial discourtesies become intentional slights. Any criticism becomes personal.

Ramsdell believed this oversensitivity to be an exaggeration of any insecurity latent in the personality. It may also arise from the tension of an identity that does not yet fit. The deafened adult, if he is to find any peace, must integrate his new and unwelcome characteristic into an acceptable picture of himself. The task is no easier than that facing the parent forced to accept that a beloved child is not now and never will be perfect. For the person struggling to deny some incontrovertible but unpalatable truth, malevolence is everywhere; any encounter masks the possibility of disclosure, both to oneself and to the world at large. Those uncomfortable with the truth about themselves see malice in the faces of others, reflecting what they themselves feel.

If the permanent impairment is to be essentially physical rather than psychic and spiritual, the individual must come to accept it. Both those who have experienced the journey, like Mulrooney, and those who have studied it, like Ramsdell, agree that honesty is ultimately the only balm that heals. This is not to say that the process of surrendering the former identity occurs all at once or, indeed, ever completely ends. "The new identity," Mulrooney writes, "is found neither in denying one's past life nor acting like a congenitally deaf person, but in the altered life situations of everyday experience."[6] Each individual's experience reflects his own past and present: the nature and extent of his loss, the abilities and resources he brings to the crisis, the structure and strength of his character, the help he receives from old and new friends, and his own understanding of the meaning of his situation.

In this regard what a person first hears about the loss can help or hinder the process. For some people like Nanette Fabray the diagnosis itself is a major trauma. She was already a star when she discovered she could not hear. In fact, she had been losing her hearing gradually to otosclerosis at least since her early teens. This unsuspected disability colored her short and frustrating school career. Not knowing she couldn't hear, she never guessed why her grades never topped C, no matter how hard she worked. But somehow her deteriorating hearing never prevented her from learning to sing and dance well enough to achieve fame in her early twenties.

She was touring with a musical when she finally found out. In the Chicago theater the orchestra sat under the stage, not in an open pit where she could see them. She came on stage for the first performance in this unfamiliar house and "literally could not hear any of the music at all. Ordinarily I could hear some of the music—I could hear them when I sang, I could hear them when I danced. But now the conductor's signaling to me and I haven't heard a sound. So I started to sing, and I was on key, and finally the orchestra followed, but I couldn't hear anything. I went downstairs to talk to the conductor at intermission. I said, 'I can't hear the orchestra. I can't hear a thing.' He said, 'I can tell that.' He knew because I never took my eyes off him, I was so frightened."

A doctor hastily chosen from the yellow pages gave a cursory examination with a tuning fork. He announced that the musical star at the beginning of her career had only five more years to hear, and consequently, only five more years to speak. "When you lose your hearing you'll lose your speech too," he said. "In about five years you'll be deaf and dumb."

"The fact that his diagnosis was cruel and wrong was terrible at the moment but a good thing in the long run," Fabray says now. "The important thing was that it was such a catastrophic shock that it opened my mind to the idea that there was nobody I could turn to. I knew nobody, I knew nobody under the age of a hundred who had a hearing problem. I knew nothing about it, I had never heard anything about it."

Thus began her long journey to an acceptance of her impairment. "Deafness until very recently was a closet kind of handicap," she says. "Older people still have real hang-ups about it. At first I hid it for a long time, but at last I had to get a hearing aid. And I began talking about it for my own therapy."

But the first reaction was terror and paralysis. Many years later she attended an awards banquet honoring her work on behalf of the hearing-impaired. "Sitting at the table with my own ear doctor," she recalls, "was a doctor from Chicago. He said, 'Do you remember when you came and got your test in Chicago?' My heart sank. He said, 'Yes, you came to my office.' I said, 'Are you the one that tested my hearing in Chicago years ago?' And finally I said, 'I had a very bad experience.' 'Yes,' he said, 'when you came to my office you were in quite a state of shock. You had heard from somebody else that you were going to lose your speech.' Well, to this day I don't remember my second visit. I don't remember that I went to get another opinion. I was so traumatized by the first visit that I never heard what he told me."

For Fabray, adjusting to her loss meant making it part of her public personality. Gradually the press began to ask about it and she began to answer freely. "I was very severely criticized for this," she says. "People said I was using a handicap to attract attention." But she viewed her access to publicity as a way to increase understanding. "I wanted people to see that you could be young and successful and have a problem and not be destroyed by it."

Before she could say this convincingly, however, she had to believe it herself. "And that took time." "The human reaction to loss is grief," writes Jean Mulrooney,[7] and the process of adjusting to a handicap has been likened to that of mourning a loved one. Just as some people never fully recover from bereavement, some never adjust to the new realities and requirements of their lives. "They use it as a crutch," Nanette Fabray says, to seek and demand extra attention and warmth, to explain away problems or failures, or to exempt themselves from duties or expectations.

The attitudes that accompany a disability eventually become habitual. When an operation restored her hearing Fabray faced an adjustment nearly as demanding as when she lost it. There were small annoyances like being disturbed and distracted by background noises hearing people take for granted. The rubbing of the bedsheets kept her awake at first. Beyond this, however, she had to discard her "deaf speech mannerisms." She habitually mumbled "huh?" whenever anyone spoke to her; because she always missed something said, she forced people to repeat themselves. Now she had to train herself to hear and understand the first time and to try to believe that she *could* hear. After a lifetime of professional singing, she took lessons again to learn to control consciously all the things she had done with her voice without knowing it.

Handicaps terrify the non-handicapped largely because we cannot imagine how life is possible without the faculties we so depend on. Like the parent who watches a deaf child too closely, we do not fathom the depths of possibility of the human organism. How can deaf people do the things that hearing people do? How can they travel abroad, for example? More easily, in fact, than the hearing, because they have generally cultivated the arts of communicating without speech and generally feel no embarrassment at using them. How can they work, dance, play musical instruments, compete in sports? We can't guess, but hearing-handicapped people have done them all. The challenge that lies before the newly deafened, even more than learning new skills, is exploring the limits of the possible. Fear of stigma keeps many from admitting their problem, then meeting the people and making the effort that can help. Age and isolation keep others from trying. The road is long and difficult and has many lonely stretches, but many people have traveled it in courage and dignity.

CHAPTER 7

History

The true history of deaf people can probably never be written. What has come down to us is the history of their treatment at the hands of the hearing. Like the peasants and the poor who lurk unseen around the margins of the history books, the deaf for most of recorded time left no records. Indeed, they are more invisible than the teeming common people of past ages because they left even their folklore in a medium few hearing people understand, the many diverse and largely local systems of sign language. Recently deaf writers have begun gathering anecdotal materials about the deaf American past, but these efforts can reach no farther back than the memory of those now alive. Journals and books published by educated deaf people extend little more than a century into the past. The memory of nearly all past generations is therefore irremediably lost, leaving behind not even a "dead" but written language as witness. What knowledge we have of deaf people in various epochs comes primarily from the testimony of hearing contemporaries, who generally knew little about them and understood even less. History written from reflections, like anything else read in a mirror, often comes out backward.

Even this distorted picture, however, can help us see the present more clearly, help us untangle the absurdities of our own time. The present state of the deaf world makes very little sense without a knowledge of the passionately contentious past and its profound intellectual, emotional, and social legacies to the present and the future.

The reflections we have from ancient times are scant indeed. Quintus Pedius, the first deaf individual known by name, does not appear until imperial Rome. He was the son of the consul of the same name, and a trained painter. He had no speech, apparently, and his contemporaries expected him to have none, for the ancients assumed muteness to be a necessary concomitant of deafness rather than its result. Aristotle, in a widely mistranslated statement, wrote, "Those who become deaf from birth also become altogether speechless. Voice is not lacking, but there is no speech." Because many took "speechless" to mean "stupid," the authority whose word ruled Western thought for over a thousand years appeared to state that the congenitally deaf were necessarily congenital morons. The ancient physician Galen, whose medical texts exerted as great an influence in their own field, believed that hearing and speech were controlled by a single portion of the brain. Injury to this area meant destruction of both faculties. Other worthies of the time concurred. Pliny the Elder, for example, opined that "there are no persons born deaf who are not also dumb."[1]

These theories had far from theoretical consequences. The Greeks exposed to the elements babies deemed defective, and the early Romans countenanced the destruction of such children until the age of three. Ancient Jewish law was the first to accord the deaf any specific protection in the command "Thou shalt not curse the deaf." The Talmud distinguished between deaf-mutes, who were legal minors unable to own property or form contracts, and people who could either hear or speak but not both, who enjoyed more privileges. The sixth-century Roman Code of Justinian made finer distinctions among five classes of the communication-impaired. Those congenitally both deaf and mute exercised none of the rights of citizens, nor bore any of the obligations; guardians handled their affairs. Adventitious deaf-mutes who could write were free to handle their own business and to marry. Congenitally and adventitiously deaf people who had speech enjoyed full legal rights, as did hearing mutes.

Beyond these scant legalisms, we know essentially nothing of the lives of the hearing-handicapped in those times. In one of his dialogues Plato refers to "present mutes" who communicate using "the hands, head, and other parts of the body," so we may assume the use of gestures or signs. It also seems clear, from the example of Quintus Pedius, that some members of wealthy or prominent families managed to obtain education superior to what must have been the lot of most of their deaf contemporaries. Until the eighteenth century, in fact, the sons of distinguished houses were the only deaf to be educated. Aristotle's theory seemed to imply that the whole idea of educating the deaf was probably fruitless, and we can assume that few such attempts were made during the centuries when the Greek philosopher's word reigned as fact.

The early Christian Church allowed sign language weddings; this implies the existence of sign systems capable of expressing fairly abstract ideas. It is not clear, however, whether the deaf lived clustered in communities of their own or as scattered individuals among the hearing.

The next deaf person in Western history does not appear for hundreds of years. In his sixth-century chronicle of Christian England, the Venerable Bede describes what appears to be a speech lesson given by St. John of Beverly to a mute young man. The deaf English author David Wright observes that the technique closely resembles that used by his own teacher more than 1,400 years later. Whether the boy was truly deaf we cannot say, but Bede obviously regards St. John's feat as miraculous, indicating his estimate of the educational potential of mutes. Life for the deaf in the Middle Ages could hardly have been other than brutal and squalid. In that religion-obsessed time the Church barred them from communion because they could not confess aloud, and the influence of the Justinian Code barred them from inheriting under the rules of primogeniture.

It was this latter consideration, rather than any desire to free their minds or save their souls, that appears to have prompted the first organized efforts to educate deaf people. The idea that this might be possible began percolating about Europe in the sixteenth century. In 1528 a book by Rodolphus Agricola, a Dutchman, mentioned a literate deaf man. About the same time the Paduan physician Girolamo Cardano suggested that the deaf could learn by associating written symbols with objects or pictures. He had the revolutionary insight that language did not depend on speech, and thus laid the theoretical foundation for teaching the deaf.

By the 1550s the Spanish monk Pedro Ponce de León had put the theory to a successful test. Born in 1520 in Valladolid, he joined the Benedictine monastery of San Salvador, where, legend has it, he encountered a deaf and mute youth barred from becoming a postulant by his handicap. After teaching this man speech and reading, Ponce de León took other, well-authenticated students and had similar success with a number of them, but they came from the nation's greatest houses, not from the lowest ranks of religious orders.

Ponce de León lived in Spain's proudest age, when a small and haughty nobility controlled huge estates and the vast wealth flowing from the Americas. These families took a keen, sometimes desperate interest in maintaining their lines of succession. Congenital defects including deafness, however, were not rare when marriages often joined close relatives. Inbreeding combined with the legal disabilities of deaf-mutes to confront a number of families with an heir barred from his inheritance. Thus, some influential members of the aristocracy interested themselves in Ponce de León's work; learning to speak entitled a deaf man to inherit.

Ponce de León may have worked for the sake of his students' immortal souls, but their parents sent them for the sake of their temporal estates. Although scattered deaf individuals in other countries seem to have mastered reading and writing during the sixteenth century, systematic education of deaf people first developed in Spain. Ponce de León's technique has not come down to us, but contemporaries attested to its success. Students of his apparently learned to read, write, and speak well enough to take part in worship, serve in the military, even sing a bit.

When he died in 1584, two of his countrymen, Juan Pablo Bonet and Manuel Ramírez de Carrión, continued the work. In 1607 Bonet, then almost thirty, entered the service of the Constable of Castile, Juan Fernández de Velasco, three of whose brothers had studied with Ponce de León. Don Juan died in

1613, but his widow retained Bonet as secretary to the new Constable, her four-year-old son Bernardino. Another son, Luis, then three, had lost his hearing the year before and Bonet found him a tutor in the person of Ramírez, who had previously worked as secretary to another deaf nobleman, the Marqués de Priego. Ramírez taught the boy from 1615 to 1619, when he returned to his previous employer. Bonet then took over the boy's tuition, probably using methods cribbed from Ramírez. In the next year he published an epoch-making book about his efforts, *Reducción de las letras y arte para enseñar a hablar los mudos*. Others, including Ramírez, had written about successes teaching the deaf, but Bonet's work was the first to disclose a method. How much of it represented Bonet's originality and how much he had stolen from Ramírez, Ponce de León, and others caused some controversy, but no one can dispute the influence this book would have over centuries to come.

Bonet began with a one-handed manual alphabet—essentially the same one used in America today—which the deaf student and his entire household had to learn and use. After mastering the alphabet the student learned to pronounce each sound, then to combine the sounds into syllables and, later, words. Finally he learned to make grammatical sentences. Bonet understood the value of lipreading, but did not believe it could be taught.

Regardless of who had originated the method—Ramírez and Bonet's dispute was merely the first of many among members of their profession—it worked. That is, it worked in the close to ideal conditions the Spanish sixteenth century offered: intensive individual instruction over a long period; selected and highly motivated students and families; and a well-paid, dedicated, resident teacher. Using it, a number of deaf Spanish aristocrats astonished their fellows.

Contemporary accounts spread word of these marvels throughout Europe and others tried their hand at the work. In England, Drs. John Bulwer, John Wallis, and William Holder and Mr. George Dalgarno all published books on the education of the deaf during the 1600s, the former three basing their works on their experience as teachers. Dalgarno's effort, more theoretical than the others, incorporated the thought of Comenius, who in the 1650s wrote an influential book on pedagogy advocating less rote learning and more dependence on the child's own experience.

On the Continent, Johann Konrad Amman, a Swiss resident of Amsterdam, became a successful teacher and published books on his methods in 1692 and 1700. He firmly believed in oral techniques, relying heavily on lipreading supplemented by the use of touch and mirrors to teach articulation. Unlike Bonet, he drilled his students in lipreading. Amman's importance lies primarily in the wide influence of his writings; L. W. Kerger and Georg Raphel, for example, spread his ideas to Germany, where they formed the basis of what came to be known as the German system.

One of the most brilliant of all teachers of the deaf emerged about this time in France. Jacob Rodríguez Pereira, a Sephardic Jew born in Portugal in 1715, began in Bordeaux by teaching his deaf-born sister to speak. Aristocrats sent their children to him, and eventually word of his skill reached the King, who hired him to instruct a deaf godson, Saboureaux de Fontenay. Unlike most of his predecessors, Pereira depended on his teaching for the bulk of his income. Thus, like many of his contemporaries and successors, he regarded his methods as trade secrets and bound his students to secrecy. Pereira's family tried to carry on his work after his death in 1780, but his secret, which may have depended as much on his personality as on technique, died with him.

In Britain, however, another oral teacher did succeed in founding a family dynasty. In 1760 Thomas Braidwood (also born in 1715), until then an Edinburgh math teacher, undertook to train a boy deafened at three. He successfully imparted speech using oral methods, and then took other deaf students and advertised his results. He tried unsuccessfully to find public support for his school, but his reputation spread, aided in part by the visit of Dr. Johnson. In 1783 Braidwood moved his school to London and his work eventually expanded sufficiently to support John Braidwood, a nephew who became his son-in-law, and Joseph Watson, another nephew. The Braidwood family monopolized teaching in Britain for half a century, and their extreme reluctance to divulge their methods would have far-reaching and ironic consequences for America.

Scientific interest in deaf education had grown markedly since the days of Ponce de León, and teachers and techniques had multiplied, but the essential pattern had not changed. Private teachers taught a few handpicked students who could afford handsome fees. For deaf children of more modest means there was no education at all. Indeed, almost nothing is known of the lives of deaf people who did not study with one of the illustrious masters; how they lived, worked, or communicated are matters of conjecture. The pupils of the great teachers apparently succeeded as often as not in finding a place in the hearing world, or, more accurately, the only ones we hear of succeeded in doing so.

About the time that Braidwood was finding his feet in Edinburgh, Charles Michel de l'Epée was taking in Paris the most revolutionary step since Ponce de León. Epée was an abbé; born in 1712, he had had a mediocre career as a Catholic cleric. When he was almost forty he happened to meet a Parisian family with two deaf daughters. True to his calling, he immediately perceived the situation in spiritual terms: unless the children learned something of the Catholic religion they would lose their souls. Their parish priest had attempted to teach them using pictures, but he had died, leaving them without a spiritual mentor. Epée decided to take up this work. He made up his methods as he went along, but eventually taught the girls to read and write. By chance he learned of Bonet's book, and especially of the manual alphabet. He learned Spanish in order to study it. Bonet and Amman were the "torches" that guided his work with the growing numbers of pupils that came to him.

In 1760 he opened a school in Paris supported largely by his own funds. This modest institution had a double significance. It was the first school anywhere to offer instruction to deaf children regardless of means, and it was the first substantial community of deaf people known to history. Working among numbers of deaf children, Epée made a startling observation: many of them, especially those from deaf homes, communicated by means of gestures that appeared systematic. This implies, of course, that a sign language existed among the deaf of Paris, essentially unknown to the hearing population. Other local dialects probably also existed wherever settlements were large enough to include significant numbers of deaf persons. During the first years of his school Epée collected the signs, which he believed to be the "mother tongue" of the deaf. For pedagogic purposes, however, he wanted a sign language that resembled French, so he augmented the existing signs with others he called "methodical" signs. These indicated such grammatical points as gender, tense, or number.

Epée broke with tradition not only methodologically but philosophically. Possibly influenced by John Locke's *Essay Concerning Human Understanding*, Epée surmised—much as Dr. Johnson had done in passing—that deaf people could bypass speech entirely and use visual symbols as the basis of their communication and thought. He recognized the practical value of speech, and even attempted to teach articulation to some of his students, but as their numbers grew apace with his interest in signs he abandoned the effort as impractical. Good oral results demand close work over a long period. But Epée accepted all comers, and his classes sometimes numbered as many as sixty children. Unlike anyone before him, he took as his goal to give many deaf children some knowledge of language, albeit silent, rather than giving a small number a mastery of speech.

Even more importantly perhaps, he permitted the deaf community both to establish its own identity and to surface into the consciousness of hearing society. His detractors argued that his silent method condemned the deaf to isolation in their own enclaves. But these critics ignored the fact that the vast majority of these common children had no hope of obtaining any oral training whatever, let alone of succeeding. Nonetheless, the existence of a specifically deaf community has lain at the core of the methods controversy for two hundred years.

Epée's methods produced quick, flashy, and shallow results. His sign system permitted him to train children to take dictation in perfect French, Latin, Italian, and Spanish and to translate them back into perfect sign. That they could understand very little of what they so glibly rendered did not strike him as a serious flaw. His own disciple and successor, Abbé Roche Ambroise Sicard, wrote that "he led them from the unknown to the unknown."[2] On another occasion Epée chided Sicard for insisting on "training writers but my method can only produce copyists" and counseled him to "content yourself modestly with the share of glory you see me enjoying."[3]

But if Epée's methodical sign language, consisting of natural signs and French grammar, was awkward, complex, and ultimately not very useful, his work had another, profoundly important linguistic consequence. By bringing the deaf together in a community he provided the soil where natural sign language could grow and flourish. Linguistics calls a "natural language" any language that occurs spontaneously in the daily interaction of a human group, so the term thus perfectly describes the conversational sign of Epée's students. From the early years of the Paris school and, indeed, up to the present, sign language has existed in two distinct but related forms, the colloquial usage of deaf people among themselves, which may not resemble any national speech, and the formal or educated form, which consciously does. The Parisian colloquial grew in subtlety and power into a real language of a real community.

It was not this achievement, however, that brought Epée the glory he bragged of to Sicard. And indeed, it was worth bragging about. His students performed sleights of language before the leading personages of the day, and kings, nobles, scholars, and divines all marveled. Would-be teachers flocked from all over Europe to study his methods, and his influence spread throughout France and beyond. It was just this fame that instigated his public controversy with the German Samuel Heinicke in 1782. A devout pure oralist born in 1729, Heinicke is recognized today as the founder of the "German method" based primarily on Amman, just as Epée is recognized as the founder of the "French method." Heinicke opened Germany's first deaf school in 1778 under the patronage of the Elector of Saxony and became a vocal proponent of the philosophy of integration of the deaf into general society through speech and lipreading.

The two men ultimately asked the Zurich Academy to arbitrate their dispute, and the referees found for the Abbé. It is not clear, however, that they could judge the merits of the case objectively. Heinicke viewed his methods as trade secrets and divulged very little of them. The decision, furthermore, convinced neither disputant, nor any of their supporters; the debate continues, with essentially the same arguments, even couched in some of the same phrases, to this day. Indeed, one of the truly remarkable aspects of the history of deaf education is how little real technical progress has occurred in the centuries of furious argument. Every method hailed as revolutionary in our own time, be it auditory training, the simultaneous method, mainstreaming, even cued speech, has been tried at least once, and in some cases repeatedly, in the past. But as the argument is at bottom philosophical—almost religious—rather than technical, it shows no signs of abating.

Foreign detractors notwithstanding, Epée was a hero in his native country. His school successively enjoyed both the patronage of King Louis XVI and the approval of the Revolutionary National Assembly, which proclaimed it the Institute Nationale des Sourds-Muets (National Institute of Deaf-Mutes). And the Institute's exemplary reputation helped Epée's successor survive the anticlerical fervor of the Revolution.

Epée died the same year the Bastille fell and leadership of the school passed to Sicard. In an astute and typically Gallic gesture, the authorities chose the new director by a contest in which several teachers each entered a prize student. Sicard's protégé, Jean Massieu, won and the Abbé left his school in Bordeaux to take up the post in Paris. While a young priest in Bordeaux, Sicard (1742–1822) had been sent by his archbishop to study with Epée and had returned to establish a school in his home diocese. As we have seen, he did not entirely agree with his mentor's goals or methods. This had to do in large part with the man who won him the directorship.

Massieu had spent a rural boyhood as one of seven deaf-mute siblings. Although he received no education until almost fourteen, he used manual signs from an early age. Within a year after coming to Sicard's attention the boy had learned to write and Sicard had learned a good deal of his sign language. Unlike Epée, who taught writing by associating words with signs, Sicard began with objects and taught French not as an exercise in translation but as a language in its own right. As Massieu learned the French names for fifty objects a day, Sicard learned an equal number of signs. But unlike Epée, he did not attempt to impose a Frenchified grammar on this natural language of signs. "As a foreigner cannot teach a Frenchman the French language," he wrote, "so a man who speaks should not get involved in inventing signs."⁴ Like his teacher, however, he wrote books describing his method and issued a dictionary of signs.

Although much of Epée's clanking apparatus of methodical signs fell into disuse, the school he founded continued as the most important center of the French deaf community. Gradually that community developed a conscious tradition and a far richer and more flexible vocabulary. Through one of its most distinguished members, furthermore, it set the pattern for deaf education in the United States as well.

This country got off to a relatively late start. While other countries were setting up their early schools for the deaf, the United States had more pressing chores on its hands. Deaf people hardly appear in the turbulent record of colonization and independence, although they must have been present. One of the earliest deaf Americans definitely documented was, like his Roman counterpart, an artist. A revealing coincidence, this similarity of calling; for these men, both their profession and their disability encouraged keen visual observation. Joseph Brewster, Jr., was born deaf into the family of a Connecticut physician in 1766. He apparently had little formal artistic or academic training, but, according to the diary of one Reverend James Cogswell, he was literate and apparently communicated by manual signs and by notes. He had become a skilled portraitist by his young manhood, traveling about Connecticut to seek clients, and later followed his brother, Royal, to Maine, where he pursued a highly successful career as an itinerant portraitist. He never married, apparently, or established his own household, but he left a large body of work in the towns of coastal New England. After his death his work passed into obscurity, regarded, like others of its type, as an old-fashioned oddity. Only renewed interest in primitive (that is, untrained) American painting revealed his true standing as a significant talent. By the late 1970s his work was consistently commanding record prices at major art auctions.

Of the fate of less gifted deaf people we know almost nothing. They had very little opportunity for education because the first school for the deaf on these shores was not founded until the second decade of the nineteenth century. Until then, well-to-do children, including a nephew of President Monroe, went to Europe for help. During this period the Braidwoods controlled four schools in Britain (at Edinburgh, London, Birmingham, and Hackney) and the alcoholic black sheep of the family tried to extend their empire to the New World. Between 1805 and 1815 John Braidwood, the grandson of Thomas and son of the John who was the old man's nephew and son-in-law, attempted several times to start a school in Virginia, at the urging and with the support of one Major Thomas Bolling. Each time, however, Braidwood's drinking torpedoed the venture. He gave it up entirely in 1818 and died a drunkard the following year.

Had Braidwood been a sober man, and had one or two other things happened slightly differently, the whole history of deaf education in America would have taken a different course. But in 1815, just about the time that John Braidwood made his last floundering attempt, a young Connecticut cleric became aware of the girl next door.

In the emotional history of the American deaf, the meeting of Thomas Hopkins Gallaudet and Alice Cogswell probably shines as the most radiant single incident. Nearly seventy years later, deaf people from every state commissioned Daniel Chester French, the leading portrait sculptor of the age, to commemorate this legendary turning point. The poignant and powerful statue shows the young minister, a half smile of pleasure and anticipation on his lips, teaching the small girl the first letter of the manual alphabet. Her eyes are wide with wonder, her body tense with longing, her face grave and innocent. He knows, and she glimpses, that this is a moment fraught with destiny. Copies of the statue stand both at Gallaudet College and at the American School for the Deaf in Hartford in mute but moving testimony to the deep sense of debt and reverence that is Thomas Gallaudet's memory.

In 1815, however, he was a twenty-seven-year-old preacher, nine years out of Yale College and recently graduated from the seminary at Andover, Massachusetts. She was the nine-year-old daughter of his neighbors, deaf since two from a disease that appears to have been meningitis. Like the Abbé de l'Epée, Gallaudet tried to instruct the girl and succeeded in teaching her a bit of reading and the manual alphabet from Sicard's book. But her education occupied a distinctly minor place in the young pastor's life until a local group approached him with a proposition.

Alice came from a family of means. Her father, Dr. Mason Fitch Cogswell, was one of Hartford's leading citizens, and he turned his considerable financial, social, and intellectual resources to easing his daughter's plight. With a group of ministers (perhaps including the Reverend Cogswell?) he undertook a census of deaf children. They turned up about 80 in Connecticut alone and surmised that there were at least 400 in New England and perhaps 2,000 in the whole United States; more than enough, Cogswell thought, to justify a school on this side of the Atlantic. He proposed the idea to a group of ten civic leaders meeting in his home in April 1815. Specifically, he wanted a school in Hartford. They raised a fund to send a teacher to Europe to investigate the latest methods. Gallaudet seemed the natural choice, and after a bit of hesitation he agreed and sailed for Britain the following month.

He immediately repaired to the Braidwoods, and was soundly rebuffed. Neither in Edinburgh nor in Birmingham nor in London would family members or employees (who had paid a £1,000 bond of silence) consider teaching their methods to a potential competitor of John's. They proposed that Gallaudet accept a contract to teach at one of their schools or, failing that, to have John or another Braidwood teacher run the American school. During the time that Gallaudet was wondering how to proceed he happened to hear about a demonstration by Sicard, Massieu, and another of Sicard's students, Laurent Clerc, who were visiting London. Intrigued by what he saw, he met Sicard, who immediately invited him to study in Paris. Gallaudet, favoring oral methods at this point, demurred at first and tried prodding the Braidwoods a bit more. When that proved fruitless he traveled to Paris to look into what Sicard had to offer.

He spent two months in what David Wright calls a "crash course in the silent system"[5] under Massieu and Clerc, and like many a sign language student to follow, found his progress dismayingly slow. Hartford awaited, and the projected school. Finally, however, he persuaded the suave Clerc to abandon his beloved capital for the ruder precincts of Connecticut and, in August 1816, after more than a year away, he sailed for home.

The passage took nearly two months; Gallaudet studied sign and Clerc English. Then they spent a number of additional months traveling to various states to raise support. The fund they collected ultimately totaled $17,000, including $5,000 from the state of Connecticut. On April 15, 1817, Gallaudet and Clerc welcomed the first seven students—among them Alice and the fifty-one-year-old Joseph Brewster, Jr.—to the American Asylum for the Deaf at Hartford. Although not the first school for the deaf in this country, it was the first permanent one and arguably the most influential. Gallaudet and Clerc did in Connecticut what Epée had done in Paris; they permitted the deaf community to solidify and flourish. Clerc's sophisticated French sign language became the medium of instruction and ultimately an important component of the American sign dialect. To this day sign language in this country retains a markedly French cast; American signers can communicate fairly easily, if not perfectly, with French signers. British sign language, on the other hand, springs from other roots and is a totally foreign "tongue."

Like Epée, Clerc and Gallaudet actively spread the gospel of their method. Within the next few years some twenty other schools opened in various states, many of them country residential asylums, and many teachers made the pilgrimage to Hartford to be initiated into signs and the method. Graduates also spread about the country as teachers, and direct intellectual descent from Clerc still carries great prestige. Even today elderly deaf people claim with pride that they studied with students of the master, just as early Muslims defended their versions of doctrine by the authority of hearing it from the lips of one who had heard it from the Prophet. In the mid-nineteenth century signs held undisputed sway in the United States. Schools essentially ignored the teaching of oral skills.

The reaction set in somewhat earlier in Europe than in the United States. In most of Western Europe the silent system, along with other aspects of French culture, had arrived with the French conquerors. With Napoleon's defeat at Waterloo, however, all things French passed out of favor and appeals to local nationalism came to the fore. Thus the "German system" of strict oralism found sudden respectability. In Britain, meanwhile, the oral schools that had once brought glory to the name of Braidwood had gradually degenerated into asylums as overcrowded and poorly staffed as those that brought fame to the name of Dickens. Even in France the standards of teaching fell and fell. As the early Industrial Revolution advanced, more and more rural poor converged on the cities, and the handicapped, who had previously been cared for at home, increasingly became public charges to be warehoused as cheaply as possible in asylums.

The Germans were among the first to the attack. Johann Baptist Graeser (1766–1841) undertook what today's educational innovators hail as mainstreaming. In the early 1820s he experimented with deaf classes attached to ordinary schools at Bayreuth, where the deaf children would learn alongside their hearing agemates after mastering oral skills. The idea spread to other towns, but did not succeed anywhere. The deaf children simply could not keep up. Other leading German oralists were Victor Jager and Friedrich Moritz Hill (1805–74), the former influential through his writings, the latter through his teaching. Hill had studied with Pestalozzi, the Swiss teacher who reintroduced Comenius into educational thinking. Like his spiritual mentor, Pestalozzi favored the "mother method"—learning language and other skills as a child does from his mother. Hill translated this into a natural method of oral instruction, and through the many teachers he trained, spread this philosophy to many countries. An example of his influence is David Hirsch, who taught for many years in Amsterdam. Through him Hill's thought spread to Italy, in the person of the Abba Balestre, who visited Hirsch in 1861. Balestre then converted to the oral camp Abba Giulio Tarra, who headed the Milan school for the deaf and later chaired a pivotal meeting of educators.

Also through Hirsch's students Gerrit van Asch and William van Praagh, Hill's thought made a beachhead in England, where Van Praagh ran a small school for deaf Jewish children under the patronage of the Baroness Rothschild. His work proved so successful that it eventually inspired the founding of a college for oral teachers in England, and thus helped rejuvenate the moribund oral education descended from the Braidwoods.

Even in France, the heartland of the silent method, dissatisfaction reigned. Dr. Jean Itard, famous for his work with the mute "wild boy of Aveyron," had attempted auditory and oral training at the Paris Institute and willed a fund for an advanced reading and writing class in which sign was prohibited. The class supported by this bequest started in 1842, but it is not clear how closely it adhered to the donor's terms. Jean-Jacques Valade-Gabel, however, a student of Pestalozzi, taught at the Institute during the 1820s and 1830s. He later became Inspector General of Institutions for the Deaf in France and in that post helped prepare the ground for the growth of oralism.

The middle years of the nineteenth century also saw growing dissatisfaction in America. Like earlier efforts for deaf education, these began in New England and also centered on a deaf girl, an inspection trip to Europe, and some strong personalities. The tour in question was undertaken in 1843 by Horace Mann, the prominent educational reformer, and Dr. Samuel Gridley Howe, both the head of the Perkins Institution, the Boston school for the blind where Annie Sullivan would later train, and the teacher of Laura Bridgman, a deaf-blind prodigy. The men visited German oral schools and returned convinced that banning signs and concentrating on speech produced much better results. Hartford had experimented with speech training for adventitiously deaf children in the 1830s; when Dr. Harvey Peet and the Reverend George Day, respectively of the New York Institution and the American School, made their own trip to Germany, they came away less impressed. They acknowledged that some students might benefit, particularly those who lost hearing after developing speech, but generally found the German system inferior as a total system of education.

Nonetheless, Hartford began to feel the pressure and in 1857 it hired Miss Eliza Wadsworth to teach speech full-time. Perhaps this move arose from a genuine interest in fostering articulation, but it may have been intended merely to forestall Massachusetts from transferring subsidized students to some other school. As interest in a strictly oral school grew Hartford resisted with all the political muscle at its command.

Then in 1863 the little deaf girl, again the daughter of a prosperous, able, and influential man, entered the story. That year Mable Hubbard, age five, lost her hearing to scarlet fever, and her father, a well-born and well-connected attorney, began to interest himself in education of the deaf. Like other parents of his social class, Gardiner Greene Hubbard particularly wanted his child to learn to get along in polite hearing society, and he rejected the essentially manual training offered at Hartford. Along with the parents of two other post-lingually deaf girls (one a Cushing and the other the daughter of Rhode Island's governor) among others, he petitioned the state of Massachusetts to establish an oral school. Opposition from Hartford helped to defeat the idea that year, but in 1867 a small private oral school was opened in Chelmsford, Massachusetts. Hubbard persisted in petitioning the state, however, and by chance the governor received his request at the same time that he got an offer from one Thomas Clarke, a banker, to donate $50,000 toward the establishment of an oral school. In October of that year the Clarke School for the Deaf, then and now one of the finest of its kind, welcomed its first class, which included Mable Hubbard.

Clarke narrowly missed being the oldest permanent oral school in America. In March of the same year a much less socially prominent group established the New York Institution for Impaired Instruction, ancestor of the present-day Lexington School. In 1864 Hannah and Isaac Rosenfeld had set up a small private oral school. When they decided to admit children of poor families along with the more well-to-do they had to reorganize it. Like Clarke, the newly expanded institution took its inspiration from the German model; Bernhard Engelsmann, formerly of the Vienna Hebrew School for the Deaf, served as its first director. In 1870 New York State began helping to support the school, but it never matched Clarke in the size of its wealth or the prominence of its supporters.

Foremost among that distinguished, moneyed company for more than a century has been the family of Alexander Graham Bell. The future inventor of the telephone and husband of Mable Hubbard began his career as an oral teacher of the deaf and retained a passionate interest in the advancement of oralism the whole of his life. He was one of a pair of strong-willed, opinionated rivals who dominated American deaf education in the late nineteenth century and to a large extent set the terms of the debate as they exist today. The other was Edward Miner Gallaudet.

As Donald Moores has pointed out, Bell and Gallaudet were very like one another and very representative of their age. Self-confident Victorian worthies and centers of admiring circles of followers, they were roughly contemporaries, Gallaudet being born in 1837, Bell a decade later. Both had hearing-impaired mothers; Mrs. Bell spoke and used finger spelling and Sophia Fowler Gallaudet attended the American School and used sign. Both sons therefore grew up with strong feelings on the oral-manual controversy. Furthermore, they both followed distinguished fathers into careers in deafness. Bell's grandfather, Alexander Bell, and his father, Alexander Melville Bell, were well-known elocution professors in Edinburgh. When poor health forced the family to move to Canada, Alexander Melville brought his method of Visible Speech and Alexander Graham taught it at the Horace Mann School, an oral day school founded in Boston in 1869; at Clarke; and even at Hartford. A system for teaching articulation, Visible Speech consisted of written symbols representing the sounds. Each symbol, somewhat resembling a character in a mysterious foreign language, showed the positions taken by the tongue, teeth, and other speech organs while making the sound in question. The method did produce results, but it was cumbersome in practice, requiring children to master a whole separate alphabet, and it eventually passed out of use. Clarke dropped it because the children took to communicating by tracing the symbols in the air.

Both Gallaudet and Bell achieved great success very young. Thomas Hopkins Gallaudet had died in 1851, depriving the four-teen-year-old Edward of the chance to go to Yale. But at twenty the young man accepted the invitation of the Washington, D.C., philanthropist Amos Kendall to run the Columbia Institution for the Deaf and Blind, a new school in the federal district chartered by Congress in 1857. In 1864 Congress authorized the Institution to grant college degrees, and Gallaudet, at the age of twenty-seven, became president not only of Columbia but of the National College for the Deaf and Dumb, ancestor of Gallaudet College, then and now the world's only liberal arts college solely for the deaf. For nearly a century it was the world's only college for the deaf, period. Like Howard University, also supported by federal subventions, the college was a Civil War-era benefaction for the deprived. The mood of intense nationalism, historians suggest, encouraged the country to put its conscience money into good works with "national" in the title.

Bell, meanwhile, was beginning his teaching career and later undertook the experiments that culminated in the telephone. Contrary to legend, he was not attempting to invent something to benefit the deaf when he called to Mr. Watson that he wanted him. As a young man in Boston, Bell had won Mable's heart, but he did not win her hand until the device succeeded, financed largely by her father. A business association with Gardiner Hubbard and other canny partners insured his financial future, and the award of the prestigious Volta Prize by the French government symbolized his international stature.

The prize, commemorating the scientific pioneer Alessandro Volta, had more than a symbolic result. With his 50,000-franc prize money, and an additional $100,000 of his own funds, Bell established the Volta Bureau "for the increase and diffusion of knowledge relating to the deaf" in Washington in 1887. This was only one of Bell's many philanthropies in support of oral education. He also participated in founding the American Association for Teaching Speech to the Deaf, which ultimately combined with the Bureau to form the Alexander Graham Bell Association for the Deaf, one of the world's leading proponents of oralism.

Bell and Gallaudet, now bearded and opinionated as befitted their prominence, at first enjoyed friendly relations as fellow Washingtonians and allies in the cause of the deaf. Gardiner Hubbard introduced them and Bell received an honorary degree from the college in 1880, a year after he moved to Washington. Gallaudet spoke and wrote in favor of oral training as a supplement to sign and instituted some oral training at his schools. Eventually, however, a personal fissure developed and it grew into what can only be described as a feud. The philosophical disagreement came to a head over Bell's "Memoir upon the Formation of a Deaf Variety of the Human Race," which denounced both manual schools and deaf teachers as encouraging marriage among the deaf and thus the propagation of deafness. Each man, furthermore, accused the other of personal and political deceit. Bell, for example, testified before Congress against allowing the college to train teachers; he failed to inform Gallaudet of his intention to do so. Gallaudet, for his part, blackballed Bell from the Convention of American Instructors of the Deaf, which he headed until 1917. Efforts to merge this group with Bell's AATSD foundered; historians differ about where to lay the blame.

The two disagreed basically and heartily about the purpose of educating deaf people in the first place. Gallaudet had spent his life living and working in the French tradition of signing schools that fostered a deaf culture and community. Bell opposed such schools and the community they foster; he wrote his controversial "Memoir" arguing on the basis of the new science of genetics that deaf people should be integrated into general society for the good of future generations. (He neglected to notice that close inbreeding among the hearing appears to cause as much congenital deafness as marriage between deaf people.)

Personal grievance thus joined with philosophical dispute to produce the intense rancor characteristic of the oral-manual controversy in America. The entire emotional load carried by the argument certainly does not trace back to these two proud, prejudiced, and self-righteous men, but personal and family loyalties run very deep in the small universe of those seriously concerned with deafness, and each of the two leaders founded a constellation of institutions that still revere his memory and carry on his work as a duty to both the past and the future. To this day publications of the Bell Association invoke the words of the founder. Edward Miner Gallaudet, though long dead, still remains an almost palpable presence at the college that bears his family name. Had these two men reached some sort of personal accommodation, their intellectual heirs still might not agree today, but they might find it possible to communicate without seriously, angrily, and continuously questioning one another's motives. A minor but typical incident gives the flavor of their relationship: the dispute surrounding the late publication of a 1978 report by the Office of Demographic Studies at Gallaudet. When the federally funded document failed to appear at the expected time, a Bell Association official publicly charged that Gallaudet had "suppressed" it because it tended to support the oralist argument. Officials at Gallaudet, on the other hand, maintained that the reason was a re-analysis of the data by outside experts to prevent misinterpretation of the results by the oralists. The final version did seem to give less support to the oral argument than the earlier one, but it carried the imprimatur of important scholars with no stake in the outcome. The point is not the statistical accuracy of this particular study; it is the inability of either side to ascribe anything but base motives to the other.

Bell's money and name helped finally to turn the tide in favor of oralism, and even before he became a leading figure the trend had been running strongly against sign language as a means of instruction both here and in Europe. Certainly the manifest failure of the silent and simultaneous methods to produce good readers, writers, and speakers counted heavily, but that was probably not all. The French scholar Bernard Mottez believes that, in Europe at least, national politics played a part. The 1870s were years of nation building on the Continent; the most important countries were struggling to form unified nation-states out of constellations of local loyalties. This movement doomed a number of particularisms, most especially the regional dialects, which had to give way to the official national tongues.

Thus sign language, the dialect of the deaf, appeared anti-nationalistic, possibly even unpatriotic. And indeed, Europe's deaf people had long enjoyed good communication across national borders. The drive to make oral education universal was thus in part a drive to make deaf people good Germans or Frenchmen.

The emotional and political climax of the European movement for oralism came in 1880 at the Congress of Teachers of the Deaf in Milan. Over 150 delegates attended, with Edward Gallaudet and his brother Thomas, an Episcopal minister and founder of St. Ann's Church for Deaf-Mutes in New York, representing the United States. The Abba Tarra, whom we have already met as a follower, thrice removed, of Friedrich Moritz Hill, gave the emotional keynote address. As the priest closed his remarks the cry *"Evviva la parola!"* (Long live speech!) echoed through the hall. The Gallaudets stood almost alone as holdouts against the stampede to pure oralism; the resolution, passed by 160 to 4, states: "The Congress, considering the incontestable superiority of speech over signs in restoring the deaf-mute to society and in giving him a more perfect knowledge of language, declare that the oral method ought to be preferred to that of signs in the education and instruction of the deaf and dumb."[6]

In the wake of Milan every country except the United States went over to pure oralism as national policy. Even France, the birthplace of the sign method, shifted in 1886. Only in the United States did sign language remain a medium of instruction, and then generally only for slow students in the upper grades. By the early years of the twentieth century American schools that did not practice strict oralism used the "combined method": oral instruction in the primary grades, with sign language acknowledged and permitted (but not taught) among the "oral failures" beginning in early adolescence.

As in all great power struggles, more than philosophy was at stake. The nature of teaching naturally determined who could qualify as a teacher. Until the late 1860s American schools held deaf teachers in high esteem. Laurent Clerc, for example, earned more than Thomas Hopkins Gallaudet, despite the administrative responsibilities Gallaudet discharged in addition to teaching. As comprehensible speech and the ability to impart it became the criteria for success, however, deaf teachers quickly lost ground. In 1870 they accounted for over 40 percent of all teachers of the deaf in America; by 1895 their share had dropped to 22 percent and by 1917 to 15 percent. The shift involved more than numbers of jobs. Deaf teachers were banished from the classrooms of the early grades and the academically able (or orally able, which was often taken as the same thing). They gathered in the ghetto of vocational courses for "oral failures." Teachers like Clerc, cultured deaf people who communicated in sign, disappeared from both the classrooms and the imaginations of young deaf students.

Many count the watershed year of 1880 a dark time for the manual deaf community, but it was also a dawn. As interest in the oral approach grew among educators, parents, and some deaf people, the passionate attachment of other deaf people to their sign language culture never diminished. In August 1880, a month before the educators convened in Milan, between 250 and 300 deaf people gathered in Cincinnati to found the National Association of the Deaf. The meeting grew out of suggestions published in the *Deaf Mutes Journal,* the most important organ of its type at that time.

By the 1880s three generations of deaf Americans had passed through schools for the deaf and a cadre of young leaders had graduated from the college. They had their first success at large-scale organizing in 1851, with the founding of the New England Gallaudet Association of the Deaf. Difficulty of travel discouraged larger meetings for several decades but the idea recurred frequently in print. When the 1880 convention successfully convened at Cincinnati's Bellevue House Hotel, many noted with pride that the meeting had been organized entirely by deaf people and took place in a public hotel rather than a school for the deaf. It meant that organized deaf people could act on their own, independent of their hearing friends.

As Leon Auerbach implies in an article on the Cincinnati meeting, the two great conventions of 1880 may be more than coincidence. Deaf people obviously felt themselves distinct within, if not apart from, the general hearing society. It was precisely to hamper the growth of a separate deaf culture and consciousness that the hearing educators passed what Auerbach, a deaf college professor, terms "that infamous resolution."[7] But hearing people held the power in the deaf educational world and oral methods came more and more to dominate teaching, both here and abroad, in the following decades.

Deaf people continued their efforts at organization, however. The NAD grew to include state sections and its magazine, *Silent Worker,* became probably their single most important organ. (The name was changed to *Deaf American* during the Communist witch-hunts of the 1950s.) In 1901 the National Fraternal Society of the Deaf (the "Frat") began issuing insurance to deaf people denied coverage or charged higher premiums by regular companies. By the 1970s its policies in force numbered well over 10,000. Other deaf groups include a network of athletic organizations, including a deaf world Olympic federation, local social clubs, and religious associations and churches representing all major denominations.

But despite their growing solidarity in the late nineteenth and early twentieth century, the influence of deaf people was nearly totally eclipsed. In 1900, for example, Edward Gallaudet again crossed the Atlantic to an international congress of teachers of the deaf, this time in Paris. "As the hearing professors presented paper after paper in support of oralism," writes psychologist and historian Harlan Lane, "the deaf professors, meeting separately, resolved repeatedly in favor of sign."[8] The hearing congress refused to meet jointly with the deaf on the grounds that French, not sign, was the official language of the meeting; that some hearing delegates knew no French appeared to weaken this argument not at all. Lane asserts that "the language problem was indeed a pretext for excluding the deaf";[9] the chair rejected even a summary of the deaf section's proceedings. Gallaudet vainly pressed for recommending that the instructional method fit the capacities of the students rather than for prescribing oral training for all. He attempted, with no greater success, to have the report favoring speech labeled as the resolution of the hearing group rather than of the congress at large.

Renewed interest in oral training did not grow out of mere obstinacy, however. It arose in part because of the nature of the student population. Until antibiotics and vaccinations became widespread by the late 1940s, school-age deaf children included a high percentage who had lost their hearing after achieving speech or at least after having been exposed to it. Surveys of cause of hearing loss doubtlessly had even wider margins of error in the past than they do today, but data incontrovertibly show that a smaller proportion of deaf children than now had profound losses from birth. The three girls whose parents led the drive for Clarke, for example, were all adventitiously deaf. Speech and speechreading training promise better results for such youngsters than for the pre-lingually deaf.

A further spur to interest in oral methods was the discovery that residual hearing could be exploited in many cases. Traditional oral training had emphasized lipreading, but as early as 1761 the French Academy received evidence that training could improve some deaf children's ability to make out sounds, and in 1767 the great teacher Pereira advocated training those with residual hearing to listen to words. Jean Itard's experiments in the early 1800s convinced him of the value of such training and motivated him to leave his bequest for oral training at the National Institute. The Whipple Home School for Deaf Mutes (later the

Mystic Oral School), established in 1869 in Connecticut, became the first American school to adopt the auditory approach.

Not until the early 1900s, however, did this method begin to receive widespread attention. Dr. James Kerr Love in Scotland demonstrated that most deaf children have some residual hearing. In Vienna, meanwhile, Dr. Ferdinand Alt conducted experiments that culminated in 1900 in the first electric hearing aid. In 1914 the otologist Max Goldstein founded the Central Institute for the Deaf in St. Louis and there elaborated his acoustic method of stimulating residual hearing.

In retrospect it is obvious that the slow development of hearing-aid technology hindered efforts to train residual hearing. Only in the 1940s were hearing aids small, cheap, and accepted enough for really widespread use among children. Early in that decade the Dutch government issued aids to all deaf preschoolers in the country, and with surprising results: many who previously would have gone to special schools for the hard-of-hearing or deaf proved able to attend regular schools. This discovery encouraged some teachers to adopt an extreme form of auditory training called the unisensory method. It expects the child, using a hearing aid, to gain initial mastery of language through hearing alone. Like other enthusiasms of the past, this method produced some outstanding results, but it did not prove to be the general solution its advocates had hoped and it offered little or no help to older people whose hearing had not been trained at the crucial developmental stage. Nonetheless, its undeniable benefits for many deaf and hard-of-hearing children have made early use of hearing aids and auditory training standard in all types of treatment for hearing-impaired children.

An equally large change took place during the 1940s and 1950s almost unnoticed. The nature of the deaf school population changed. Modern medicine essentially wiped out most of the traditional causes of hearing loss in childhood. The recurrent earache, mastoid infections, scarlet fever, measles, and other childhood diseases became rarities. Ironically, though, antibiotics and advanced medical techniques began saving more and more youngsters who would previously have died, meningitics and the extremely premature or defective. The deaf school population, therefore, became harder to educate, with a greater predominance of pre-lingual losses and multiple handicaps. Unlike the school populations of fifty years ago, students at state residential schools in the 1970s were often more than 90 percent pre-lingually deaf.

As teachers struggled with this more demanding type of student, doubts about the efficacy of the old methods began to grow, slowly at first and in widely scattered places. By the mid-1960s, however, a number of forces united to bring a new movement to the surface. The Babbidge Report on deaf education, issued by the U.S. Department of Health, Education, and Welfare midway through the decade, sent the educational world reeling with its stinging attack on decades of failure. The great rubella epidemic of 1963–65 produced a huge bulge of deaf and otherwise handicapped children. In different parts of the country individual parents, teachers, and administrators began to express their private doubts. And the idea of cultural pluralism was in the air; the black civil rights movement had brought to national consciousness the possibility of pride in ways of life unlike the white American norm.

Scattered schools began to experiment with manual methods. Louisiana revived the Rochester method, developed in upstate New York in the nineteenth century; it consisted of simultaneous speech and finger spelling. North Carolina shortly followed suit. In 1968 the Santa Ana, California, special education program became the first in the country to adopt true simultaneous communication: speech and sign language used together. But then, Santa Ana had in Roy Holcomb the country's only hearing-impaired program supervisor. That same summer the Maryland School for the Deaf under David Denton began teaching sign language to preschool children and their parents. Just as the new wave mounted to sweep the country, Holcomb gave it a dynamic name, total communication.

Just exactly what this title means has never been exactly clear. To many it means a method: using all means of communication at one's command, including voice, signs, finger spelling, and hearing. To others like Denton, it means an outlook as well, "an unequivocal acceptance of deaf people as people, [a belief that] the language of signs is legitimate, that it belongs, that it is *the* cultural language of deaf people and the best possible tool that we have to become part of their existence and as a consequence to grow with them."

News of these doings spread through articles, editorials, and word of mouth. Interest in sign language had been growing in the 1960s anyway, especially among parents who had long been told that encouraging manual communication would damage their children. Nanette Fabray tells of organizing a sign language class in Los Angeles at about this time and advertising it in the newspaper. Over five hundred people appeared to claim the thirty places and fights broke out among many desperate to be included. It took the police to restore order.

The interest in total communication finally resulted in a national gathering in April 1971 in Memphis. This "tripod" conference included professionals, parents, and—for the first time in generations—deaf adults, and matched the Milan Congress in emotional fervor. Eyewitnesses describe it as a "celebration" with dramatic scenes of tears and embraces. Researchers such as Schlesinger and Meadow presented findings emphasizing the importance of early unambiguous communication. Delegates hugged, wept, and sang together in sound and sign. Teams of people who had attended the Memphis meetings then spread the word in regional meetings for parents, teachers, and deaf adults.

The effect of these meetings on deaf education was as stunning as that in Milan almost a century before. The private oral schools stood by their customary methods, but total communication swept through the public systems like a prairie fire. Within a few years state schools and local day programs across the country had adopted it, either as the sole basis of instruction or as one of several parallel tracks. Oralists, naturally, bemoaned the spread of the system they had fought for so many years and pointed, often quite justifiably, to deficiencies in various programs.

A very serious problem has bedeviled the movement since its beginning: the many advocates, writers, and practitioners of total communication have never agreed on exactly what it is and how it should be practiced. Nor is there any substantial agreement on what version of sign language ought to be used. Large numbers of teachers had to learn sign quickly, and standards vary widely among and even within programs. In the rush to the new bandwagon, many educators appear to have forgotten valuable elements of the oral programs they formerly practiced.

But the speed of the change should surprise no one familiar with history. Psychologist Harry Bornstein describes deaf education as "a field which has traditionally resolved the uncertainties and ambiguities of communication with adherence to rigid orthodoxy. There was a right method and there were wrong methods. It is hardly any step at all to move to a new orthodoxy."[10]

But the change represented more than philosophy. As at Milan, careers and jobs hung in the balance. As the pendulum swung back toward the skills of the manual deaf, their numbers on faculties began to grow. In 1960 only 503 deaf teachers worked in the nation's schools, nearly all in state residential institutions. By 1973 their numbers had more than doubled, and more than a third taught in public day classes and freestanding day schools. For the first time in generations higher administrative positions became reasonable goals for deaf educators. For hearing faculty members the power shifted between generations. Those few who possessed good signing abilities, or who could acquire them quickly, usually the younger people, found themselves at a sudden and considerable advantage over older, more conservative colleagues.

For some educators, the change was simply too great. It meant reversing the values of a lifetime, embracing the anathema of many years. In describing his experience teaching at a signing school the Reverend Thomas Arnold, founder of a famous oral school in Northampton, England, had written many decades ago: "It seemed like being among a people who spoke another language, lived a different kind of life, thought and felt unlike ourselves. . . . The sign method made them strangers and their teachers had to become like them to understand them."[11]

That, people like Denton argue, is precisely the point. Accepting sign language implies accepting deaf people as a distinct and valid cultural reality. At its philosophical extreme total communication calls on hearing people to become, to the extent possible, like the deaf; to enter, as relative novices, a new cultural world; and to relinquish forever any claims of special or superior knowledge. No hearing person not born of deaf parents can ever know sign language as well as a deaf person who has grown up using it daily and colloquially. Hearing people therefore can't remain arbiters of correctness. Total communication programs generally use sign language forms compatible with spoken English, which most signers consider hybrids or even bastards, instead of the pure forms of American Sign Language used colloquially by the deaf community. From being the model, indeed the definition, of linguistic correctness, English is demoted to one of several alternate language forms.

If the oral movement took stunning body blows, however, it kept its feet. In the early 1970s a series of lawsuits and acts of Congress granted all the handicapped important new rights in access to education and public facilities. Culminating in Public Law 94-142, the Education for All Handicapped Children Act of 1975, this trend continually strengthened the ability of handicapped children and their parents to demand education from the local authorities rather than at special schools. We will discuss these developments and the issues surrounding them in detail in a later chapter. Briefly, however, the new body of law encourages school authorities to educate handicapped children in the regular schools to the extent possible. This new approach is called, with the particular inelegance of bureaucratic jargon, "mainstreaming," because it includes the handicapped child in the so-called educational mainstream.

A further aid to the oralist cause, although not at first conceived as such, was the introduction in the late 1960s of cued speech, a communication method designed to facilitate lipreading and English acquisition. Developed at Gallaudet College by physicist Orin Cornett, cued speech has enjoyed relatively greater popularity in strongly oral Australia than in the U.S., but its use in public and private schools is growing here. Cornett envisions students using cues for the first years of life and the first years of schooling, but entering the mainstream of public school by junior high age. When he introduced his system, however, staunch oralists at the Bell Association and elsewhere saw only the hand signals the system uses and overlooked its ultimate goals. With use, however, cued speech has gained increasing respect in oral quarters, although it has not gained widespread approval among deaf adults.

Thus, American deaf education in the late 1970s rushed eagerly off in all directions. No clear trend emerged from this welter of techniques and policies. The only constant was the continuing oral-manual debate. Oralists saw grave dangers in total communication; manualists saw perils no less dire in mainstreaming. Both camps forecast the failure and ultimate demise of their rival's newest enthusiasm, but only after serious damage had been done to many children. "They'll sell a whole generation of children down the river," said both an official of a prominent total communication school about mainstreaming and a national officer of the Bell Association about T.C.

In the early years of the national commitment to integrating the handicapped into regular education, the effect on the deaf community cannot be clearly discerned. The enrollment at the state residential schools, long the backbone of deaf cultural transmission, appeared to be changing somewhat. More and more children handicapped only by deafness now get their schooling closer to home, so the percentage of multiply handicapped in the residential schools has risen. But only the future can tell whether mainstreaming of severely or profoundly deaf children will work.

In this atmosphere of growing confusion, only one trend undeniably leads toward the advancement of deaf people. Starting in the 1960s, opportunities for higher education increased dramatically. Until that time Gallaudet was the only college in the world specifically equipped to educate deaf students, and the lack of flexible higher education severely limited the economic prospects of deaf adults. After many years of agitation by deaf leaders and hearing allies, Congress established the National Technical Institute for the Deaf, which opened at the Rochester Institute of Technology in New York State in 1968. One of several colleges of a polytechnic university, NTID offers training in technical subjects at levels ranging from post-secondary terminal courses through the doctorate and beyond. In the late 1970s it enrolled more than nine hundred students.

To meet the growing need for vocational and introductory programs like those offered by junior and community colleges the U.S. Office of Education and the Rehabilitation Services Administration established programs for deaf students at St. Paul

Vocational Technical Institute in Minnesota, Delgado Junior College in New Orleans, and Seattle Community College in Washington State in 1968–69. The California State University at Northridge also undertook to open its programs to deaf students in 1964. These six programs, all receiving federal funds for the purpose, together provide a nearly complete range of liberal arts, technical, vocational, and professional courses from the freshman level through post-doctoral work. By the late 1970s close to 90 percent of deaf school leavers were attending some post-secondary educational program, a drastic and promising change from the situation less than a generation before. Under the provisions of Section 504 of the Rehabilitation Act of 1973, which requires equal access for the handicapped to federally supported programs and facilities, many other colleges and universities undertook to educate deaf students. In an economy increasingly dominated by service occupations and technological expertise, therefore, the next deaf generation appears to have some realistic possibilities of escaping from the shrinking vocational ghetto that had constricted their elders.

Equally striking was the change in national atmosphere. Starting in the 1960s American culture had begun to acknowledge and accept the value of cultural expression and experience different from the white middle-class norm. Along with other racial, religious, and ethnic minorities, the deaf community has emerged somewhat from the shadow of "differentness," at least enough to demand television programs captioned or signed for their benefit, or to support the rise of professional deaf theater in the sign language idiom.

Sign language on television caused the predictable dissension along traditional lines, but another technological advance had the paradoxical effect of bringing all elements of the deaf population together in a common effort. At the Bell Association convention in Salt Lake City in 1964, Robert Weitbrecht, a deaf engineer, demonstrated a new invention, an acoustic coupler allowing ordinary telephones to transmit signals from a teletype machine. Weitbrecht's device transformed the teletypewriter's output of electrical signals into sounds which could be translated back into electric impulses at the other end, and breached at last the prison that Bell's great invention had ironically constructed for deaf people. Deaf-run organizations to collect, manufacture, and disseminate the devices, and the teletypewriter (TTY) and other telecommunications devices for the deaf (TDD), soon revolutionized many lives. In addition to fostering a small industry and improving the lot of individuals, the invention had salutary effects on the deaf community at large; hearing-impaired people of all persuasions recognized their common need, and work to advance the spread of the TTY involved the first large-scale cooperation between the two camps since the days of Bell and Gallaudet.

Significant as these changes were, however, they did not alter the basic facts of life. Hearing people still knew little about the deaf community but still controlled its most crucial institutions. The communications controversy still split the hearing-handicapped into hostile factions. Educators still periodically announced "innovations," each of them promising the "answer."

Probably a single observation can sum up the experience of deaf people in this country and abroad: how little true progress has occurred and how many years have gone by in futile wrangling. A number of useful techniques, systems, and devices have been developed, of course. The technology of identification, measurement, amplification, and telecommunications steadily advances. At least dim awareness, if not clear understanding, has dawned on the general public. Knowledge among parents, physicians, and educators is growing. But still, the core of the problem, the oral-manual controversy, is no closer to resolution than when Heinicke and Epée squared off two hundred years ago; generations have passed in the issuance of windy proclamations and fervent declarations of belief rather than in the research that would convince scientific investigators and produce usable results. Educational "breakthroughs" present the same solutions time and again. Today's enthusiasm for early identification can be traced at least to 1852. Finger spelling for young children, rediscovered in the early 1960s, was proposed by Dalgarno in 1680. The Englishman Arrowsmith proposed mainstreaming in 1819 and Germany tried it on a large scale, but without consistent success, in the following decades. German schools had also attempted something very like total communication and the

Danes used a system resembling cued speech over seventy years ago.

Generations of educators have made their careers on "solutions" that solve only selected parts of the problem, on theories that fit only selected facts, on philosophies whose effects bear on other people's lives. And still, in the last quarter of the twentieth century, four hundred years after the scientific study of hearing impairment began, the most basic questions remain unanswered. Parents and teachers searching for practical answers find only partial ones. The field of deaf education remains one of the great scandals and shames of education; and it is the hearing-handicapped, burdened by prejudice and bad schooling in addition to their disability, who bear the consequences.

CHAPTER 8

The Evidence

If necessity is the mother of invention, then ignorance is the mother of dogma. People invent maps of belief for areas their knowledge cannot penetrate. The Polish anthropologist Bronislaw Malinowski spent the years of World War I interned on the Trobriand Islands off New Guinea, watching Stone Age tribesmen fish and navigate, and he made an arresting observation. Their magic and religion began where their science and engineering left off. The Trobrianders needed to understand and thus feel in control of the areas most crucial to their existence, luck in fishing, safety on the ocean, success at farming. In some aspects of these subjects they had knowledge based on experience and observation, what we would call empirical evidence. When a tribesman fished from the beach or constructed a canoe he based his work on principles that Malinowski, a trained physicist, could appreciate; but much of what they wanted to know lay beyond their inadequate attempts at science. When they set off on a trip they knew how to navigate but not how to guarantee good weather. They had maps for the former, but for the latter they could only appeal to their gods.

Even where their data stopped their need to know did not, so they invented explanations of the things they couldn't really explain and then invested their explanations with the emotional energy of their need. Thus, Malinowski concluded, the real difference between magic and religion on the one hand and engineering and science on the other was not the motives that required them or the logical processes that produced them, but the data base where the reasoning began. For Malinowski, magic and religion, both deeply felt but unempirical ways of knowing, fill the same need as what we call science: They make the unknown less frightening and more predictable. When people need very much to understand something beyond the power of their real knowledge to explain, they invent an explanation, invest it with the strength of truth, and cling to it like grim death.

Malinowski learned this watching sailors of outrigger canoes, but he might as well have studied teachers of the deaf. The whole history of deaf education since the founding of the first schools has been a war of religion, a battle of belief between two brands of magic, neither of which, in fact, has ever made a very impressive empirical showing. That this desperate struggle should take place in so intellectually torpid a field as pedagogy is in itself noteworthy; the combatants have railed against one another with the righteous fury of crusaders for generations. It is difficult to think of another pedagogic dispute where passions run so high. The progressive-traditionalist battles of the 1930s were mere skirmishes by comparison. The conservatives of the 1960s surrendered to "relevance" without, relatively speaking, firing a shot in their own defense. But both oralism and manualism resolutely refuse to die.

This is an unorthodox situation but hardly a mysterious one. The passion matches the importance of the stakes. Both sides believe, and rightly, that the battle involves something infinitely valuable, the happiness, the futures, perhaps even the souls, of innocent children. We have already quoted Kathryn Meadow's observation on the origin of the dispute, but it bears repeating. "The oral-manual controversy is about the emotional experience of having a deaf child." It is about the deeply irrational experience of wanting the best for a child, as all parents do, and not having any true empirical basis for deciding how to go about getting it. It is also about the deeply troubled consciences of professionals who wish to guide parents to a safe path through the quagmire. Thus, it is about what happens to the rationality of people who, year after year, decade after decade, see their efforts fall short of their promises, but who must still continue making those promises to parents in bitter despair. After one has led a generation of innocent and desperately vulnerable children along a certain perilous and painful road, only a rare person can even entertain the possibility of being wrong.

It may be that in recent years a new generation of practitioners has appeared on the scene, educated more eclectically and blessed with a new open-mindedness. There are numbers of younger practitioners who sound more pragmatic, more flexible about techniques, and more determined not to waste their careers in fruitless wrangling. But these people will have to be very strong indeed to surmount the venerable ramparts they have inherited. Even in ruins the old fortresses have high walls and deep trenches separating them. As in many countries with histories of ancient struggles, the structure of this situation makes it difficult for common decency to flourish across the old barricades. Each camp maintains its own training programs, journals, and professional, parents', and deaf people's associations. Even publishing houses carry the banner of one or the other camp. And researchers, of course, are easily identified by their past work and associations. A new generation might be able to make peace, but it will have a lot of forgetting to do first.

Not surprisingly, the field has attracted few disinterested researchers. It is difficult, in fact, to imagine an atmosphere less congenial to the ordinary run of academic investigators. The questions at issue are profoundly important and very large, the base of knowledge is small and not very solid, and the vast majority of the literature fails to meet the most elementary standards of objectivity. Daniel and Agnes Ling and Gail Pflaster, after reviewing "several thousand" books and articles, report despairingly that they "found relatively few that were more than simple statements of faith, philosophy, and opinion."[1] From across the barricades Donald Moores concurs. "Most of the literature cited as research," he writes, "involves description, defense, and praise of a program by a person who has developed it or is in some way closely related with it. With the exception of a possible audiogram or tape accompanying a lecture, no data are presented. . . . Given such a climate, most researchers prefer to investigate other questions."[2]

These problems only increase the unlikelihood of attracting first-rate researchers to the field. The central questions about deafness, unfortunately, do not generally hang out in academically very prestigious neighborhoods. Many of the practitioners and most of the researchers come out of special education departments, ordinarily housed in schools of education, which the tonier denizens of academe tend to regard as shantytowns best left to their own devices. Audiology is one of the technologies on the hazy borders of medicine that are predominantly populated by women, unfortunately usually a sure sign of low academic prestige. A very high proportion of the practitioners enter the deafness field for personal, rather than strictly professional, reasons. Often the children or siblings of deaf people, they arrive with strong methodological biases based on personal experience and family relationships. One important researcher of the last generation, for example, is reputed to have developed his influential theory of deaf intellect because of his dislike for his deaf father. Whether or not the story is true, the fact that well-informed people credit it hardly testifies to a very high standard of objectivity, on the part of either the researcher or his critics. It is probably no accident that at least two of the most rigorous and original recent thinkers in the field, Hans Furth and Daniel Ling, came to it inadvertently. Furth's interest developed out of his work on Piaget. Ling, already trained in electronics and music, needed a reason to live in Manchester, England; he found it by enrolling in the department headed by Sir Alexander and Lady Irene Ewing, two leaders of British oralism.

The very desperation motivating much of the research further discourages impartiality. Writes psychologist Edna Levine: "Most, if not all [investigators] have been driven to research out of deep frustration with the unchanging status of the deaf over the decades, and with the futility of expecting traditional educational methods to improve the situation."[3]

We badly need research because we have very little reliable information on very crucial issues. These include the differences among people in using the various sense modalities for gathering information and the effect of early intervention programs on intellect and communication. Objective research on manual communication only began to appear during the 1950s. And on the crucial question of the effect of manual communication on the development of speech, Daniel Ling, a careful if committed researcher, states that the evidence is "at best equivocal."[4] Weak evidence creates special problems in a field rent with passionate disagreement, Ling believes. "If anyone already holds an opinion, then the evidence for rejecting that opinion has to be very strong. And at the present moment there really isn't strong evidence for manualists to reject their view because of oral success or for oralists to reject their view because of manual success. We come to this not with biases, because biases are fair . . . we come to this not with biases but with prejudices."

Into this wasteland of confusion venture the parents of a small child, often knowing so little of the field as to be unaware of the existence of the controversy. But because everyone agrees on the vital (if ill-understood) importance of the early years, some decision about education must be made quickly. Ling, Conrad, and others believe that the choice may be even more crucial than present workers, in their ignorance, think it is. If we knew more about the functioning of the nervous system, they argue, we would see that early training may influence lifetime styles of processing sensory information.

It seems apparent, even from the confusing evidence available, that some children do better under a given educational regimen than others. The problem is, however, that no one can predict with any exactitude which severely or profoundly deaf child is likely to flourish and which will fail in a given program. The basis for the choice, the Lings and Pflaster say, is "philosophy and hope." Serious philosophical argument can be made in favor of either an oral or a manual approach. It helps in getting some grasp on the situation to state clearly the arguments and their supporting evidence. Even if we will sometimes appear to be grasping at fog, we will outline the main points and the information their advocates muster in their support.

In this country at this time, it is something of a misnomer to talk of an oral-manual controversy. No responsible authority on either side denies the importance of speech to those hearing-impaired people able to achieve it. Rather, the controversy separates those who advocate a strictly oral approach and those who would augment speech, speechreading, and auditory training with early exposure to manual communication. Not every program styling itself total communication (TC) provides adequate oral training, of course; some, indeed, honor its importance more in the breach than in the practice. The central issue of the debate is not about a choice between speech alone or sign alone but about the effects of combining them.

The argument of the oral camp rests on a simple idea. English speech is the common mode of communication in this society and to participate fully a person must master that mode, as well as reading and writing. Advocates further imply, and some state, that many or most deaf people can master speech, if properly trained. And finally, they assume that hearing society is where deaf people should seek their personal identity and most important relationships. "Deafness," writes Winifred Northcott, president of the Bell Association, "can be reduced from a handicap to the level of a defect that still permits full and independent living."[5]

To achieve these ends oral educators prescribe an "oral" or "talking" environment in which the child communicates, both expressively and receptively, in spoken language only. Thus, it is argued, he learns language through residual hearing or lipreading or both and he learns to speak clearly enough for others to understand him.

The importance to the deaf child of learning English is more than academic, the oralists argue; or, put another way, it is very academic indeed. Success in this society depends on schooling; success at school depends on a detailed mastery of English. Reading follows from speech and so does writing. Small details of grammar carry important conceptual distinctions; knowing the difference between active and passive, between past and future, between conditional and present, spells the difference between being able to reason in English or not. It is vital, the oralists argue, that the child learn English as his first and major modality of expression and thought. It must be his major modality because he must know it as perfectly as possible. It must be his first modality because learning it takes more work for a deaf child than signs and thus is less attractive. Latham Breunig distinguishes the "steep and thorny way" of integration into hearing society from the "primrose path of letting these skills deteriorate through excessive espousal of manual communication."[6]

Central to the oral-only or oral-first philosophy is the idea that a child permitted to sign before mastering speech, or before speech has become an obvious impossibility, will not learn to speak well. In its least sophisticated form it argues that laziness will rule. "A kid will take ice cream every time," says Kenneth Lane of the Bell Association. More sophisticated proponents, such as the Lings, argue from their suspicions about the structure of the nervous system. They worry that speech and sign conflict because they present the individual with more stimuli than he can effectively handle.

This is a serious argument advanced by serious students. The individual has only so much attention, the brain only so much short-term memory capacity; when modalities compete for limited space, part of the message may be lost. Were the functioning of the nervous system better understood, more decisive evidence might be available on this point. For now, the argument rests on studies that appear to show that hearing-impaired children receiving messages simultaneously through speech and sign attend more to sight than to sound. When sign is present, the Lings and Pflaster argue, it rather than speech claims the bulk of the attention. Even when the person has so little hearing that messages arrive exclusively by sight, they argue that signing can still damage oral skills. Watching the signs may keep the person from attending to the lips, and good speechreading skill is vital for communicating with hearing who do not communicate manually.

The evidence on this point is confusing, to say the least. Deaf adults skilled in both speech and sign can and do follow both hands and lips. "You said X but you signed Y," they might tell an inexpert signer. Ling's own evidence indicates that the hearing-impaired person who combines speechreading with residual hearing gets substantially more of a message than one who depends on either hearing or sight alone. Why one type of visual information should conflict with hearing while another enhances it as yet lacks a totally convincing explanation.

One possible reason is that speechreading is a close, if incomplete, visual analogue of speech. The lips transmit only a fraction of the information, but everything they send forms part of the speech message. The same is not true of signs. A person may sign in English word order and add elements representing English grammatical modulations, but if he uses signs in their standard meanings many will not coincide perfectly with English words. For example, a single sign can mean "sorry" or "apologize" or even "apologetic." Another single sign can mean "talk" or "chat" or "converse." Conversely, the single English word "right" can take the form of three different signs, for the senses "right turn," "human rights," and "correct." Exposure to signs does not provide exposure to purely English usage in the same way that speechreading and audition do.

Furthermore, receiving a known language in two modalities is probably quite a different thing from learning it that way in the first place. The skilled adult—perhaps adventitiously deaf—has two large vocabularies, one of words, one of signs, which he need only compare. The child who is first building them faces the problem of mastering two systems of usage at once.

If the child is to learn to speak clearly he must learn to listen closely to subtle sound shifts and gradations that hearing people do not consciously hear at all. If he can depend on visual cues to get the entire meaning of the message (instead of cues only to individual words), then he is less likely, it is argued, to do the hard work of training his residual hearing. Without learning to use every bit of hearing that remains he will neither learn to speak clearly nor develop a knowledge of English detailed enough to support good reading and writing. These arguments go a long way to distinguish speechreading from sign as a visual modality, but they still do not completely answer the Lings' argument that visual communication per se may compete with hearing for neurological space.

Nonetheless, the oralists argue, to assure the greatest possibility of mastering English, the child should be exposed to no gestures or signs until his spoken language is secure. (Or until the effort is given up as a failure. "One is duty bound to give the child a system of communication that works and through which he can learn," Daniel Ling says.) Then, if he wishes, some oral advocates say, the oral success can learn signs to communicate with manual deaf people as he would a second language. And if oral teaching does not succeed, he can be switched to a gestural program before serious harm is done. Teaching speech exclusively at the beginning thus gives the child the widest range of options, the oralists say; it permits him to succeed at speaking without depriving him of the chance to learn sign later. And modern technology and techniques provide a better chance at oral success than in the past. Remarkably "deaf" youngsters have proved to possess surprisingly large amounts of trainable residual hearing.

Those who reject this position argue not so much from philosophy as from experience. In the past and, to a depressing degree, in the present, oralism simply has not kept its promise to large numbers of children. Conrad, for example, tested very close to the entire population of English pre-lingually deaf fifteen- and sixteen-year-olds who had no additional handicaps. These youngsters had ten years of strictly oral training, and 85 percent had hearing losses in excess of 85 decibels. He found the usual academic and communicative disaster. Of those with hearing losses less than 65 dB, half read less well than the norm for children aged 10 years 8 months; of those with losses greater than 85 dB, half read worse than the norm for children aged 7 years 6 months. Nearly half of all students read below 9 years and only 6 out of 360 read at their age level.

Nor did they have very good oral skills. After years of training about half lipread worse than an average hearing child of their age with no training. Only 10 percent of the profoundly deaf spoke well enough to be easily understood; their own teachers—presumably sympathetic judges and experienced decoders of deaf speech—rated about half very difficult to understand. More than 70 percent of the profoundly deaf fell into that sorry category. Conrad suggests that most of these unfortunate young people had no mother tongue—no linguistic system that they knew intimately and could use with ease. "These results worry me," he writes.[7]

The children in this study, of course, do not represent the best in oral teaching. Ling claims a success rate of nearly 60 percent for children with unaided losses in the profound range, and some of his pupils do very well indeed, well enough, in fact, to enter the French immersion program required of children from many English-speaking homes in Quebec province. And the children in Conrad's study do not represent the most modern methods; they began their education in the early 1960s. But they probably represent a realistic average level of performance. The best teachers take only a handful of students. Most children receive training that is quite mediocre indeed.

Critics of oralism base their case most strongly on the presumed harm done to the child who fails to develop adequate communication skills. Moderate oralists suggest that the child be switched to another method if pure oralism proves inappropriate. But when and how does this change take place? And what does it cost the parents and teachers to admit that the time has come? Ultimately, of course, for legal, bureaucratic, and moral reasons, the choice belongs to the parents—the people perhaps least equipped to make a rational choice. If the parent has come to believe that speech development equals "success," then introduction of manual communication must equal failure. If the goal of education is to make a deaf child appear to communicate "normally" in hearing society, then adopting sign language or cued speech means that the parents must accept the fact that their child may be permanently "abnormal" (a fact that they should have accepted long before). Freddy Howard's plight is far from rare; his mother is extreme but not unusual.

A highly skilled and conscientious teacher will know within months—certainly within a year or so—whether a child's progress promises a reasonable hope of success. Even with good progress, a deaf child needs as much time to develop speech as a normally hearing one—ordinarily at least three years from beginning of training. Still, teachers tell grim stories of parents who refuse to give up, those who, like Freddy Howard's mother, cling year after year to increasingly vain and damaging hopes. Although some teachers will simply advise parents that they have nothing more to offer a child, others will continue as long as the family continues to insist or to pay.

Changing approaches also depends on the teacher having the detachment and intellectual honesty to admit that a case falls short of expectations and that a new method—and a new teacher or school—is required. In so highly charged an atmosphere a teacher may lay off a good deal of blame or guilt onto the parents—for not providing a proper oral environment, for not cooperating actively enough with the teacher, or simply for not being "committed" enough.

Finally, the possibility of change depends on the assumption that the child and his family can "always" learn sign. Running through the oral argument is the implicit belief that learning sign is somehow "easy." That it is easier for deaf people to learn than speech does not on its face indicate that mastering sign presents no difficulties, especially for the parents. Like any foreign language, sign takes years of work to achieve real fluency; neither hearing nor deaf who seriously try to learn it find the task trivial. The Maryland School for the Deaf, a TC school with an extensive sign language program for parents, found that only about half of the mothers could sign sentences after six months of studying with a teacher who visited once a week. Forty percent had some usable individual signs, and 10 percent had no usable signs whatsoever. Only half of the fathers knew any signs, a quarter managing sentences and a quarter using only individual words. Parents get better as time goes by, but not all become proficient, and those who come to the task disappointed and unwilling are even less likely to do well. If it is determined that a child should use sign, then his parents should make the effort cheerfully and with hopeful hearts. Steady application will produce heartening results. Hearing adults *can* learn to communicate well in any one of a number of sign systems, but they must be willing to spend time and care on the project.

A final criticism of the strict oral approach is the amount of school time devoted to learning communication rather than the information and skills other children get in school. At best, oral training is exacting and time-consuming; at worst, excruciatingly tedious. Under best modern practice, a child with considerable residual hearing whose loss is discovered early and who immediately receives proper amplification and highly skilled training ought to have a fair command of English by normal school age. Even this child will require additional speech work during his school years, and most children, of course, receive something less than ideal treatment.

Shortly after World War II the Soviet Union junked pure

oralism in favor of what it called "neo-oralism," known in America as the Rochester method; this combines speech with simultaneous finger spelling. During the late 1930s the Russians had concluded that the traditional oral approach did not work, mainly because it equated language with speech and viewed the child as a passive creature who learns language by imitation. The Russians hoped that adding finger spelling would allow children to express themselves in language earlier, more freely, and more spontaneously. To date they have been pleased with the results. They begin finger spelling when the children are very young (this was Bonet's method too); preschoolers learn in two years what used to take at least three. Three-year-olds can learn to finger-spell some words in a month or two; two-year-olds may take up to half a year. Formerly a child of seven might know 200 words; children this age now sometimes know 2,000, Moores reports. American work with the Rochester method appears to bear out these results.

Rather than harming speech, the Russians believe that finger spelling helps. Russian is, of course, a far more phonetic language than English (almost any language is) and the children gain a good deal of phonetic information from finger spelling. The claims for neo-oralism, in fact, resemble those made for cued speech in this country. By providing relatively clear visual information on the structure of the spoken language, both Russian finger spelling and cued speech permit the child to learn language in a manner similar to that of the normally hearing child, assuming, of course, that everyone around the child uses the system. But small children may lack the dexterity for finger spelling; nonetheless, it doesn't seem to impede speech development, the Russians believe, and may even aid speechreading. Children do appear to pay some attention to the lips and to sound as well as to the hands.

Part of the reason that sorting out the oral-manual controversy is so confusing is that the arguments run in a circle. Modern manualism arose as a reaction to the manifest failure of traditional oralism. But before it was tradition, oralism was innovation, the nineteenth century's answer to the failure of the combined and silent methods to give children everything they needed. And Epée adopted sign language because he perceived the impossibility of giving worthwhile oral training to large numbers of pupils.

Not surprisingly, total communication advocates base their position largely on the perceived deficiencies of the oral method. They cannot argue that their method is better at attaining the oralists' goal, mastery of spoken English; not since Epée have most educators viewed sign as a practical device for conveying the finer grammatical points of the majority language. Some in the manualist camp believe that sign language can be modified to serve the purposes of perfect English syntax, but their view does not appear to predominate. Rather, most advocates argue for total communication over oralism on the grounds that it does less harm.

As Conrad's data and other research (and ordinary observation) show, run-of-the-mill oral teaching has not provided most deaf children with a usable means of communication, either expressive or receptive, and the psychological, familial, and intellectual results of this lack, as we have seen, can be very severe. Early manual communication, its advocates maintain, gives the child a ready means of communicating without hurting his chances of learning to speak.

This, the effect of sign language on the development of speech, is the crux of the argument. No responsible educator or deaf leader denies the great value of oral skills to deaf people of all ages. Many merely question the price that pure oralism asks the child to pay for them.

Several researchers who have looked into the question maintain that they could find no negative effects of sign. Hilde Schlesinger and Kathryn Meadow, for example, offer cases of young children exposed to simultaneous spoken and signed English who use both codes appropriately and switch between them properly when talking to various people. That is, they use sign with those who understand it and speech with those who do not. Schlesinger reports that one child with considerable residual hearing in the lower range modulates verbs differently in the two modalities while using both simultaneously. Thus, he correctly says "playing" while correctly signing "play." Furthermore, this child's speech has markedly improved since he began signing at two and a half years. Up to that time he had acquired some speech, but, as is normal for losses of his type, had considerable difficulty with consonants. Sign language apparently allowed him to stabilize his language knowledge and thus speak more clearly. Studies of this kind, of course, raise questions about the value of anecdotal reports, which remains moot. Nonetheless, such reports constitute a substantial portion of the literature.

Schlesinger and Meadow report from a joint study that as children advance in their knowledge of simultaneous communication, their use of speech, either alone or with signs, gradually increases and their use of signs alone decreases. They argue that the child learns to talk more quickly when he has something to talk *about*. Establishing early communication by any means possible helps parents and teachers nourish curiosity and sociability and gives the child the incentive to communicate and the subject matter to work on. Even brief contact with children in total communication schools proves that they clearly understand the communicative value of speech; they generally try to use their voices, however inexpertly, with hearing people. A number of authorities contend, furthermore, that children who use signs early read, write, and speechread as well as those who do not. We have already noted that the children of manual deaf people appear to do better in school, a result made even more striking by the deaf parents' relatively low socioeconomic standing.

A great tangle of research results argues for and against particular points in the debate, but little of this work both meets high methodological standards and has wide applicability. The basic dispute persists because the two sides are arguing past one another. The oralists base their argument on technical outcomes, the manualists on psychological ones. Daniel Ling worries whether "those taught by both speech and sign can learn to speak as well as those taught by speech alone or can learn to sign as well as those taught to sign alone."[8] "It is hard to see how one could prefer a situation in which 90% of the deaf do not know language and perhaps 4% are excellent in both aspects of speech to a situation in which 90% of the deaf conceivably would have linguistic competence and possibly only 30% would be proficient speech artists," Furth retorts.[9]

Both overstate the case. Talking about "sign alone" is a red herring; no American schools teach a purely manual program, although some provide very inadequate speech training. And the vast majority of intellectually normal adult and adolescent deaf know some sign language; here Furth inadvertently equates language with speech or assumes that deaf people will not learn sign unless taught it at school.

The relation of the deaf person to the language he uses in daily life forms another, and rather subtle, argument in favor of manual communication. Aaron Cicourel and Robert Boese believe that, however good a deaf person's command of verbal language might be, he can never speak it like a native, or, put another way, it cannot be his native language. By this they do not mean that it cannot be his first and only language, but that he cannot have the complete, unconscious, intuitive familiarity with all its possibilities that marks a mother tongue. Native fluency requires an ability to monitor and evaluate one's performance, they say, and a control that makes the performance automatic and perfect. Regardless of the degree of excellence in syntax, vocabulary, and pronunciation, some subtleties of expression will escape the deaf person: intonation, loudness, timbre. No matter how detailed the receptive ability, something will elude the deaf listener or speechreader. Whole areas of word play, fine distinctions of social standing or intention based on slight variations of accent or timbre, the vast realm of expression implicit in the term "tone of voice," all these escape the person who cannot hear accurately. Not only does he not hear them in others' speech, he cannot reliably duplicate them in his own. To the proposition that a deaf "master of language" is "equally at home in both deaf and hearing society," Ben Schowe, Sr., profoundly deafened in his teens nearly seventy years ago, replies, "Let us not indulge in flights of fancy."[10] The English performance of deaf children resembles that of bilingual children "tested in their non-dominant language." Unlike the Spanish-dominant child, "too many deaf children are not dominant in any language."[11]

But, argue Cicourel and Boese, the deaf person can completely control the resources of sign language. He can accurately perceive other people's messages and reliably monitor his own. Thus, everything the language can express—irony, emotion, social position, plays on words—is potentially within his repertoire. Deaf people can attain a perfectly native fluency in sign language—hearing people can too, but rarely have the chance—and that means that they can achieve the ease and confidence of expression that one knows only in his native tongue. (Nobel laureate Isaac Bashevis Singer, after more than forty years using English, has a native speaker check all his translations from Yiddish to make sure that the tonality, the "feel" of the words is exactly right.) Native signers using oral methods feel the same relief on meeting a fellow signer, Cicourel and Boese maintain, as a traveler running across a compatriot in a foreign land. They can both relax and feel "real" by talking in the "real" language, the language of dreams, passion, and emotion, of unconscious ease and genuine intimacy.

We know little about the emotional value of the different language modes of deaf people; indeed, so ethnocentric are the hearing that the expressive communication of the deaf has hardly been studied at all. But for what scattered anecdotal testimony is worth, several "oral successes" have acknowledged the emotional value of sign language. "I envy their ease of communication," Sally, a profoundly deaf American with superb oral and written skills, says of the manual deaf. E. M. Sheavyn, an orally raised British deaf woman who came to manual communication rather late, has written: "It was a revelation to me. . . . I realized how silly my attitude had been all along and on meeting old school friends who communicate manually again I saw them as happy and well balanced people."[12]

Many responsible oralists advise, or at least do not discourage, deaf people who have mastered speech to learn sign, but they often underestimate the commitment of both emotion and time that such a project requires. To learn sign well means spending a great deal of time with deaf people; to gain fluency in the colloquial means being accepted almost as one of them. The attitudes that permit a child to resist learning sign in his early years may not change easily, and manual deaf people resent or envy one who previously rejected them. "I sincerely believed at the time that the oral method was the best way for the deaf to become integrated into the hearing world," Sheavyn writes. "Vanity and false pride prevented me from mixing with other deaf people."[13]

So while the oralists argue that manual communication isolates the deaf from the hearing, manualists argue that strict oralism isolates the deaf from themselves and their fellows. Sally spends nearly her entire life among hearing people; she knows only a little sign language and none of the colloquial. "Oralism is socially isolating," she says. She cannot use the phone, and she has no TTY because she knows no one to call. Never truly at home among the hearing, she is no more at home among the deaf. "Sadly enough," writes the adventitiously deaf David Wright, one of oralism's most brilliant successes, "the main case against the 'pure oral' system also rests on the isolation of the deaf person who has been educated by this means."[14]

To argue that the total communication approach can solve certain shortcomings of oralism is not, however, to assert that most existing programs provide a complete answer for deaf children. Many schools, in their enthusiasm for sign, have purposely or inadvertently neglected speech training. Few teachers have the technical skills needed to cultivate good speech. Attitudes fostered by the long and bitter controversy disparage the detailed work and arduous practice required, and even the goal itself. Nonetheless, this situation might improve if parents vigilantly demand good speech training as part of TC programs. It is a simple fact that deaf people who speak do better in the world at large than those who do not. Income correlates with speech ability, and so does education and vocational standing. We don't know, however, that the relationship is causal; good speech and good educational attainment might both result from some third factor, like good residual hearing or adventitious loss. The way to guarantee oral success, Conrad writes, is to be "very intelligent and not very deaf."[15] But within the realistic limits of each child's ability, good speech is well worth cultivating. Much of the blame for the present deplorable level of oral skills must go to incompetent or ignorant teaching. Those who care about deaf children owe them a chance at good speech training.

For a satisfying life, however, most deaf people need more than speech. Bell railed against deaf marriages a century ago, but then and now deaf people who marry overwhelmingly marry one another. Even staunchly oral adults generally find mates among the hearing-impaired. Sally's husband is hard-of-hearing.

Latham Breunig married a Clarke classmate. Deaf marriages don't arise out of some mystical attraction between the hearing-impaired, but because most people marry someone with similar social values and from a similar background. The products of schools for the deaf, mainly "oral failures," form cohesive communities in most American population centers. The "coherent social entity of the deaf" (Ben Schowe's term) stands out distinctly from the great "deaf aggregate" consisting of all those afflicted with seriously impaired hearing. Most deaf adults really need both types of communication, and they need fluent, colloquial sign to develop relationships of satisfying intimacy.

If nearly all deaf children end up learning some sign language anyway, then it makes sense, manual proponents argue, to learn it right in the first place. Children kept from learning systematic signs often invent their own, which, as we have seen, cause other problems. A major study of the communication of Dutch and American deaf schoolchildren by Bernard Tervoort, a scholar not especially sympathetic to the linguistic claims of sign language, found that those exposed to standard signing use clearer, more precise signs. The other children did not sign to one another any less; they merely did it haphazardly.

In practice, oral and manual skills probably do not conflict. Sociologists Paul Furfey and Thomas Harte studied deaf adults in and around Baltimore, most of whom had been educated either at the Maryland School for the Deaf before it went over to total communication or at strictly oral day schools. The combined method, that sloppy amalgam formerly tolerated at the state school, seemed to prepare people with early profound losses better for adult life. The state school graduates communicated better with the deaf and no worse with the hearing than the oral school products. A few had very good oral skills, but the average person could not communicate easily with the hearing and some had no oral ability at all. Surprisingly, however, most of those with average or better oral skills had average or better manual skills as well.

"One of the principal findings in the present study is the importance of manual communication in the social adjustment of the deaf," write Furfey and Harte.[16] "Oral and manual communication are not alternatives between which the deaf man must choose. They are both useful."[17] Despite the hopes of their parents and the promises of their teachers, the vast majority of deaf children and adolescents will grow up into culturally deaf adults. "If they escape total isolation, the oral schools deserve no credit."[18] Although total communication hardly existed as a movement when Furfey and Harte drew these conclusions, they prescribe early exposure to sign along with competent oral training as the most flexible, and ultimately the most useful, educational regimen for deaf children.

In the long run, of course, the whole controversy is about social outcomes, and in this country, at least, always has been. American education of the deaf has always had a markedly pragmatic cast. Schooling for the average deaf child meant learning a trade rather than learning to speak, and the leaders of the movement for oralism understood the distinction. Hubbard and his supporters did not especially care to give all deaf children a chance to speak; they wanted to assure their own wealthy, wellborn daughters an entree into polite society. He told a joint committee of the Massachusetts legislature in 1867, "If the child were of poor parents, I would not attempt articulation."

"Let it grow up in silence?" a surprised legislator asked.

"No, sir," Hubbard answered, "I should send it to Hartford."[19] But the controversy has so long concentrated on methods of schooling that the combatants have forgotten that other factors may be at work. Like Poe's purloined letter, this fact is so obvious that it becomes invisible. The biographies of deaf people who have succeeded in fulfilling their parents' vocational hopes offer some suggestive clues. Deaf people of conspicuous achievement—conspicuous in the deaf community, at least, although not necessarily among the hearing—are successful upper-middle-class professionals and business people, perhaps not particularly well known outside deaf circles, but substantial people of comfortable means and similar to tens of thousands of hearing counterparts.

Surveys show that many of them have good oral skills, but nearly as many use sign language with deaf friends. They went mainly to schools for the deaf; those from hearing schools mostly have post-lingual losses. Over half the sample could hear until the age of twelve or later. Nearly all went to college, and most had degrees. And most significantly, nearly all came from educated families of the upper middle or upper classes. Thus, they had behind them cultured homes; concerned parents; money for tutors, books, special schooling; influential connections; family traditions of achievement. They were, in a word, children who would have ended up in the professional classes anyway, and except for hearing loss they differed very little from the other sons of doctors, lawyers, businessmen, and officials with whom they associated professionally every day.

It's been said that if the dirty secret of the Victorian age was sex, the dirty secret of ours is class. Enlightened people may discuss bodily functions in Anglo-Saxon, but we allude to social inequality only in Latinate euphemisms. Nice people would no more bring up social privilege in mixed company—in the presence of their social inferiors, that is—than nineteenth-century gentlefolk would have discussed reproduction in the drawing room.

Maybe this is why the oral-manual controversy has so consistently, even resolutely, ignored social origin, everywhere else recognized as the most obvious factor in social outcome. Or perhaps concentrating on the depravity of one's opponents has obscured everything else. Perhaps, indeed, the combatants knew their own best interests. Once the discussion takes social origin into account, pedagogy becomes less crucial and the traditional positions rather harder to maintain.

This, at least, is what a very large study of the outcomes of deaf education concluded. The Bell Association accused Gallaudet College of suppressing and then doctoring the results, but the conclusion stands. The Office of Demographic Studies at Gallaudet painstakingly catalogued the audiological, sociological, and educational characteristics of a random sample from a national census of 10,509 students representing many degrees of hearing impairment. The early reports implied that orally trained children do somewhat better—marginally better—on academic tests than the manually trained. But the researchers insist that this interpretation distorts their truest and most important conclusion, so they worked their results over again to emphasize what they felt was truly at stake.

And this, after centuries of dispute, is that *the difference in communication mode cannot in itself account for differences in outcome; sociological and physical characteristics do.* "Hearing impaired children who communicate differently are also different on a wide range of other educationally significant factors," write Carl Jensema and Raymond Trybus. "Thus, for example, children who use much speech and those who use little speech are very different children: the latter have much more severe hearing losses, come from lower-income families, use a hearing aid less, etc. To say that these two groups differ in achievement scores therefore says little about the contribution of communication patterns to those achievement differences."[20]

Consider those words with care. They should surprise no one who knows anything about American society. We all know that where in society a child starts out largely determines where the adult he becomes will end up, regardless of the dogma of equal opportunity or the promises of educational innovators. The fact is that deaf children, like all children, are shaped by the socioeconomics of their families.

The relationship between speech and status is clear, just as Gardiner Hubbard knew it was. To this day, the richer the parents, the more speech the child will be exposed to, both at home and at school, and the likelier he is to attend preschool, wear a hearing aid, and use speech himself. Not only parents but teachers act differently toward children of different social classes. Poor and nonwhite children see less speech, both at home and at school. Perhaps, the researchers suggest, teachers want to expose children to the communication modes they believe most appropriate to their futures; but perhaps simple prejudice is to blame.

The relationship between signs and socioeconomics is less strong but still apparent. Sign use tends to increase as social status drops, although the correlation is not nearly as solid as that between speech and social origin. Because the survey was made during the school year 1973–74, however, it may not reflect the full extent of total communication now in use among the middle class.

A second set of variables clusters around the nature of the child's hearing loss. The better his hearing, the more and better he speaks and the more he uses a hearing aid.

The study uncovered a further surprise: very few children live in a "pure" communication environment. Homes and schools do not necessarily use the same modes, and most children have to adapt to a variety of communication styles.

"Put simply," Jensema and Trybus write, "the study means that once the effects of hearing level, family income, hearing aid use at home or dormitory, preschool attendance, and type of present educational program are accounted for, the remaining differences in achievement for groups which differ in communication style (high vs. low speech use, high vs. low sign use) are trivial."[21] But, as the Bell Association rightly stated, those differences do argue in favor of speech. Children who use a lot of speech do a bit better on achievement tests than those who use little, but sign use, in itself, appears to have no effect. Children who use little sign appear to do no better than those who use a lot.

So on the vexed issue of which communication method leads to good academic performance, this study perforce declares a draw. "These results do not mean that communication methods can never make a difference," Jensema and Trybus write. "It is entirely possible that an experimental study pitting best practice of method A against best practice of method B with 2 equivalent groups of children could show a superiority of one method or the other in children's achievement scores."[22] But this doesn't invalidate the results of studying messy actuality rather than hypothetical ideals. It is probably impossible to find the two "equivalent groups of children" differing only in communication method.

So the controversy comes down, in the end, to matters of values and style. The belief that early exposure to sign language damages speech acquisition can at best receive the old Scottish verdict of "not proven." But the converse, that early manual communication does *not* damage oral skills cannot be proven either, if only because logic does not permit proofs of nonexistence. The question at last is what sort of risks one is willing to accept in exchange for what sort of benefits: possible damage to speech in exchange for easy and early communication, probable social isolation in exchange for the possibility (or hope) of apparent normality. Beyond this, all the jargon and ideology merely attempt to clothe ignorance in the robes of science. The most basic, and probably the most bitter, fact remains. At the present state of concrete knowledge, it is essentially impossible to predict with certainty which method will most benefit a particular profoundly or severely deaf child. Parents must clearly consider the probable outcomes (rather than the promised ideal) of an educational or communications choice and must understand that they are choosing emotionally as well as intellectually. They must choose with their eyes open and trained on the future rather than focused on foreclosed hopes or the dead past.

But because adults do the advising and the choosing they, rather than the children, bear the doubt and the guilt. The children, and the deaf adults they become, each know the truth of the controversy, the blazing, irreducible truth of their own particular and painful childhoods. The truth of years invested in labor, inching arduously to the point of doing what any normal four-year-old can do with ease; the truth of years consumed in fruitless boredom, finding true communication, true expression, only by stealth. The Lings are right when they say that the deaf are not the best judges of educational methods. Deaf people's memories may burn too harshly for objectivity, their achievements may be too hard-won. But the hearing are not the best judges either, because they have to live with neither the process nor its result.

But like Malinowski's fishermen, the experts have nonetheless transformed their unsureness into certainty, and according to their several understandings they explain the motives of their adversaries. It's revealing that the oralist cause has been championed most ferociously by people professionally trained in deafness work, while most interested parties from elsewhere—social workers, psychologists, psychiatrists, sociologists, and the like—line up on the other side. In other words, the oralists make the promises, but dealing with the failures—in clinics, psychiatric wards, social service agencies—tends to make people into manualists. This strongly psychological orientation has given the manualist camp many more members skilled at devising colorful explanations of other people's motives, and they have produced a small but emphatic literature on the psyches of oral teachers.

Psychologist McCay Vernon believes that resistance to sign language relates in part to a person's reluctance to recognize his own repressed feelings. Psychologist Harry Bornstein suggests that teachers are bookish people whose only power arises from manipulating words, so they reject a language invented by uneducated people and lacking a written form. Psychiatrist Lars von der Lieth believes that normal people derive satisfaction from feeling superior to and protecting the handicapped and resent the idea that their "wards" can do just as well without them. Sociologists Cicourel and Boese ascribe the pathology theory of sign language to pure ignorance of its structure, powers, or use. Historian Bernard Mottez puts it down to distrust of cultural pluralism.

Oralists tend to be more straightforward in their explanations. Sign language permits deaf teachers to hold and protect their jobs, they say. It is necessary because residential schools have neither the knowledge nor the energy to provide good oral training and because deaf people have neither the stamina nor the discipline to eschew the "primrose path."

But most people probably find themselves in one or the other camp for reasons far more complicated than these theories allow. Spend even a short time among deaf people of either persuasion and their hearing friends and you will sense at least superficial differences. Good signers are very demonstrative people. Americans generally distrust physical demonstrativeness, but to sign well, you have to surrender yourself—arms, hands, head, eyes, features—to the message. And you read signs not by concentrating intently on the elements but by letting the whole wash over you. Good oral skills, on the other hand, demand constant tension—continuous, if unconscious, attention to sound production and an almost unbelievably acute observation of other people's tiniest movements and sounds. Speechreaders watch the face in a particular, tireless way—a steady, unblinking gaze focused slightly below the speaker's eyes—and they work constantly at intricate guesswork. Whether the two approaches to communication attract different types of people in the first place, or whether the demands of the method cause the differences, is impossible to say. It is probably no coincidence that people's signing style resembles their handwriting. Tight, precise signers tend to write in small, neat hands; expansive signers' script rambles around the page.

So what have we learned from this long recitation of data and results? Mainly that the experts know very much less than they willingly admit. In the central dispute, whether early manual communication damages speech acquisition, no one can marshal totally convincing evidence. On the larger question, of which approach best suits deaf children, the most important considerations lie in the realm of values, not that of techniques. Many people have taken their prejudices—an emotional attraction to the deaf subculture, or an equally emotional rejection of it—and clothed them in the robes of theory and certainty. The real debate is not about methods but about values, not about techniques but about the direction of lives.

And the real marvel, of course, is the debate's intensity. It has emotional energy enough to have raged for two centuries, and it rages on. Malinowski probably had the answer: anguish, desperation, and terror at one's ignorance have fueled many another engine even more fearsome than this.

CHAPTER 9

Talking to the Eyes

Suppose you are sitting by a closed window, watching the leaves of a nearby tree moving in the wind. The pane blocks out the sound, and they seem to bob silently, twisting and fluttering on their stems. If you now open the window and close your eyes, the soft rustle can tell you just as well that they are moving. Human beings are meant to have two ways of knowing what is happening to that branch too far away to touch, two different means of surmising that a breeze has disturbed the leaves. These two means do not tell you exactly the same things, even though both might convey the same bare fact of leaves in motion. Only one tells you of the soft scratching, and only one lets you know how the leaves twist and dance and show their light-colored backs.

Getting information through the eyes is not the same thing as getting it through the ears, and that is the crux of the communication issue and of the central problem of all deaf people everywhere. They do not—they cannot—receive all the kinds of information that normally hearing people do, yet they need to know about their world just as badly. Just as no poem can be a symphony or tell what a symphony tells, just as no painting can convey what's said in dance, no gestural language can truly translate an oral one, or vice versa. They are different media, as music and verse are, even as clay and wood are, and they take the shape of thought, even of the same thought, very differently. Understanding the differences between them means stretching the mind and senses in unaccustomed directions, and acquiring a certain amount of technical information at once detailed and abstract. But only this exercise will permit an understanding of deaf people's concrete options in communications or provide the slightest glimpse of what it is like to live in their world.

Our species has been using sound to transmit detailed information since before we were human; physical anthropologists believe that the demands of speech may well have set the direction for human evolution. We are built to speak and hear; human ears and human nervous systems do things specifically useful to human beings. Other species have auditory systems that do things we do not need done. Some animal ears pivot to locate specific sound sources very exactly. Some connect directly to the autonomic nervous system to permit instantaneous response to danger, much as we unthinkingly and automatically pull our hand from a hot surface. We, however, do not survive by using our hearing to evade predators. We survive by catching and decoding words.

We are also built to see. The human eye is meant to do certain specific things very well, but different things from what the ear excels at. We learn from our eyes most of what we know about space, the objects in it, and their positions relative to ourselves. We can isolate certain objects and observe them in great detail, making the fine discriminations required, for example, in reading. We can scan large areas and follow particular movements at great distances. We can shift our focus instantly from far to near or the reverse, picking out exactly that thing we most want to see.

Every normal human being thus possesses two superb and specialized distance senses, each brilliantly designed to provide particular types of necessary information and each exquisitely adjusted to complement the other. Ordinarily they work together close to perfectly, but if one fails, the other must take on an unaccustomed load, which it is less than perfectly adapted to bearing. Without sight you would have to use hearing to find out about space, as a blind person is guided by small variations in the sound of a tapping cane. Without hearing you would need to use sight to find out what sound tells other people. And since the most important use that human beings make of sound is to convey information symbolically through language, you would have to find a visual substitute for the human voice.

America's deaf have traditionally attacked this problem with two visual strategies, speechreading and sign language. A third technique, cued speech, though numerically trivial today, shows signs of increasing importance tomorrow. Each of these systems tackles the task in a different way and each has particular advantages. But like everything else in this vexed field, each also has the vices of its virtues.

Speechreading is the act, art, skill, feat, of deciphering language from the visible motions of the speech organs. People both in and out of the field have traditionally called it lipreading and those outside it generally still do. The new term, recently come into use, emphasizes that more than lips are involved. Mouth movements, facial expression, even glimpses of the tongue moving behind the teeth, all tell something of what is being said. Residual hearing can also play a part, and a skilled speechreader can even use grammatical context to guess what is likely to come next. The very best speechreaders are linguistic Paderewskis, practicing a dazzling virtuosity that permits them to follow, indeed to participate fully in, adult conversations lasting for hours. They move among hearing people without obvious strain, mastering social and business situations alike. Meeting one of them, an unsuspecting hearing person may well conclude that deafness can be fully conquered.

As in all virtuoso performances, the skill is in making it *look* easy. Reality is something else again. Constant problems dog the constant speechreader. He misses out, he misinterprets, he misunderstands. " 'Where's the baby?' 'I put it in the dustbin.' "[1] "Paper" and "baby," David Wright intimates, look exactly the same. So do hundreds, even thousands and tens of thousands of other words and phrases. Only 30 percent of English sounds appear unambiguously on the lips; the rest must be guessed from contexts, probability, or sheer, blind luck. A skillful speechreader need not "read" every sound to catch a message, of course, just as a hearing person can miss a phrase or two and still catch the gist. Many social situations are helpful set pieces, the clichés following upon one another like lines in a well-rehearsed play. "How are you?" "Fine, thanks. Yourself?" "Oh, fine." Sometimes enough hearing remains to fill out what one sees, but this still doesn't change the reality of unrelenting close observation and continuous guessing. The constant speechreader lives the life of a riverboat gambler. He's dealt some hands that are easier than usual, and faces some players more transparent, but every conversation is still a game of bluff and figuring the odds.

Even catching every word and syllable, however, doesn't deliver all of a spoken message. The features that linguists call supersegmentals—stress, intonation, and intensity—get lost without sound, and they often carry the real information. A simple phrase like "no kidding," for example, can cover possibilities from wonder to derision. The face might mirror the underlying intent, of course, but then again it might not.

So high is the element of guesswork that some have called "speechreading" a misnomer. One does not read speech, whose essence is sound, claims researcher Roger Falberg; one reads facial movements, "a by-product of speech," something not even intrinsic to the message. Sound carries the real message and is sufficient to that task. That is why normally hearing people can understand speech as well on the telephone as in person. The word "reading," Falberg writes, "seems to imply a certitude and exactitude which is simply not present in lipreading."[2] "Lip-speculation" describes the skill more accurately, he suggests.

Complicated though we have made it sound, the reality is more complicated still. Some individuals are easier to speechread than others and some situations make the job more or less difficult. One master who can tell a New Yorker from a Bostonian by lip movements admits that some New Yorkers and Bostonians are difficult and that all Britons are close to impossible. Thus, some who rely on speechreading come to depend on trusted hearing friends to act as "oral interpreters" in unfamiliar situations. One "oral success" in her thirties goes everywhere with her mother, whose lip movements she can confidently interpret. A profession of oral interpreting has developed to fill the needs of oral deaf people attending lectures or meetings.

Beyond its visual challenges, speechreading assumes a knowledge of the language being deciphered. It is thus close to useless for learning a language. "For maximum progress in speech and speechreading," writes Orin Cornett, the inventor of cued speech, "the deaf child needs to think in spoken language, or at least its visible equivalent."[3] A child born with little or no hearing might not even know that speech sounds exist. He has no idea that the lip movements are supposed to have any meaning, so he never sees any meaning when he watches. It is no wonder, then, that the best speechreaders are usually verbally gifted and adventitiously deaf, or have substantial residual hearing.

As a method of conveying messages, speechreading makes poor use of the possibilities of sight. Each individual movement conveys very little information. The movements themselves are difficult to decode because they vary only slightly from one another and they carry only part of the message. The ratio of "noise"—extraneous stimuli and distractions—to signal is high, and so is the anxiety level of the reader. Manual communication takes much better advantage of the properties of vision. It packs more information per symbol. The symbols themselves are much more distinct and diverse and easier to separate from "noise." In short, sign language is a symbolic communication medium specifically designed for transmission by the human body to the human eyes. The reader interprets the thing itself, not its shadow.

As we enter the realm of gestural communication it is well to expect an encounter quite unlike that with an individual foreign language. Whole families—indeed, whole phyla—of communication systems cluster under that single rubric of manual communication. The possibilities are as broad as those of the oral realm. Just as one can speak or speechread English, French, Swahili, or Pig Latin, manual language comes in many different forms. Deaf people may be skilled mimics or mimes, and can frequently communicate across national boundaries more easily than the hearing, but specific sign languages are in no sense universal. Different countries and regions have sign languages quite as distinct as their spoken ones. Interestingly, just as the trail of English across the world tells the history of the British Isles, the genealogy of sign languages reflects specifically deaf cultural history. American Sign Language owes much to nineteenth-century French sign, and even today American signers can understand a good half of a French sign conversation without great difficulty. British sign, on the other hand, is totally foreign to Americans, who, by the way, communicate fairly easily with the Irish deaf because of the work of French religious orders in Ireland.

If we imagine the many forms of manual communication used in this country spread across a spectrum, at one end we would find techniques that barely rate as linguistic, and at the other, codes that reproduce English morpheme by morpheme or even letter by letter. At one extreme lie attempts at communication that have none of the systematic features of true language; these include pantomime, imitation, "body language," natural gestures such as yawning or wiping imaginary sweat from the brow. Next come symbolic gestures understandable to only a particular small group; these include what deaf people call "home signs," the private manual codes of particular families who know little or no standard sign language; signs used at particular schools; the spontaneous inventions of children; and signs used in very localized areas. Besides having very small publics, these systems are often quite crude, lacking many devices that permit a wide range of sophisticated discourse.

Reaching the center of our imaginary spectrum, we find the American Sign Language, which is both truly linguistic and widely understood. After English and Spanish it may well be the most commonly "spoken" language in the United States. Only an estimated 10 percent of the pre-vocationally deaf are truly comfortable in English; ASL or Ameslan is the native "tongue" (in Cicourel and Boese's sense) of most of the rest. ASL struggled very hard to gain even the limited respectability it now enjoys. Many leaders, Bell prominent among them, have denounced it as primitive, iconic, concrete, and incapable of abstraction. By this they meant that it has no grammar discernible to the rules of English syntax; that a number of signs began as imitations of the things they represent, a kind of manual onomatopoeia; and that it appears closely tied to the physical. Bell went so far, Moores reports, as to elaborate these criticisms in a lecture at Gallaudet

College, which his student audience followed through a sign language interpreter. The irony appears to have escaped him.

The reasons for Bell's attitude, which remains common even today, run deeply into history, but their result has been that no one undertook serious research into manual communication until William Stokoe, an English professor newly arrived at Gallaudet, began poking around in the early 1950s. By 1960 Stokoe had published claims based on linguistic research that ASL met the technical requirements of a true language. He and his co-workers had to reinvent descriptive linguistics as they went along, and several centers in addition to Gallaudet are now contributing to a growing body of knowledge about the structure of ASL.

We will return to the specific features of ASL presently. For the moment, it suffices to note that it is a developed human language filling the needs of the community that uses it, although it has virtually nothing in common with English. This in itself constitutes no linguistic criticism; Chinese has very little in common with English either. But the difference creates problems because ASL users must deal with hearing people who are profoundly and unconsciously ethnocentric about their mode of communication. Even spoken languages that differ markedly from the Indo-European model have been denigrated as "inferior." Chinese, for example, carries the oldest continuous cultural tradition on earth and has served at various times as the vehicle of the world's highest civilization, but some Western writers have termed it "primitive and iconic" because it is written ideographically instead of alphabetically and because it does not inflect as European languages do. Scholarly minds generally rejected the idea that a system developed mainly by people without speech, who use gestures rather than words, could be other than worthless mumbo jumbo.

To communicate with hearing people, therefore, the deaf cannot depend on ASL. To the hearing, language has always meant ordinary speech; from the days of Epée, the first hearing man to take sign language seriously, hearing people have tried to bend signs to their own purposes. Epée invented the hybrid—some say bastard—form of sign language, and American teachers have followed his example. Today the lingua franca between manual

deaf people and the hearing is sign English, which uses standard
ASL signs in the word order of English. Many of the specific
grammatical and inflectional markers of English (verb markers,
plurals, and the like) do not appear, because sign has no way of
expressing them economically, but the general sense of English
sentences is preserved. Hearing people can learn to express
themselves in sign without the arduous training that mastering a
wholly different diction and syntax would require, and deaf people can approach English through their own favored modality,
their hands.

Indeed, sign English will probably take on new importance as
a generation grows up using it as a home language. For the first
time significant numbers of hearing parents are raising their deaf
children to sign, and these children do not learn ASL at their
mother's knee. Mother generally uses a version of sign language
closer to her own native tongue, English. This might substantially change the linguistic picture a generation from now. As
total communication spreads, sign English spreads with it, and
may well serve as the native language of ever larger numbers of
the rising generation.

Satisfying as its use may be in emotional terms, this quasi-
English falls short of some important pedagogic goals. Using it
teaches deaf children bad English. It gives them no practice in
inflecting words to express number, tense, gender, voice, or case.
It handles pronouns and modifiers awkwardly. It cannot distinguish clearly among parts of speech and it confuses vocabulary
acquisition. One of the great and constant goals of deaf education in all its guises has been to teach an adequate command of
the national language, at least in its written form. When the
schools began to move toward total communication, therefore,
teachers began to seek ways of making sign language serve this
purpose. In the late 1960s, a century and more after Sicard and
then the Gallaudets had discarded formal versions of sign language that closely mimic spoken tongues, a movement began to
develop a manual English exactly mirroring the spoken grammar. A number of scholars have proposed systems, each with a
cheery acronym and a set of rules that distinguishes it, sometimes confusingly, from its competitors.

To return to our imaginary spectrum, we find, at its extreme of

Englishness, two main forms of gestural communication, cued speech and the Rochester method of pure finger spelling. In the latter, Bonet's one-handed manual alphabet survives as a manual Morse code. Finger spelling is used very sparingly in ASL for words that have no corresponding signs, and more and more frequently as the code approaches English.

This typology gives some orientation to sign language, but explains little of its true nature. The greatest obstacle to understanding it is at once simple and insurmountable. Conveying the experience of ASL to those unfamiliar with it taxes the resources of English to its limits. One might as well try to re-create in words the sensation of hearing a symphony. It is not hard to explain the differences between the woodwinds and the brasses or to outline the structure of the strings or the function of the percussion, but no amount of intellection can duplicate the rolling, palpable sound as it fills the consciousness. One can only say that communicating in sign is unlike communicating in any kind of speech. Signs demand a different kind of attention flowing through unfamiliar channels. It seems—physically feels—as though the brain stores a vocabulary (manulary?) of signs in a different place from where it keeps caches of foreign words. Signs seem to pop, fully formed, from low in the back of the head, just above where the neck begins. Words in foreign languages squeeze from somewhere high in the back and to the right. A hearing adult learning to sign can almost feel a vivid energy moving down dark, narrow passages, dusty from disuse, and rolling on through a whole balky apparatus of channels and connectors that only unwillingly come under control. It is physical and intellectual at once, like playing checkers while ice skating, perhaps. When the signs are coming well, they almost seem to bypass consciousness—that is, they bypass the hearing version of consciousness, that silent speech track running in the head. They move as if by their own will through hands and arms that gradually rebel and begin to ache. Learning to sign is not only a linguistic task; it is also a motor skill, and unwilling muscles must be forced until repetition becomes habit, just as they must to learn vibrato or double crochet. Adults forget that speaking is a motor skill too, and that thousands of trials and corrections went into getting "sh" or the "th" in "through" just right. Good deaf signers have decades of practice backing their agility and hands so limber that rheumatism in the fingers is a genuine rarity. But hearing adults begin awkward and finger-tied, inhibited as much by their stiff muscles as by their fear of appearing foolish.

But if sending signs is disconcerting, receiving them rocks the very foundations of our habits. Perhaps radar operators or airplane pilots must pay such close attention to a rapidly changing visual field, but most people have never concentrated on their vision so profoundly in their lives. The signal moves and alters and one must catch it, remember it, and keep abreast of it, all the while riffling through the memory to discover what it means. The close scrutiny we're used to—that used for inspecting tiny objects, or the tight focus used to track far-off moving ones, or the steady concentration used to catch a sudden, expected event —will not do. Hanging too tightly to the specific visual image prevents catching the message, just as listening to the words of a foreign language inhibits understanding what they mean. The attention must be automatic and even unconscious, because the message is the important thing. One must concentrate raptly and also completely relax. Only time and a great deal of practice teach the skill of how to watch.

It's no wonder hearing people become obsessed or subtly repelled. Having to learn sign robs a hearing person, particularly an adult, of his sense of social competence even more profoundly than immersion in a spoken foreign language. Whether the individual grasps the experience as an expansion of consciousness or rejects it as a threat to confidence depends on personality and motives. But hearing people can do it, given time and application, just as one can learn to type or tap dance or master any other skill. Hearing adults are unlikely ever to be mistaken for "natives," of course, but many foreign immigrants who speak English with heavy accents still find satisfactory homes in its intricacies, its cadence, its slang. One's language need not be flawless to be satisfying and serviceable. And so the peripheries of the manual deaf community are thickly inhabited by eager squatters, hearing people converted to, seduced and intoxicated by, the power and beauty of sign.

David Denton recalls a Friday afternoon in Morganton, North

Carolina, over twenty years ago. "I was walking down the street and I noticed in the square three teen-agers, sixteen, seventeen years old—two boys in blue athletic jackets with white letters (of the North Carolina School for the Deaf) and a beautiful girl. These young people were standing there, oblivious to other things, very much in control of what was happening, and communicating in what to me was the most—words fail me—in what was the most dramatic and electric way I had ever seen. And I thought, 'My God, I can see right into these people's souls!' I had never seen such open countenances. Everything was remarkable —the kinesthetic awareness of where their hands were in relation to everything else and to what they were saying. It was truly beautiful, and I couldn't forget it." The "purity" of this conversation, of this whole mode of conversing, burned in Denton's memory and ultimately changed his life. The transparent, unguarded attention, the clarity, vivacity, and grace of disciplined, practiced hands bewitched him into an unexpected career as a teacher of the deaf, and he finally became an expert practitioner of the art that had dazzled him.

Among the hearing we see that intense gaze—oblivious to surroundings yet vividly aware—only on the faces of lovers; perhaps that's why it seems so appealing and yet so subtly threatening. It grasps on to the interlocutor's face, body, hands, entire person, as if to suck the space surrounding him dry of meaning. It creates a mutual terrain of discourse between the person signing and the person or persons being signed to. The message in a fluently signed passage—and this is perhaps the hardest thing to explain— arises much more from the context of the exchange than hearing people are used to. In speech we expect the words to carry the main burden of meaning; supersegmentals carry part of it, the face and body a smaller part still. To understand someone completely, we know it's best to see him in person, but we can still communicate nearly as well over the telephone, which robs us of visual cues, and even understand a good deal over a very bad phone connection, which even robs us of some of the words. But in ASL the context carries much of the message. Each signer puts on a small play, filling the space around him with anything or anyone he wishes to talk about, and then using signs to specify and define the relationship among these things.

ASL uses no pronouns, for instance; that is, it has no discrete items that correspond to what English speakers understand as pronouns. Instead, a signer peoples his surrounding space with those he wants to refer to. He indicates, for example, that Tom is to his immediate right, Dick to his immediate left, and Harry somewhat in front of Dick. He simply spells each person's name or gives his name-sign (a sign language nickname, often referring to some distinguishing characteristic) and points to the place where the named imaginary person stands. From then on, referring to that person requires merely indicating the appropriate place. When Tom is quoted, the signer's gaze comes from his direction; when Harry speaks, it comes from his. If a child is said to be speaking to an adult, the gaze tips upward, and so forth. As the story progresses people may move about the imaginary landscape, among the places already indicated. In conversations concerning more than one or two different people or things, ASL keeps much better track of pronouns than English; one never wonders which of two or three possibilities a particular "he" or "it" refers to.

ASL uses space the way spoken language uses sound. It is strikingly, almost shockingly, visual. Signers "sculpt" their messages, says one observer; they "paint a picture of them," says another. *Homo sapiens* descends from arboreal species and our distant primate ancestors needed very acute three-dimensional vision to survive. It is hardly surprising, therefore, that a linguistic system depending on the motion of human hands through space makes rather subtle spatial distinctions.

Even time appears spatially. The signer stands at the center of a field of time, with the past behind him and the future in front. A line running vertically in front of his shoulders is the present and thus separates past and future. One indicates the future by waving the open palm forward from the body at about ear level and the past by waving it backward over the shoulder.

If ASL had no more structure than this, it would rate as an elaborate pantomime rather than a true language. But Stokoe has demonstrated that ASL meets, sufficiently if unorthodoxly, the requirements of structure that linguists recognize.

Stokoe's argument becomes a bit technical at this point, but is worth following for the profound insight it gives into sign. Every language exists in two distinct forms. The symbolic form relates to the content of communication; the physical form is the concrete artifacts existing in time and space, whether they be sound waves emitted by a speaker, ink marks on a paper, or gestures made by a signer. The physical basis of any spoken language is called its phonology, the system that gives meaning to sounds according to a particular set of consistently applied distinctions. Of all the sounds the human vocal apparatus is capable of producing, each language selects a limited number that it regards as meaningful and ignores the rest. Then it groups those sounds into a smaller number of categories, usually not more than a couple of dozen. It regards the sounds in a given category as being the same, although they often differ quite substantially in terms of pure acoustics. We have already discussed the K's in "key" and "caught." Every language, therefore, divides the possible range of vocal sounds into a particular array of units meaningful to it. These are its phonemes.

Stokoe's first great insight into the linguistics of sign was to understand that sign languages do something comparable. They divide all the possible motions of the human hands into an array of meaningful units, which he called "cheremes," from the Greek for "hand." The various versions of a given phoneme (the allophones) can be defined along several phonetic dimensions such as place of articulation, manner of articulation, presence or absence of voicing (vibration of the larynx). Likewise the variants (allocheres) composing a single chereme can also be defined along several dimensions. The first of these is the place on the body where the sign is formed, technically called the tab. The only difference between the signs "summer" and "ugly," for example, is that one is formed on the forehead and the other on the middle of the face. In linguistic language, the two signs form a minimal pair for this feature: they differ in it and it alone, but the difference is sufficient to make them recognizably different signs. In English an example would be "cat" and "cab." The existence of a minimal pair is the technical test for the existence of a phoneme in traditional descriptive linguistics.

The shape of the hand, the deze, is the second dimension. "Summer" and "black," for example, have the same tab; both are signed along the forehead. Their differing hand shapes, however, make them a minimal pair. In "black" the pointing index finger is straight. In "summer" it is bent. The motion of the hands, or the sig, is the third dimension. It differentiates, for example, "sock," in which the two index fingers rub against one another, from "star," in which they jab forward. Recent work by some of Stokoe's associates have suggested the existence of a fourth dimension, orientation of the hands to one another. In "train," for example, the fingers of one hand lie on those of the other so that all the nails face upward. In "short," the fingers of one hand lie on those of the other so that the sides touch.

These dimensions define real linguistic distinctions to fluent signers, just as B is "really" different from V to native speakers of English. As Conrad observed, speakers trying to recall lists of words confuse items that sound similar; psycholinguist Ursula Bellugi found that signers tend to confuse signs that are signed similarly. They might confuse "China" and "onion," which differ only in hand shape, or "father" and "reindeer," which differ only in place.

Every language has rules for how to combine its phonemes into proper words; certain English sounds simply can't occur together. Likewise, the two hands work together in ASL according to definite rules. When both hands move in ASL, they properly should have the same shape. When only one hand moves and the other acts as a stationary "base," the base hand must assume one of four or five acceptable "neutral" shapes. Stokoe and his co-workers believe that these principles are so basic to the structure of American Sign Language that invented signs violating them gradually evolve toward conformity. They and some others who value the integrity of ASL find it distressing that some signs invented for English-based synthetic systems ignore the rules of cherology. Even the made-up sign commonly used for "total communication" is incorrect, Stokoe says, because the two moving hands have different shapes, one forming "T" and the other "C."

Besides rules for combining sounds into words, languages have rules of semantics, which govern how words mean what they mean. In English, for example, words ending in "-tion" are nouns indicating states, processes, or conditions. Words ending in "-er" or "-or" are often nouns indicating doers of certain actions. In much the same way the structure of a sign can give a hint to its meaning. Verbs of state, such as "know," "think," "feel," and "fear," are signed near the body, Hilde Schlesinger observes. Verbs of action are signed farther away. Many signs expressing feelings involve the middle fingers. In signs expressing doubt or uncertainty, like "if," "which," "doubt," "judge," or "maybe," the two hands move alternately up and down, like scales weighing possibilities. Also in the realm of semantics, spoken languages tend to contain clusters of words with related meanings that arise from a single root and preserve traces of it in their sound and spelling. Thus, "community," "communicate," "common," and "commune" all have the same origin. ASL has many similar clusters; a typical one relates to the sign for slavery or bondage: closed fists held crossed at the wrists. Moving the hands abruptly apart, as if breaking the bonds, means "freedom." Bringing one wrist sharply down on the other is "appointment" or "reservation." Moving crossed hands from side to side together is "custom." Tapping the upper wrist repeatedly against the lower is "work." All involve ties or bonds that limit or diminish the individual's freedom.

The idea that sign language is "concrete" or "incapable of abstraction" probably arose because many signs begin in physical mimicry. But sign language is abstract the way good poetry is abstract—"it resorts to the specific in order to intuit, apprehend, and express the abstract," in the words of Eugene Berman.[4] "He maketh me to lie down in green pastures," sings one of the sublimest verses in English—a line utterly specific, totally concrete, and because of that more resonant and expansive than any treatise on theology could be. Critics who comment on sign language without attempting to know it from the inside draw unjust conclusions about its powers. No English translation can express the sum of undertones and overtones in a sign language phrase, any more than it can for a French one. We know that verbal languages "lose in translation." Sign language, by comparison, nearly vanishes.

Other misunderstandings arise because sign language appears to offer a very scant choice of words. It has very, very few synonyms and single signs may encompass several English words. But sign language does not need an array of distinct signs to express the differences among "large," "big," "huge," "enormous," or "pretty," "beautiful," "stunning," "gorgeous," for example. The signer can vary the sign in many expressive ways: slowing it down or speeding it up, forming it tightly or expansively, smoothly or abruptly. He can change the expression of his face or the posture of his body. Nuances in English arise from using exactly the right word; in ASL, from making the sign in exactly the right way.

Modifications of a sign do more than expand the signer's vocabulary; they also provide the structure of his sentences. This may be the hardest aspect of ASL grammar to explain. English speakers think of syntax as a matter of stringing elements out in time; signers think of it as superimposing elements in space. Understanding English depends on catching syntactical clues as they flash by. It's easy to miss many of them, and even fluent speakers often do. But the language gives us many chances to understand; it generally signals a single grammatical point more than once. In technical terms, English has a highly redundant grammatical structure. It gives us repeated chances to find out facts such as number and tense. A simple sentence like "They are deaf," for example, signals that it is plural twice in three short words. Every verb must carry a tense marker, so that we have many chances to find out when something is supposed to be happening. Pronouns carry number, gender, and case to help us make sure of both what we're talking about and how the words function in the sentence. We probably don't need all the available information to decipher a message, but the high redundancy takes a considerable load off the listener. We don't have to catch every element of every word, and even though there's no predicting which particular element of any utterance we may miss, we still get enough to understand.

But sign language doesn't happen nearly as fast as speech. The hands can't transmit signals as quickly as the mouth and the eye can't apprehend them as quickly as the ear. But the vivid context of communication means there's less chance of some important fact like number or tense slipping by unnoticed. Sign language doesn't need many of the redundancies of speech; indeed, many small, discrete visual images tend to confuse rather than clarify a message. Articles, prepositions, case endings, and pronouns—

what Schowe calls the "colorless words"—thus disappear as
grammatical elements, along with the verb "to be," auxiliary
verbs, and tense and number inflections. Rather than accreting
grammar by piling on words and word elements, ASL carves it
out of space or melds it into signs. We have already seen how
space can substitute for pronouns. It can also do the duty of
some adverbs and prepositional phrases. Questions of agency
and beneficiary—of who did what to whom—resolve easily in
space. "I gave it to you" moves from me to you; "You gave it to
me," from you to me. The direction of the moving sign "give"
clearly shows the difference. The same goes for the difference
between "Tom hit Jerry" and "Jerry hit Tom." We know where
each man is standing and can watch the direction of the blow. "I
watched them" has symbolic eyes peering from the teller's direction; "They watched me" has them staring at him.

Internal modifications of signs meet other grammatical needs.
Adverbs of manner—slowly, quickly, quietly, sadly—show in how
the sign is formed. So do variations on verbs; tendency, habit,
and repetition are all expressed by specific modifications of the
verb. How many times the sign is made distinguishes singular
from plural. Some hand formations can serve as either nouns or
verbs—"airplane" can be "fly," "food" can be "eat," "chair" can
be "sit." A smooth action versus a choppy one shows the
difference. And in a small number of specific cases a sharp snap
of the wrist turns a sign into its own opposite. Thus "good" can
become "bad," "I know" become "I don't know," and "I want"
become "I don't want." A negative facial expression and a shake
of the head can also negate an utterance even if no specific negative element is used.

The looseness of sign language word order has probably
caused more misunderstanding than any other element of its
grammar. It appears to have no particular rules about which
signs must precede or follow others, and many critics have concluded from this that it has no grammar. In English, unlike some
other languages, word order is absolutely crucial to meaning.
English is not a highly inflected language as verbal languages
go; most words in and of themselves carry relatively little information about their function in the sentence. Except for a very
few situations, a word's position in the sentence provides the

basic information about its relationship to the other words. In most highly inflected languages, on the other hand, word order makes relatively little difference. Each individual word carries much more grammatical information. Every Latin noun, for example, carries a case marker. Nearly every Latin verb carries person, number, tense, voice, and mood. It is almost impossible to pronounce a Latin word without indicating its role in the sentence. One can essentially toss the words of a Latin sentence in the air, read them where they land, and still make out the meaning. Spanish sentences often omit a subject because the verb contains it implicitly. Hebrew possessives and participles indicate number and gender, also eliminating the need for some subjects. And these languages are somewhat looser than English about where certain sentence elements must go. American Sign Language does, however, have a few word-order rules, and because these appear to resemble French they also confuse English speakers. Adjectives, for example, usually follow rather than precede nouns.

ASL, however, does not correspond perfectly to a highly inflected verbal language. A good deal of its implicit information is communicated by the context rather than by internal changes in the signs, technically known as modulations. Exactly what this means is not easy to explain to those who have never seen a sign conversation, but it has to do with the quality of attention that so captivated David Denton. Sign conversations are intensely personal. They occur *between* people to a much greater extent than is customary in speech; indeed, the space between the "speaker" and the "listener" is usually alive with the people or things being discussed. The speaker constantly monitors the listener's comprehension and uses him as part of the sentence's frame of reference. Sign language is strongly directional—direction has grammatical meaning. This means that the point of view of the person receiving the signs means almost as much as that of the person sending them. Together they define the grammatical relationships in space.

The mere denotation of the words, their strict definitions, does not exhaust the meaning of an English sentence, and neither does it in ASL. A whole system of visual supersegmentals provides additional information on emotion, intention, and social context. Some of these elements are informal, like facial expression. Others, however, are as highly structured as an English speaker's use of intonation to signal the intention to continue, to pause, or to solicit the other person's opinion. Hearing signers often ignore this level of communication and get a false impression of deaf signers. An English question has a particular melody and if he doesn't hear it a person may fail to realize he is supposed to answer. A signed question also has a characteristic shape: the face has a questioning expression and the hands either keep the form of the last sign or move outward toward the watcher. Returning the hands to neutral repose, however, signals more to come, just as the characteristic melody of a declarative sentence telegraphs the speaker's intention to continue speaking. If a hearing signer finishes a question by returning to repose, a deaf signer may not realize he is expected to respond.

A whole other realm of speech expression also has its parallel in sign. Hearing speakers play with language for many expressive purposes, both with the meaning and with the very physical stuff of sound. Fluent signers do the same sort of thing for the same purposes. They can distort or reverse the meaning of signs for irony, mockery, elegance, or humor. Make the sign "college" upside down, for example, and it indicates a person conceited about his education. Make the sign for "perfect" imperfectly and it means about the same thing as the famous parody poster "THIMK."

If any further proof were needed that ASL is indeed a language, researchers tell us that it appears to convey information about as efficiently as spoken English. Telling a given story usually takes many fewer discrete sounds than words but about the same length of time. If one signer translates a paragraph from English to ASL and another translates it back, it emerges very close to the original (assuming, of course, that both know English).

Like every other language, sign language both expresses and encompasses the life of a specific community. Anthropological dogma holds that all languages are capable of expressing everything their users need expressed, and, indeed, everything that other languages can express. But ASL strikes many English speakers as highly limiting. English says many things easily that are just plain difficult to sign. The sign vocabulary is relatively small and relatively specific. This is not to say that sign cannot discuss philosophical abstractions or theological concepts, but that it does so less easily and less precisely.

An interviewer once asked Isaac Bashevis Singer whether he didn't find Yiddish a difficult, restricting language to write in about the modern world, belonging, as it does, to a dead time and an archaic culture. Well, Singer replied with a twinkle, it is true that Yiddish presents modern novelists with problems. If one wants to write about airplanes or atomic bombs, he's going to have trouble. But if he wants to write about scoundrels, fools, misers, and bores, well . . . there's no language with a subtler, more nuanced vocabulary. Sign language may barge clumsily among intellectual distinctions where English treads delicately, but English stammers about emotions where sign language flows eloquently. Languages express the world of the people using them. If sign language can't say some things easily, it is because deaf people do not generally discuss them, not because the language is inherently incapable of doing so. Cultural change always produces new developments in language. Thus, the growth of higher education for the deaf has meant new demands on sign language and new efforts to develop technical vocabularies. Already academics at Gallaudet, NTID, and elsewhere have forged boldly into the untried field of academic and instructional signs. If they have not yet succeeded in producing jargons as clotted and opaque as those of their counterparts at colleges for the hearing, the fault can only lie in the relatively short time they've been working at it.

Like other living languages, sign language provides an accurate picture of the community that uses it. The imaginary spectrum of sign language systems that we discussed earlier, for example, is more than a linguistic curiosity. It is an accurate map of the life of the deaf community.

Stokoe early perceived that the variety of different sign language types in use simultaneously in America is not accidental, nor does it indicate sloppiness or imprecision. Instead, he argues, manual communication in America is an example of the phenomenon linguists call diglossia. This means the permanent and simultaneous existence of two forms of the same language. It is not bilingualism, where two different languages are used by different groups within the same society, like French and English in Canada. In a diglossic situation the two different forms of the same language appear within a single group but in different social situations. An imperfect example might be the case of black dialects of American English, which are often used among black people who wish to emphasize their social solidarity. Many of these same individuals, though, also know the standard form of English spoken in the society at large and use it in situations when they wish to emphasize their participation in the general society. This analogy must be used cautiously, as it is not exact. Indeed, American examples of true diglossia occur only rarely. The entire trend in this country has been toward assimilation to regional or national standard norms. Some Southeast Asian languages fit the type far more exactly, having different vocabularies and even different grammatical constructions for conversing with different degrees of social superiors and inferiors.

We can begin to explore the social structure of sign language by returning to our imaginary spectrum. Everyday communication among American manual deaf people does not generally use all the versions of communication we mentioned. It spreads across a somewhat narrower range. The two extremes of this narrower continuum are "pure" ASL in a form that uses very little finger spelling and virtually no English-based constructions on the one end and the moderate forms of sign English—signs in English word order but without most grammatical inflections—on the other. Between these extremes lie a number of intermediate possibilities, some clustering closer to ASL, some closer to English. Although different persons feel most comfortable at different points along this continuum, many customarily use forms from both ends—in effect two different dialects of sign language—in different social situations.

The English-like end of the spectrum contains dialects connoting education, worldly sophistication, and correctness. Coming closer to the world of the dominant culture, they are closer to the power and allure that world represents. Like court language, academic jargon, and other high-flown palaver, they are considered suitable for formal occasions and for people one does not know intimately. Essentially, they are the forms used when outsiders—

hearing people—are watching and in situations that call for company manners.

The ASL end of the spectrum contains the forms many deaf people use among themselves. They imply intimacy, "insideness." Indeed, being permitted to learn and use ASL is prima facie evidence of insider status.

The social world of ASL is the world of home and intimate friendships. Very few hearing people except the children of deaf parents ever enter it; thus very few hearing people learn enough ASL to use it fluently. The polar forms of sign language not only result from but also symbolize the basic separation of the inner social world of the deaf community from the hearing world. If a hearing person enters a conversation between deaf people, the language usually shifts closer to English. "In this way," observe Markowicz and Woodward, "hearing people who sign at the ASL end of the spectrum might find themselves subtly forced to use a more English-like form if that more accurately reflects their perceived social position."[5]

"Nativeness" in a language implies understanding the society that uses it. "Native" signing—fluent use of the forms closest to ASL—so strongly implies close involvement with the deaf community that specific grammatical constructions can serve as social markers. Linguists Carol Erting and James Woodward found that signers who tend to negate certain verbs with the snap of the wrist, who consistently use direction for expressing agency, and who indicate plurals by repeating verbs, most likely are deaf themselves, have deaf parents, and learned to sign before the age of six. Those who hear, have hearing parents, and learned to sign later, use these ASL patterns much less often.

Sign language diglossia is a real, permanent, and significant feature of the linguistic scene. Unlike much American bilingualism, it does not die out as succeeding generations become more fully American. It endures because it serves a genuine social function and meets a genuine cultural need. True diglossic situations persist because the forms differ in function and people feel strongly about the differences. The forms do not merge because emotions forcefully keep them apart.

American deaf people have felt strongly about their native sign for a long time, and it has proved extraordinarily resilient. It has also changed gradually and systematically, though, as all natural languages do. Historical linguists can spot trends similar to the great shifts that separated the European languages from their ancient common root and gave them their modern forms. Grimm's law, for example, outlines the consistent movement of English and German consonants. Signs also tend to move over time; Woodward believes they drift toward the base of the throat. He reports several that have shifted slowly but decisively from the outer reaches of the signing field toward this linguistically central point. "I don't care" used to be signed over the forehead; it now appears over the nose. "Young" once occurred near the waist, but now it is made near the shoulders. "Happy" has moved from the left to the center of the chest. This drift toward the center probably forms part of a more general trend. Many signs begin as imitations of some physical act or feature. "Happy," the open hand tapping the chest, showed the rapidly beating heart; "female," the thumb grazing the chin, showed the bow on an eighteenth-century lady's bonnet. But as time passes the actions become more and more abstract, more purely symbolic, and the relationship of the sign to its physical origin becomes, in Moores's word, increasingly "opaque." People forget the old, literal associations, just as English speakers have forgotten that the word "sad" long ago meant "full."

After a century or more of fairly steady evolution, the pace of change in ASL appears to have picked up in the last decade or so. English presses in ever more insistently as educational opportunities improve and new English-based signs become more and more common. Sign order among the younger and better educated appears to be moving closer to English. New "initialized" signs regularly appear. These use the hand shape of a letter to specify one particular English meaning from a traditional sign's range of possibilities. "Freedom" and "liberty," for example, have the same movement, the breaking of bonds, but to make the former, one uses the F hand, and to make the latter, one uses the L. To some extent initialization may limit the growth of the sign lexicon; representations of English words increasingly substitute for new items that might use more fully the expressive resources of pure sign.

Older signs gradually pass out of use, but regional, racial, and generational differences still persist. Black signers use a number of forms unknown in general white signing. Southern signers, like speakers, use more archaic forms than Northerners. The better educated and the young use more of the newer signs.

Because languages generally evolve at a predictable rate, linguists can look backward to learn something of their history. Glottochronology, the study of linguistic changes over time, has helped scholars trace the paths of many spoken languages as they have grown, divided, and influenced one another. Linguists know how rapidly vocabularies tend to change, and which words best resist alteration, so they can fairly accurately estimate when two related languages separated. They can sometimes discover previously unsuspected connections.

These principles apply to sign languages too. Working from old reports and recollections, linguists see that ASL has changed internally at a steady, expected rate for a century or more. Legend has it, of course, that Laurent Clerc brought his French Sign Language to Connecticut, taught it to the American deaf, and thus was the "father" of the present ASL.

But glottochronology tells a different story. If ASL truly landed on these shores in 1817 it ought to resemble its French ancestor much more closely than it does, Woodward claims. The differences that actually exist are "wildly discrepant." They imply a separation of over a thousand years longer than we know to be the case. The biggest changes appear to have happened in the early decades of the nineteenth century and they're not the kind caused by simple evolution. Something very different from the legend must have happened in 1817.

Instead of simply transplanting French Sign Language to America, Woodward and others believe, Clerc and Gallaudet began to create something entirely new, a genuine American hybrid. FSL did not take root in empty, virgin soil; it barged into a field already occupied by indigenous, local signs. We know, for example, that the deaf painter Joseph Brewster, Jr., used signs long before he studied at Hartford. We know nothing about them, however, or about who else used them. But FSL had great prestige and offered real social and economic rewards to those who learned it. People adopted it quickly, but also used some of their old signs. Thus, FSL mixed with its existing competitors to form a new crossbred language, one that included elements of both old and new. In technical terms it became creolized. Creoles usually occur, Woodward writes, when a culturally dominant language comes into contact with less prestigious ones. The type case is the Caribbean, where African slaves of many nations had to adapt abruptly to the French or English of their colonial masters.

And so it was during the early days at Hartford. Clerc and Gallaudet, two cultural colonizers—foreigners, Woodward says, to the native deaf population—began to gather people together from the many scattered and isolated cities, towns, and farms of New England, people who used a host of very localized sign systems. The teachers began to instruct their charges in a new language even more foreign than the local argots were to one another, and the native deaf people had to adapt all this into a single, usable system. "Some of us have learned and still learn signs from uneducated pupils, instead of learning them from well-instructed and experienced teachers,"[6] Clerc wrote in 1852, corroborating, Woodward claims, the process of creolization. Late in his life the great teacher bemoaned the degeneration of the elegant signs he carried from Paris into the graceless ones we saw in Hartford.

So American Sign Language, Woodward believes, is truly American and only partly French. He sees its roots running deep into the experience of the unlettered native deaf people of New England, who instructed Clerc and Gallaudet, and of the deaf of France, who taught Epée and Sicard. "It seems more than a little ethnocentric," he writes, "for us 'hearies' to maintain the myth that two men, Gallaudet, a hearing man, and Clerc, a foreign deaf man, founded ASL as we know it. It seems time to give just a little credit to the American deaf people who drastically modified (if not creolized) FSL to satisfy their needs."[7]

If deaf people modified French Sign Language for their own use, hearing people have attempted to modify ASL even more drastically for theirs. The pidgin English sign language that serves as the general lingua franca between hearing and deaf is, like all pidgins, a synthetic language and, like all pidgins, it lacks much of the richness of either of the languages it merges. Its fidelity to English word order robs it of the spatial resources of

ASL; its acceptance of standard signs robs it of the semantic and syntactic precision of English. And efforts to make sign language carry the full grammatical baggage of English move it farther and farther from the sources of its expressive strength.

The new sign systems closely mimicking English are almost totally synthetic; particular educators and scholars invented them and gave them names. The first two major American entries, *Seeing Essential English* (known as SEE 1) by D. A. Anthony and others and *Linguistics of Visual English* (LOVE) by D. J. Wampler, appeared in 1971; *Signing Exact English* (SEE 2) by Gerilee Gustason and others appeared the following year. These systems all have the same goal, to transform grammatical English into a visual counterpart based, to the extent possible, on American Sign Language. They attempt to transmit to the deaf child learner all the detailed, redundant grammatical markers of correct speech and writing: all pronouns, articles, conjunctions, verb and noun modulations, the whole inflectional paraphernalia that ASL does without and expresses badly. The various systems have their own particular rules and premises, and this is not the place to discuss their characteristics in detail. Their creators all faced similar conceptual problems, though, and the solutions they separately arrived at tell much about the problems involved.

From a pedagogic standpoint, English words have three basic aspects: a meaning, a sound, and a spelling. Traditional signs intersect with English words on the plane of meaning, and they do so inexactly. It's generally said that signs stand for concepts, not words. In a system that would replicate English, however, signs must be made to stand for words; the child's exposure to signs must reinforce accurate knowledge of English vocabulary. Let us take as a case in point the word "right." Someone who knows English thoroughly knows that this single spelling and pronunciation covers at least four separate meanings: "right turn," "civil rights," "right ahead," and "you're right" (and maybe even "right on"). In addition, he knows that the same pronunciation but with different spellings covers at least three other meanings: "rite," "write," and "wright." But how to convey this knowledge, or even part of it, to a deaf child? ASL and sign English have a different sign for each of these meanings.

In transforming signs standing for concepts into motions sub-
stituting for words, the developers have generally opted for the
rule of two out of three. If they share any two of meaning,
spelling, or sound, then two different versions of a word come
under the same sign. Thus, "right turn," "civil rights," "right
ahead," and "you're right" form one big group based on sound
and spelling. This group excludes "rite," "write," and "wright."
This choice violates the integrity of both sign and English, but it
violates English somewhat less. The developer of each system
then contrives a vocabulary based on his interpretation of the
needs of young children, some emphasizing similarities based on
English words and others similarities based on concepts. Each
developer also constructs a system of grammatical markers, usually based on the manual alphabet, which permit signers to indicate unambiguously elements such as "-ing," "-ly," "-s," and
"-ed."

Obviously, the developers of synthetic sign languages do not
agree perfectly, and that has become a serious and growing
problem. As total communication has spread, English-based sign
systems have proliferated, sometimes invented and usually
taught by people with no profound understanding of sign language. The psychological, pedagogical, and linguistic effects of
this mounting confusion are far from clear. Some observers like
Louie Fant, among the most eloquent of hearing apologists for
ASL, believe that unless schools also systematically cultivate natural sign language, the deaf will suffer both linguistically and
psychologically. He fears that ASL might degenerate "into a
plethora of local dialects" unless children learn to use it properly,
and that teachers' tolerance of sloppy ASL signing might be
taken as tolerance of sloppy language in general. And finally, he
believes that teaching ASL in school programs "precludes hypo-
critical attempts to gloss over the fact that deaf people are
different from hearing people. It rejects the notion that the more
successfully a deaf person can approximate the behavior of hearing people, the worthier a human being he becomes."[8]

Many educators committed to total communication believe
that deaf children should ultimately become bilingual in ASL
and signed English, and that ASL can serve as a medium for
teaching English, just as bilingual programs for the hearing can

use the home language to teach the national one. But this goal requires a sizable body of bilingual teachers who know what the children understand about language before learning English and who can use this understanding for building a usable grammar. Such bilinguals are far too rare to meet the needs of the schools, and training programs have done little to increase their numbers. And indeed, the children in most good-sized schools or programs for the deaf come from so many different linguistic backgrounds that their teachers can usually assume very little common knowledge. The sign language situation will probably become murkier and murkier as total communication spreads. We won't know for another half generation whether making sign imitate English actually produces deaf children who handle the national language any better than their predecessors could.

Two other systems exist for transmitting English with the hands. One, the Rochester method, has been used on and off since the late nineteenth century. It consists of spelling out every letter of every word on the fingers while speaking at the same time; the Russians call it neo-oralism. The system gives the deaf person two chances of apprehending the message as it flashes by on the lips and the hand and some individuals develop remarkable skill at both sending and receiving. Even very young children can often put it to good use, at least as a receptive medium. Before they understand the hand shapes as strings of letters, they seem to grasp them as strings of signs. Indeed, every skilled finger speller sees the flux of finger movement the way a skilled reader sees a procession of printed letters: as meaningful composites rather than as individual items. Experienced finger spellers don't see sequences of letters which they then must aggregate, but whole words. They learn to predict (guess, really) from context and to catch entire words by catching their beginnings and endings.

This skill takes time to develop, though, and depends, as communication becomes more complex, on reading ability—on knowledge of words and their spellings. Sending finger-spelled messages is far easier than receiving them. The basics take only a few hours to learn, but developing any degree of speed is no trivial task. The hand must make very precise movements in very rapid succession and should reflect both the rhythm of speech and the integrity of the words. And the hand is simply not as agile as the mouth. Three hundred letters or sixty words a minute seems a realistic rate for reasonably skilled sending and receiving—not a bad speed for typing, perhaps, but less than half as fast as a fluent speaker's 150 words per minute.

A method developed more recently attempts to solve this problem by presenting English syllable by syllable rather than letter by letter. Orin Cornett invented cued speech at Gallaudet in 1966 in an effort to give deaf children the chance to learn English the way hearing children do, from consistent use in daily life. Most deaf children now acquire most of their English in the classroom. Like the Rochester method, cued speech uses the hands in the service of oralism; Cornett wants to provide the most accurate picture of English possible and enhance the child's speech-reading skills at the same time.

Speakers of English, Cornett reasons, perceive the language as a system of sounds. To achieve a native speaker's grasp, the deaf child must learn it that way too. But the deaf person's most available clues to the English sound system, those from speech-reading, are ambiguous and incomplete. The problem is to make speechreading yield up the information hidden in the mouth and throat. With a mathematical exactness derived from his training in physics, Cornett analyzed the relationship of speech sounds to mouth shapes and decided that the main problem arises because most mouth shapes can stand for more than one sound. The speechreader who did not already know the language has no way of telling which of several visually identical possibilities the speaker was pronouncing at any moment. If the speaker could somehow signal this information visually, the speechreader could receive the message in its phonemic entirety. So Cornett developed a system of eight hand shapes that can be held in any of four positions relative to the face. These by themselves do not stand for sounds; they have meaning only when combined with information on the speaker's lips.

The shape of the speaker's mouth indicates, for each syllable, one set of possible consonants and another set of possible vowels. For example, the syllables "hoe," "suh" (as in "sun"), and "rah" (as in "rot") appear identical on the lips. The hand cue, formed near the face, gives the information that pinpoints the correct choice. The hand's shape indicates the correct consonant and its position indicates the correct vowel. Thus, hundreds of possibilities narrow instantly to a single certainty. As long as those around a child cue consistently he receives a correct and unambiguous picture of the phonemes composing speech. He also learns to concentrate on the lips, so that, it is hoped, he will speechread people who do not cue more skillfully than he would otherwise.

Cornett invented cued speech so that the deaf children of hearing parents can learn to communicate in their parents' native language. He believes sign language is an unrealistic medium for the family life of adults who are not themselves deaf. It's pure fantasy, he says, to expect most hearing parents to become fluent signers. "How much time can you expect parents to spend with deaf people?" he asks. Hearing parents can learn cued speech in a matter of days, Cornett claims, and their children will benefit from being raised in a language their parents know profoundly.

It is one of the great ironies of the past decade that oralists at first rejected a method so earnestly dedicated to their deepest goals. "The Bell Association really missed the boat on cued speech," one observer commented. Only recently have influential members of the oral camp come to appreciate its value in conveying phonetic information visually. Some argued at first that watching the cues would distract attention from listening. (Why hand motions but not lip motions should have this effect is not entirely clear.) Cued speech is a much better system than he originally thought, admits Daniel Ling, who now views it as a possible approach for children who lack sufficient residual hearing to succeed through a mainly auditory-oral approach.

Cued speech does deliver on many of its promises. The scattered programs that have used it in this country and in Australia have found that children achieve a good receptive grasp of English syntax and semantics and learn to read well much sooner—"just as Cornett claims," says Ling. Scattered evidence also seems to indicate that cues do not interfere with speechreading of uncued speech, as oral critics feared, but actually enhance that ability, as Cornett predicted.

But it is what cued speech does not promise that worries its critics. Like some other systems designed to teach a child English by pouring examples into him, it does not offer equally good ways for him to get his own linguistic efforts out. The profoundly deaf child who knows only cued speech may well have no unambiguous means of expressive communication. Unless he can speak clearly, he himself must cue. He probably can't monitor his own vocal production very accurately, and thus can't guarantee that he moves his lips properly, and without accurate information on his lips, his own cues are meaningless. Ironically, the very feature that makes it so useful as a receptive medium hampers it as an expressive one. Critics also doubt that small children have the dexterity to make the cues unambiguously. "Baby sign" can be understood because hand shape carries only part of the message, and signs are made over rather large areas of the face and body. The distinctions of hand shape and location that cued speech depends on are minute by comparison. And despite Cornett's claim that parents can learn to send cues in only a few days, it's unlikely they can learn to read them without concentrated work over a substantial period of time. In every manual system reception is the hard part; learning to read finger spelling, signs, or cues takes practice and more practice, time and more time. For the child without a reliable voice, cued speech offers good expressive possibilities only if his parents learn to read it well.

But the most significant problems may be social. Unless a child's teachers, parents, neighbors, classmates, and playmates all cue, he has no more chance of understanding them than any other fledgling speechreader. Very few people know the system and even fewer use it. Some deaf adults have criticized it for all the familiar reasons: that it separates children from other deaf people and teaches them that success lies in being like the hearing. Old bitterness, in fact, has kept many deaf adults from seeing the system's very genuine value for teaching English. As one deaf man observed, he thought "sinus" was pronounced "seenus" until he saw it cued.

For his part, Cornett vigorously denies any intention of denigrating sign. Indeed, he claims, cued speech can help preserve sign language by relieving it of the burden of teaching English. Those of his writings intended for manually oriented audiences strongly encourage deaf children and adolescents to learn sign for social purposes. Children urgently need English as their first language, he believes, because they must master it by age six in order to keep up in school, but sign should be their legitimate and obvious second language. But the educational regimen Cornett advises—cues at home, in preschool and the primary grades, followed by total or partial integration into regular classes by junior high school—leaves little time to mingle with deaf people and learn their language, critics claim.

Success with cued speech also assumes that parents can and will use it properly. The American families who have used it to date are highly motivated and highly educated. Most of them sought out Cornett's method and attacked it with fervor. "Those kids would succeed with any method," says one deaf educator. As cued speech spreads to public school programs and to families with fewer resources and less dedication, some teachers believe the results will begin to decline. Making accurate and instantaneous phonemic identifications may be easier to learn than fluent signing, but it is still not easy, and it is quite outside the experience of most Americans.

Like other sparkling "innovations" that have flashed across the deaf education firmament, cued speech is a comet rather than a shooting star; it has appeared and reappeared. Three times in the past similar methods were tried in Europe; one skeptical Scandinavian educator accused Cornett of "reinventing the wheel." Friar Bernard of St. Gabriel, a French monk, developed at midcentury a system that showed the vowels on the lips and the consonants on the hands in twelve positions. Critics attacked his Fonodactology for telling too much and too little; the consonants were too obvious and the vowels not obvious enough. Later in the century the Frenchman Fourcade introduced plain Dactology, a very similar, but more exact, system, but it perished as a casualty of the Congress of Milan.

The Danes have the longest experience with efforts of this sort. Early in the twentieth century Dr. Georg Forchhammer introduced his mouth-hand system at the Frederica boarding school for the deaf. In seventy years it has produced mixed results. Articulation training appears to benefit significantly, but lipreading does not. In fairness to cued speech, however, it is important to note that Forchhammer's hand signals give more information than Cornett's, so the child does not learn to pay as close attention to the lips. Socially the system restricts, as very few people know it. The Danes, however, have used it profitably with a group essentially ignored by American educators, adventitiously deaf adults. As Richard Rosenthal trenchantly observes, American specialists have concentrated so intently on children that they have offered little of use to the much larger body of deaf and hard-of-hearing people who lost their hearing as adults.

CHAPTER 10

Learning to Speak

A hearing teacher of the deaf tells of being startled, one afternoon while weeding his garden, at hearing his deaf neighbor calling her grandson.

"Tommy! Tommy! Time for lunch!" Her voice came clear and true and carried far enough down the street to bring the boy on the run. She quickly signed to him, "Come wash up," and the two of them went into the house.

The eavesdropper, hidden by a hedge, sat back on his heels and gaped. In all the years he had lived next door to that good woman, in all the times he had seen her at social evenings or the supermarket or the bank, he had never heard her use her voice. He was thunderstruck. Why should a woman who sounded, to his practiced ears, better than most of the students into whom he and the school tried to pound speech, why should this woman fail to use her voice? And it was a voice that had taken no little effort to cultivate, from what he knew of her hearing loss.

He pondered and pondered, his flowers forgotten, but could devise no solution to so complete a mystery. At last curiosity overcame him and he rose, crossed the lawn, rang the light-bell at her door, and when she opened it, he asked.

"Mary," he stammered, "I'm sorry to intrude, but I simply have to know. I heard you calling Tommy just now, and you have an excellent voice. Mary, I can't understand. Why don't you use it?"

She did not move for a moment, embarrassment, reluctance, and resentment vying for her face.

"Mary, I don't want to upset you. It's just that we work so hard to get the kids to speak, and you can, and could be a model to them, and yet you don't. Why?"

At last she relented. Her signs came slowly as her mind went back many years. "I never wanted to tell this to a hearing person," she began. "I know that I have a good voice. At least I used to, anyway. I was the pride, the star pupil, of my strictly oral school. I spent years hearing how wonderful my speech was, how I was a credit to the school and its method, how I could go among hearing people with no problems at all. Of course, I never met any hearing people except those at the school. When I gave the valedictory, I spoke it, even though no one in the class could hear. Finally, I got out of school, and went among hearing people with my wonderful voice. Can you imagine my shock, my humiliation, when, as often as not, they couldn't understand me! I was so mortified that I decided I would never speak again unless I really had to. If I was going to be deaf, then I'd be deaf."

Of all the ironies in the history of pure oralism, the greatest is that it has discouraged many people from learning to speak. Manual communication took far more obvious punishment in the methods wars, having withstood nearly a century of heavy artillery bombardment, interspersed with periodic storm trooper raids. But in many places oral teaching succumbed quietly to a more insidious foe, the guerrilla army of battered refugees from the main engagement. Oralism in the schools had the big guns on its side for nearly eighty years, but manualism had the hearts and minds of most of the pupils and some of the teachers, and their secret resistance movement fought on with the inexhaustible energy of bitterness.

Like many other such attempts, the suppression of manual communication succeeded only in driving it underground and polarizing opinion. Schools for the deaf brought children together, showed them their likeness to one another, and then tried to prevent them from expressing it. Traditional oralism made the grave strategic error of setting speech in emotional opposition to sign. Most children identified strongly with sign, and thus automatically rejected speech. The decisive turn against pure oralism often happens as a young person embraces his adolescent identity; the decision grows out of his emotional development and thus lies beyond the reach of reason. Regardless of the emotional satisfactions of sign, few deaf people deny the great benefits of usable speech, but fewer can forget what they learned in their youth about its cost.

The tragic result is that some deaf people speak well, but many more should be able to and can't. Knowledge exists to help many children and adults attain markedly higher degrees of oral skill, but attitudes have kept this knowledge from spreading to many who need it most. "There is no such thing as a totally deaf child," the newest form of oral fanaticism claims; "everyone has some residual hearing." But there demonstrably *are* children who hear nothing, or next to nothing. Because their adversaries' orthodoxy ignores this fact, manualist fanatics feel justified in ignoring the equally demonstrable truth that many people with severe or profound losses can hear a good deal that might be useful.

Like other problems we have encountered, this one at first appears philosophical but ultimately proves to be technical. Only expert technique, not philosophical pronouncements, teaches people the many precise motions that go into understandable speech. Science cannot now tell us whether manual communication helps or hinders the effort; the only conclusion we can draw with confidence is that deaf children without capable and dedicated training have very little chance of learning what is for them a very demanding skill. Even with it they may not succeed. The fact that a program advertises itself as "strictly oral" does not guarantee the ability of its teachers, any more than the label "total communication" assures that students will be taught to use all the modalities at their disposal. Every child desperately needs a sound program of auditory and speech training, but he needs much more besides. Voice quality is no measure of quality of life. Parents must conscientiously weigh sometimes opposing values as they chart their child's—and their household's—course through the communications morass. But whatever road they choose, whatever philosophical home they ultimately find, they can and should insist that their child gets a chance at competent speech training.

But sadly, how much hearing a person has left and what it might be good for are often questions very difficult to answer. At present we have no good way of measuring what a person *can* hear; all we can determine is what he can't hear. The standard examination draws its conclusions from the absence of reaction rather than from the presence of potential. A tone is sounded or a syllable pronounced, a person does not respond, and the test records that he "cannot hear it." But we know nothing of why he cannot, or how close he came to hearing it, or whether, under other circumstances, he might be able to. We know nothing, in short, about the meaning of the line on the audiogram; we know only its contour and location.

But that line, Daniel Ling observes, "merely indicates the dividing line between hearing and not hearing, much as the shoreline . . . divides land from water. From this . . . it is impossible to deduce the water's depth, warmth, or its suitability for swimming or drinking."[1] One shoreline might border warm, crystal water over silky sand while another, of identical shape, could lie along cold, murky seas hiding a sharp drop to a rocky shelf. On a map the two would look the same, just as two apparently identical audiograms might disguise very different abilities to handle information in time, to perceive shifts in frequency, or to distinguish various intensities. These latter abilities, Ling believes, mean much more to the child's potential for understanding and learning speech than do mere responses to pure tones.

Many teachers have learned to believe that if a child is deaf, he cannot hear, period. But deafness is a conceptual construct as much as a physical fact. The sociologist Robert Scott notes a similar phenomenon among the blind. To many the word means a total lack of vision, although many of the legally blind can see to some extent. The difference between a blind person with residual vision and a sighted person who sees defectively may be a social definition, not the level of loss. In the world of hearing loss such rubrics as "severe" and "profound" along with shorthand expressions of the number of missing decibels represent only averages and say little about the quality, extent, and distribution of the hearing that remains.

Audiograms have another serious drawback as diagnostic tools. They are not very reliable, especially when reliability is most critical. The younger the child or the worse the impairment, the harder it is to find out what abilities remain. People who have not learned to listen may miss sounds they are physically capable of hearing.

Everyone must learn to listen, or, more accurately, to hear in a human way. We are not born knowing how to make the fine discriminations of frequency and intensity needed to understand speech. We are not born knowing that sound is symbolic. We perceive it first as a mere warning signal, much as most other animals do. A human baby with normal hearing, though, spends his waking life immersed in sound, and his immature nervous system gradually begins to impose order on the noises that engulf him. A child with impaired hearing, however, may scarcely notice the great ocean of voices all around, and when his nervous system is ready to master it, he has nothing to practice on.

The very best time to learn anything is when the body is ready. This is more than a truism; it is a physiological fact. The human infant arrives on the scene neurologically immature and needs several years to complete his growth. His cognition develops along with his nervous system. As we have seen, this statement is not a figure of speech, either; it describes a specific neurological process. As the nerve fibers mature, a sheath of white fatty material called myelin grows to encase them. Until its sheath develops, scientists believe, a fiber does not carry impulses. Until the nerve is functioning, therefore, the child cannot learn to do the things that it will ultimately control. But during the period that the sheath of a particular nerve tract is forming, the child has a particularly easy time mastering the behavior in question. A child learns to talk, to walk, and to hear when his nerves are ready, and not before. The nerves controlling hearing gain their myelin during the first year of life; during that time the child has a very special propensity for learning to hear. It comes easier, more naturally, than it ever will again. One after another the child's various nerve tracts become myelinized, the whole process following a characteristic sequence that appears to mirror the landmarks of development.

The first year of life is thus nature's own time for learning to hear, and the child who misses out may suffer a lifelong setback. Thus the crucial importance of early detection and amplification; unless a child learns to listen with sophistication and to hear with understanding he may never learn to speak with skill. Impaired children must get appropriate hearing aids quickly and use them constantly, but finding just the right aid can be a chancy proposition, even for adventitiously deaf adults with carefully diagnosed losses. Children often have neither accurate audiograms nor any conception of what a hearing aid ought to deliver, so fitting them can degenerate into glorified guesswork. Modern hearing aids have many sophisticated features designed to tailor amplification to particular auditory needs, but getting their full benefit requires a clear picture of the individual's remaining audition.

Despite these problems, however, informed opinion almost universally favors hearing aids for apparently impaired children as soon as the impairment becomes obvious. The risks of waiting far outweigh the risks of guessing wrong. Experts believe that even the mute testimony of little babies can help in making the right choice. A child whose problem is something other than deafness won't long tolerate a device blasting 90 or 100 decibels into his head; he'll simply rip out the ear molds. But if the aids do bring the experience of sound over his threshold of hearing for the first time, the reaction leaves no doubt. A deaf baby with properly fitted aids often reacts to his wonderful new toy with rapt delight. He listens happily and intently, and his own efforts at vocalization, until then unheard and unappreciated, may well increase.

It's worth noting that hearing aids for young children are now nearly always plural. The standard choice for bilateral severe or profound impairments is a pair of body-worn aids, which deliver more power than those worn at ear level. For children needing less amplification, one or a pair of ear-level aids can serve well. A body aid sits in the small pocket or sack of a harness worn across the chest. Adults often wear theirs under clothing; women may even tuck aids into a brassiere. But children need the greatest amount of sound with the least distortion; clothing both blocks out some sound and creates static by rubbing against the microphone, so children usually wear their aids outside their clothes, where parents and teachers can keep an eye on them.

Why two aids ought to be markedly better than one is not entirely understood, but experience proves that, for children at least, they nearly always are. Two aids take advantage of the possibly different capabilities of the two ears, they permit directional perception, and as one experienced teacher says, "they somehow make listening easier." She believes that the brain's blending of two signals helps filter out background noise, a major problem for the inexperienced listener.

In the long history of deaf education hearing aids are rather new. Ear trumpets, tubes, and similar devices have been used for centuries, sometimes forthrightly, sometimes ingeniously hidden in hats, hairdos, or furniture. One Portuguese king built his into a special throne. But these devices had little appeal to active children and were totally inadequate for long periods of training. The first electrical hearing aids only became available in the early decades of this century and even then were not very portable. Schools used large, cumbersome hearing aids or amplifiers for special classes in "auditory training," which many viewed as essentially a separate school subject. It's no wonder that many deaf adults have a lingering suspicion that listening is somehow something apart, just as children view spelling or grammar as subjects unto themselves. "Why did you mark me off for spelling?" many of us have asked a teacher. "This is history class."

Inadequate as they may have been, however, these classes at least offered children the chance to experience listening. In the early 1940s educators first began to realize the educational potential of portable, personal hearing aids. The Dutch authorities found, to their amazement, that many more children than they expected could attend regular schools or classes for the hard-of-hearing. These children retained enough hearing to learn to speak if sound could be delivered to them loudly enough. Many children, of course, gained nothing from even the most powerful aids, either because their hearing was seriously distorted or nonexistent or because sound could not be made loud enough for them to hear it.

This may seem puzzling in the age of high-fidelity amplification. Sound can now be made very, very loud indeed, well over the hundred or so decibels that some deaf people theoretically need. But the theoretical maximum that electronic gear can deliver is not the question at issue. To be useful sound must fall within a listener's dynamic range, which is the stretch between the softest sound he can perceive and the loudest he can tolerate. Normal ears begin to rebel at about 110 decibels; sound becomes unpleasant, then uncomfortable and increasingly distorted. In the neighborhood of 125–135, it becomes physically painful as well as permanently harmful. But impaired ears, which might most benefit from extreme loudness, often can tolerate it even less well than the normal. Many people with sensory-neural damage cannot bear sounds nearly as loud as the normally hearing can, and some suffer from recruitment of loudness, which makes small increases in intensity appear drastically larger than they really are. Some people have so limited a dynamic range that hearing aids do them little or no good; either they cannot tolerate sounds loud enough to hear or they cannot tolerate the full 30 dB range of normal speech. Modern hearing aids have features to control the gain (increase in loudness) they produce in order to protect delicate ears. But no hearing aid can alter physiological facts.

Aids must, for example, take into account that many losses are not uniform at all frequencies. If a person can hear low tones but not high ones, he can't use an aid that amplifies all frequencies equally. The amplified low sounds would mask the high ones, precisely those most badly needed to understand speech.

Hearing aids that merely amplify ambient sounds do not exhaust the possibilities. Several systems exist to deliver more specialized information. Many schools use hard-wired amplification devices (that is, large amplifiers attached by wires to earphones) for auditory exercises. With these the student listens to the teacher like a hi-fi buff monitoring his system through a headset. Loop induction systems can make an entire room, house, or playing field into a transmitter for a person wearing a specially adapted aid. With this system a wire connected to an amplifier and microphone surrounds the perimeter of an area. Inside the wire loop the aid wearer can move freely. The wire transmits a signal that can be picked up by the special aid anywhere within the loop. Churches, schools, and other facilities have found this system useful. Over larger areas, or where a coil is impractical, individual FM receivers worn by the teacher, coach, or parent can also provide a good signal to a specially designed hearing aid.

A hearing aid, however, cannot teach a person to understand any more than eyeglasses can teach him to read. Even newly deafened adults need training and experience to get the most out of their hearing aids. They must adjust to systematic distortion and they must learn to ignore the sometimes very obtrusive background noise that hearing aids deliver. A child who has never heard at all naturally faces a more serious challenge. Unlike an adult, who must learn to pick out old friends wearing outlandish disguises in a heavy fog, the child has to identify total strangers.

In addition to a hearing aid, therefore, children need constant, or at least very frequent, opportunities to listen. They need lots and lots of different sounds to experiment on and they need some hint as to how they are doing. They need, in short, people who will talk to them at levels of sound and meaning they have some hope of understanding. In TC settings, these speakers will also sign. And children need aids that work properly all the time, unlike the nearly 50 percent of school pupils whose aids, according to one survey, are on the blink on any given day.

Whether an adequate "talking environment" can properly include any systematic visual gestures is the crux of the oral-manual debate in its modern version. Advocates of the most extreme oral position, the unisensory method, maintain that learning to hear requires such deep and exclusive concentration that any visual help, even speechreading, will distract from the effort and detract from the result. Under this theory speechreading comes only after the child has learned to depend primarily on hearing. Those who hold a more moderate oral position argue that audition ought to carry the main burden, but the natural visual products of speech do no harm provided they do not become a "crutch." Even in this view, however, limited unisensory training may be useful to some children. Supporters of total communication assert that combined signs and speech provide a stimulating auditory environment and that systematic manual

communication appears to help rather than hinder language
learning.

Oralists make a variety of arguments against the last position.
Some claim that equal concentration on two sensory modes is
simply impossible, a position that, as we have seen, experimental
studies certainly do not refute, although they fail to corroborate
it convincingly either. Others argue that time is short and any
spent concentrating on sign is not spent concentrating on speech.
In the flurry of charges and countercharges, ironically, many
oralists appear not to have noticed how close the TC forces have
come to accepting their main argument. Many TC spokesmen
now fervently insist that systematic auditory training is the right
of every child. During the early rapture over sign language in
primary and preschools, however, many TC programs have done
much less than they could or should have for young children's
listening skills. But more and more of the reputable TC programs now take to heart their own claims of teaching the child
to exploit every modality at his disposal, even something as unlikely as hearing.

Even if overt anti-auditory bias has gone the way of the open
color bar, however, curious residues remain. The Model Secondary School for the Deaf, for example, an academic Xanadu on
the campus of Gallaudet College, provides every technological
teaching aid in a building of almost distracting loveliness. The
planners' good intentions shine everywhere, in the flexible and
thoughtfully organized curriculum, in the striking architecture,
in the expert teaching and lavish equipment. The school offers
almost everything that care, money, and educational theory can
provide, except a good listening environment. MSSD is a TC
school, probably the best of its kind in the world, but, following
the educational orthodoxy of the decade during which it was
built, it consists of highly flexible open teaching spaces suitable
for classes of many sizes and degrees of formality. Large galler-
ies and bays can hold more than one activity at a time, and these
spaces make for confusing listening, even for those who hear
normally. A deaf youngster would surely be hard put to follow
the traces of his teacher's or classmates' voices over the competing sounds of other class sections sharing the same room. Such a
layout represents unconscious bias. It does not actively prevent

listening, nor had the designers any such intention, but it certainly does nothing to encourage it.

If a child can learn to hear to any extent at all, he ought also to be able to learn to speak at least as clearly. "You can pretty much tell what I can hear," says one successful oralist, "by how I sound." The child can learn to use his hearing as a guide to his speaking. "The process of speech acquisition," write the Lings, "is one of progressive differentiation and control of motor movements and increasing conformity to the phonology of the community. *If the hearing impaired child is using his residual audition in the acquisition of speech, there should be a continuous, perceptible growth in the quantity and variety of sound patterns he produces from one week to the next.*"[2] The more sounds he learns to make, in other words, the more he will be able to make out, and the more accurately he learns to hear them, the more accurately he will be able to say them. Speech and hearing reinforce one another, as anyone who has learned a foreign language knows. At first it all sounds like a meaningless jumble, but gradually more and more phonemes, words, and phrases float clearly to the surface until it's possible to catch bits of meanings as they drift by. Most language students find understanding a native speaker harder than speaking themselves. Knowing a language well enough to use the telephone, that terror of pure, naked phonology, means that the whole system of grammar and vocabulary has come under control.

It's no surprise then, as the Lings write, that "the most efficient way to develop speech is through the use of residual hearing. Conversely, one of the most efficient ways to develop auditory discrimination is through the teaching of speech."[3] Some speech skills may come to some children naturally, as they imitate their hearing, but if these fail to appear they must be consciously taught. This has often meant arduous effort for scant results, endless hours of repetition yielding little more than frustration. The teaching of speech on a large scale probably ranks as deaf education's most ignominious failure.

To Daniel Ling, this generation's single most influential theorist and practitioner, these bad results are the natural outcome of bad technique. An inadequate base of knowledge coupled with slipshod teacher training has fostered sloppy analysis and low levels of skill. Most teachers, he believes, know far too little about both the properties of sound and the capacities of the human organism. To achieve success, he believes, the teacher must approach speech acquisition as a graduated series of specific and interdependent skills and not, as so often in the past, as a collection of discrete sounds. In just this way a piano student learns to move his hands and arms in certain ways, not to hit individual notes. Ling defines a skill as the ability to make a particular organ or organs behave in a particular way. Unlike many traditional teachers, he is not so much interested in teaching particular sounds as in bringing the speech apparatus under control. He views the problem like a good athletic coach: if conditioning is adequate, then specific plays will come.

Specifically, he believes that to learn speech a person must pass through a series of necessary stages. First is "undifferentiated vocalization," the vague, generalized sounds that small babies make. Next come experiments differentiating high and low, loud and soft, long and short. Then one tries holding the mouth in different shapes and producing an array of vowels. Cutting or releasing these vowels in various ways makes consonants, which, in the final stage, can be blended into clusters. These stages follow one another both in logic and in time; each depends on those that went before.

Mere physical mastery, of course, does not imply understanding. Pronouncing the sounds of a foreign language is not the same thing as speaking it. A stage of language development mastered only at the "phonetic level" (at the level of pronunciation alone) amounts to mimicking a word without understanding it. Mastery at the "phonological level" means grasping the sound's place in a system of symbolic meaning. Only the latter means that the child can use the sound in communication.

If the child progresses from the basic to the more advanced, he builds a firm foundation and retains his progress. Any attempt at teaching, therefore, must begin with a precise analysis of exactly what skills the child possesses and exactly what remains to be done. By this Ling means that the teacher must enumerate the particular skills already mastered and those that need work and develop a plan "structured to reveal not general deficits but particular faults."[4] In other words, saying that a child's speech is blurry adds nothing to a training plan; saying that he lacks specific consonants or the ability to make specific motions with the tongue lays a basis for teaching. To Ling's mind, each particular stage of development consists of a number of particular subskills, muscular motions the child either has mastered or has not. "Orderly teaching demands that training result in the cumulative acquisition of subskills, each subskill providing some immediate gain compatible with later achievement. The traditional approach was not designed to yield cumulative gains. Nor was it formulated with reference to the previous acquisition of behaviors which can serve as a base for speech development."[5]

A skilled teacher's planning thus begins with a program designed for a particular child, with recognizable milestones to mark the successful mastery of specific skills. Not only the child's speech therapist but his classroom teachers and parents should offer help appropriate to his particular stage. The exact methods used to teach a given skill might vary from child to child. In general, however, the child's own hearing is his best speech monitoring device. Failing this, many children can learn to monitor sounds kinesthetically—from their feel as they pass through the throat and mouth, just as a good tennis player knows that a shot feels bad before he actually sees it go wrong. Though less reliable and more arduous, this method still merits a try because hearing becomes less crucial to getting sounds right as a person gets better at making them and thus concentrates on them less.

If the child can make any sounds at all, Ling prefers to start by teaching the vowels, the "carriers" of the consonants. Beginning with the easier ones, such as "ee" and "oo," the child should learn to feel the contrasting positions of his tongue, lips, and jaw as he makes each one. The same holds true for consonants. Starting with the easier ones, the child learns the characteristics that tell them apart, learning first to distinguish them by manner of articulation (stop versus fricative, for example), then by place of articulation (teeth versus hard palate, for example), then by the presence or absence of voicing (vibration of the larynx). Building a structure of cumulative and compatible skills, Ling, his associates, and others have led some impaired youngsters from single sounds through words and phrases to understandable, even felicitous connected speech. His text *Speech and the Hearing-Impaired Child* turns up in schools of all persuasions these days.

Ling, a gifted teacher, has done what many of the great teachers of the past failed to do: he reduced his work to a method that others can systematically apply. Unlike Pereira, the Braidwoods, and other early masters, modern teachers try to spread the benefits of their successes beyond the small circle of those who can come to them personally. Deaf children may owe a good deal to "publish or perish"; teachers now advance their careers by writing, not by keeping secrets.

Some observers argue, though, that when oral teaching succeeds, it is the teacher and not the method that makes the difference. Henry Tobin, for example, has seen and worked with the products of many teachers and many styles of teaching. For him, the most important factor is always a dedicated person, not a plan of action. "Many fine teachers don't even know what they're doing," he says, "but they have an intuitive feel for what kids respond to, and their students do well." It's the Annie Sullivan that makes the difference, not the theory she uses. Many systems can succeed, Tobin believes, if applied consistently and with dedication (provided they include adequate oral-auditory training). He tells of a boy from a poor family in upstate New York, for example, who had everything against him except a working mother who kept at him to do what his teachers told him, and a string of devoted though technically inexpert speech therapists. "No one really knew what they were doing, but they handed the boy on as a precious, fragile jewel and made him succeed."

In every description of a fine oral teacher the same traits unfailingly appear: confidence in ultimate success, relentless dedication to the work, great force of personality. Associates and former students of Helen H. Beebe, for example, a leading American exponent of the unisensory method, describe in almost identical terms the extraordinary impression her personality makes. "She expects them to succeed. She not only puts aids on the kid, she expects them to work." So striking is the mark of a good teacher, in fact, that Tobin has stopped startled Gallaudet students on campus and said, "You studied speech with So-and-so." Their voices bore the unmistakable brand of a particular teacher.

The handful of virtuoso teachers, like all virtuosi, do all the right things by instinct. Vladimir Horowitz would probably be hard-pressed to describe or even notice all the things that go into his unique sound, but lesser pianists could certainly profit from imitating his every move. Masters produce masterpieces, but not all the time or in all circumstances. In speech teaching, moreover, there are simply not enough masters to give more than a relative handful of children a chance at a gifted teacher. Most children would do well to study with merely earnest and well-versed journeymen, but the training programs have produced far too few even of these.

Nothing shows the importance of knowledgeable teachers more clearly than the demands of auditory training. The child with impaired hearing will never hear everything that those with normal hearing effortlessly make out, but he still might be able to catch enough to understand a usable amount of speech. The phonetics of speech are richly redundant, perhaps even more so than grammar, and hints to the identity of sounds hide in many places—so abundantly, in fact, that normally hearing people ignore most of them. For the hearing-impaired, however, these hidden clues offer many second chances to know what a message says.

The amount of phonetic information a person can make out depends, of course, on the nature of his hearing loss. Speech sounds result when air moves through the highly complex passages of the throat and mouth. Each sound a person produces is a mixture of sound waves, composed of many frequencies, produced by the vocal organs. The vocal equipment that pushes this column of air vibrates at a certain basic frequency. This gives the resulting wave its fundamental, or lowest, frequency. Other vibrations are also mixed in, and these, known as harmonics, vibrate at rates that are multiples of the fundamental. If heard alone, these would sound higher than the fundamental. As the air passes through the mouth, the tongue, lips, and palate shape and reshape themselves, forming various phonemes that we recognize. Each sound is thus a specific group of frequencies, with a characteristic composition and shape. Understanding speech means recognizing these clusters of frequencies as meaningful. Vowels, for example, each consist of a specific collection of energy peaks, known as formants. Each consonant occurs because the tongue or lips stop or slow the stream of air in a characteristic way that produces specific acoustic effects.

Each allophone of every phoneme thus consists of a particular pattern of frequencies that the listener has learned to identify as a known "sound." Catching the entire pattern naturally gives the best chance at the right identification, but even part of it can give a skilled listener the answer. We understand a friend whose congested head distorts some of his consonants. We can decipher a written message in English even with every third letter missing, although a less familiar language would give more trouble. In much the same way a hearing-impaired person need not hear exactly what a normally hearing person does in order to understand speech. But he does need a consistent system that lets him identify speech sounds from the more limited information available to him, just as a person who couldn't see people's faces might pick out his friends by studying their hands.

How well a person can use his damaged hearing to decipher speech depends, of course, on the amount and kind of hearing left. Every English speech sound has at least two characteristic frequencies, one in the range of 1,000 hertz and one or more well above that. In general, the lower component carries power and the latter carries intelligibility; the upper frequencies differentiate the sound definitively from others like it. A whisper lacks the powerful lower frequencies; it's much easier to understand than it is to hear. Very roughly speaking, conductive losses tend to cut out mostly the low frequencies, leaving the upper ones more or less intact. If power can be restored, then intelligibility presents few problems in a wholly conductive loss.

Perceptual losses, however, often damage the ability to hear the higher frequencies, which carry most of the information that makes the message understandable rather than merely audible. Adapting to this type of loss involves attempting to cope with systematic distortion.

Knowing what frequencies a person can hear is thus crucial to designing a program to help him learn to hear all he is capable of. Someone who can hear clearly up to only 750 Hz, for example, can make out the prosody of speech—its rhythm and intensity—and two of the characteristic frequencies of vowels—the fundamental and the first formant, which permit some fairly good guessing—but he'll miss the second formant of all vowels, which identifies them absolutely. He will also miss all indication of every consonant's place of articulation. He will, however, be able to discern some distinctions of manner and voicing. This can at least permit him to narrow the field down a bit. Thus, lacking over three fourths of the normal range of hearing, one has some strong hints to most of the vowels and important ones to some consonants. Trying to understand speech with this little hearing is a difficult and possibly hopeless task, but even this little hearing justifies finding out how much can be done.

If hearing extends to 1,500 Hz, however, considerably more features of speech come clear: the second formants of some vowels, the manner and voicing characteristics of all consonants, and the place characteristics of some. Thus, all the vowels are discernible, along with some of the consonants. Hearing up to 3,000 Hz means that all these language distinctions can be heard instead of surmised. The important thing, write the Lings, is that a "child's ability to receive a message through his hearing is not dependent upon his capacity to discriminate or identify *all* its component sounds, but on his skill in obtaining *sufficient* cues to understand its meaning. The ways in which speech patterns vary with meaning are the child's guide in his acquisition of a cue system that permits him to decode speech signals."[6]

How can he do this? Coming events, the old saying has it, cast shadows before, and so, as it happens, do many consonants. Different types of consonants begin in different ways and have identifiable acoustic "contours." Semivowels such as W slide in. Nasals like M start with a low formant before the vowel suddenly begins. Plosives like B start abruptly. These differences can appear in the neighborhood of 500 Hz, so even if a person with little hearing cannot distinguish the individual consonants, he might learn to narrow them down to their categories. Consonants also telegraph ahead by distorting the vowels that precede them. As Daniel Ling points out, we perceive the I in "rice" and that in "rise" as the "same" sound, even though the latter takes about twice as long to say. Vowels preceding sounds like Z (voiced fricatives) are among the longest in English. You don't need to hear the consonant to know that it must be one of a specific handful. The U in "cup" and "cut" shows a similar sort of predictable difference. Say the words to yourself but leave the final consonant silent. You will easily notice the vowel's two different forms. Hearing people know this sort of thing unconsciously, but anyone trained to listen closely to vowels already knows a good deal about consonants, even those he can't hear.

Thus, Ling argues, teachers of speech must thoroughly understand the acoustics of the language they wish to teach. That knowledge, combined with a clear understanding of the student's hearing capability, can yield an accurate picture of which speech features he will be able to hear and which he can only divine by alternate means, if at all. In some cases, of course, the analysis indicates sadly limited potential, but in others it constitutes the foundation of a constructive, realistic program. This same knowledge can help the teacher know what doesn't need to be taught. To pronounce an acceptable "rise," for example, Ling believes that the elongated vowel suffices; the difficult voiced fricative may not be worth the effort some teachers insist on devoting to it. The goal is not an elusive perfection, if that lies beyond the child's abilities, but the best performance his capacities reasonably allow. "You can become so obsessed with speech that you forget the child is a child," Ling has said. If the instruction truly matches the child's abilities, he should enjoy fairly steady progress to the limit of his ability. Years of fruitless trying, à la Freddy Howard, are a sure sign of wrongheaded teaching. Realistic goals can do more than anything else to avoid the frustration and anxiety that traditionally dog oral teaching.

The technical knowledge to achieve much better average results in speech and hearing training already exists. Whether more than a relative handful of children can benefit from it depends not so much on the advance of science—although that certainly would not hurt—as on the effectiveness of teacher training. And the outlook for the next half generation at least is far from promising. Early auditory training has become dogma in both camps, but the technical skills of most teachers still fall far short of children's needs.

"Although most programs view their approach to the teaching

of speech as eclectic," concludes Donald Moores after an exhaustive study of the matter, "a better description might be haphazard."[7] Many important questions about speech acquisition by children remain unanswered, of course, but too few educators even use everything presently known. Diagnostic tests generally don't give the kind of detailed information required, and little is known about the relative value of different teaching methods. "As a general rule," Moores observes gloomily, "methods of teaching speech to the deaf in the United States have neither a theoretical nor a pragmatic base."[8]

If they lack solid underpinnings, however, the methods do not lack labels and advocates. The method in most common use today appears under a profusion of titles: auditory global, auditory-oral, aural-oral, acoupedic, natural, and, in its more extreme versions, unisensory. This method emphasizes hearing as the best teacher of speech. In practical terms, it means early and continuous amplification, a detailed and comprehensive program involving both home and school, and encouragement of any speech that occurs naturally. This method rests on the belief that understandable speech will eventually come out if enough spoken language is poured in. It relies on hearing to do this job. Good results depend on constant encouragement and reinforcement of any attempts at speech the child can make. And sometimes these efforts pay off handsomely. Our friend Sally, the oral success, and victim of a profound prenatal loss, learned to use her considerable residual hearing to listen intelligently and speak clearly on a regimen even more strictly unisensory than is now generally practiced. Advocates talk of "priming the pump so that speech will pour out." Donald Calvert and S. Richard Silverman, nationally recognized experts, believe that "the 'classroom' is the child's total environment. He is 'in school' all his waking hours."[9] And Mother, of course, becomes teacher, turning every activity and exchange into a "speech experience" to give the child the exposure he needs. With its emphasis on hearing, the auditory global method plays down, if not discourages, visual cues, although moderates do not prohibit speechreading.

The "traditional" oral approach, the one used on most of today's deaf adults, appears these days under the title of multisensory unit syllable method. It "assumes that speech will *not* develop just from the child hearing and seeing connected speech in the course of conversation,"[10] Calvert and Silverman write, and that assumption rose out of generations of children who had no hearing aids in early childhood and did not begin speech training until six or seven or later. In this method, children get formal instruction in making sounds, often in order of difficulty. Instead of working with connected phrases or sentences, it strives to produce individual syllables that might later be combined. Touch and vision also figure as teaching tools. The child watches himself in mirrors, blows out flames, fogs up panes, feels his own and other people's faces, throats, and chests. This method, happily, has passed from general use as an overall approach to speech training, but elements of it still appear in many programs based on auditory principles.

The association phoneme unit is the last-ditch position for children who have failed with the others. Here touch and vision dominate. The child is taught to associate sounds with letters. He learns them at the level of individual phonemes and only if he succeeds at simple sounds does he later combine them into syllables or words.

As Moores points out, however, these labels do not mean very much in practice. Far too many schools have no explicit policy on speech and language training because they have never thought their principles through clearly. A prominent deaf educator of the total communication camp recalls that in his school days "various teachers did various things, and nobody seemed to know what they were doing or why." This situation remains far too common today. "One thing you have to say for the strict oralists like Clarke and Central," he admits ruefully, "is that they know what they believe and practice it consistently."

Belief, of course, has not been the great lack in oral teaching; knowledge has, of both the limits and the realistic potential of people with impaired hearing. It makes no more sense to insist that "there is no such thing as a totally deaf child" than it does to assume that no child with a severe or profound loss can learn to produce and understand speech. The evidence against both propositions is too overwhelming and ignoring it has caused too much pain. Educators can no longer debate what is best for every child or even for most children. The only real question is what is best for this particular child, as an individual with individual abilities and needs. And the needs of a deaf child go far beyond developing speech. They include self-esteem, emotional security, a sense of social place. The child's personal and social growth, and not just his hearing loss, needs to be considered in developing a plan for his speech training. Ideology is a poor substitute for compassion and common sense. The experts have no infallible answers, and parents must listen to what their hearts whisper as well as to what the learned doctors proclaim.

For their part, educators belong not on soapboxes but in classrooms, clinics, and laboratories, teaching and learning. If they lowered their own voices, perhaps more deaf children would get a chance to use theirs.

CHAPTER 11

Community and Identity

Beware the dark eyes on you in the street
And the impersonal glances
Of those who pass you by—
They have no love for you, though you be their brother;
Though you should cry for pity, there would be none.

Growing in alien soil, the strange plant dies
From rocks that press too hard, that block its root,
Sent underground for nourishment in earth
That holds no sustenance for such as come
Unbidden through the tunnel of the rain.
Wherever you may go, the word shall pass
That you are stranger there, and you shall know
The unreceptive ground and fierce sunlight
In the press of hostile faces: they will shout
In a bitter voice the wisdom of the old,
Who have no will to live nor strength to die
And speak the blind prejudice of the stone,
And close the shadowy door.

Only the bitterweed can sink its root
Into the powerful rancor of the soil

And blossom forth in strong integrity,
Undaunted by a hatred. You must send
Your anger forth to rend the strangling rock
And with your strength build shelter from the sun;
And send them also
A word as bitter as theirs, as filled with hatred;
Then only will they let you pass in peace.

                                        Rex Lowman

An outwardly mild and humorous man, Rex Lowman draws these images from his Arkansas boyhood. There the bitterweed grows in hardy profusion along the roadsides and in the meadows of his memory. There also he took his first lessons in deafness and in endurance. Lowman does not willingly interpret his poems; as works of art, he believes, they must stand on their own. But he can't prevent readers from interpreting, from seeing in "Bitterweed," his best-known lines, as fine and searing a distillate of an American deaf experience as exists in English.

For the most part deaf people have lived in America, and in other countries too, not unlike Lowman's raggy weed. They have gathered along the hidden margins of the ordinary society, in stubborn and unbidden clusters, drawing sustenance mainly from their own strength. Their tenacious root has been a simple determination to endure, their "shelter from the sun," each other's company. For most Americans afflicted with early deafness, for those who belong to Schowe's "coherent social entity," the center and meaning of their lives has been the deaf community.

This small, stubborn, resolutely isolated band is also the human meaning of early deafness in America. For generations, coming to adulthood as a deaf person has meant joining the ranks of that community. For generations, seeing a child grow up an "oral failure" has meant "losing" him to the company of his own kind. This is no simple gathering of like-minded citizens; it is an exercise in essential otherness, in the assertion of difference, and the right to difference, in the face of opposition.

It's almost too easy, in these days of ethnic politics, to call the deaf community a minority group. Indeed, deaf people themselves often use the term when pressing for political goals, but in so doing they sacrifice their uniqueness to gain visibility. The cliché at once connotes too much and denotes too little, letting outsiders off easily by convincing them they understand when in fact they may not.

The deaf community, of course, shares some characteristics with the "minorities." Like them, its members carry a mark of differentness, of social shame, an undeniable sign that they are not of the first order of standing in society. Sociologists call such a social scar a "stigma," from the Greek "to prick"—as slaves and criminals were marked to set them apart. In society at large many deaf people, and many members of racial minorities, carry so great a stigma that it comes to dominate people's social perception of them; in technical terms, they carry a stigmatized master status. Each individual occupies numerous social statuses, of course—spouse, parent, employee, taxpayer, neighbor, for example—but a master status is one that overwhelms other characteristics and governs people's reactions. In segregation days, for example, the master status of Negro or colored outweighed education, abilities, character traits, age, and other capacities or attainments that a person might have possessed. The racial designation alone determined the most important things about the person's place in the general society. Race still sometimes acts as a master status in American society, although lately it has been losing power. Handicap in general, though, and deafness in particular, retain nearly all their traditional social force. Master statuses need not be unfavorable, of course: those of white Southerner or European nobleman had exactly the opposite effect on their bearers. But the designations of American minorities have nearly always involved stigma (even when the "minority" formed the numerical majority, as in parts of the old South).

The reason is that "minority" status really has nothing to do with numerical strength; it has to do with power. The majority culture—any majority culture—controls what society defines as normal—white skin, for example, or flawless English. It defines as an "outsider" anyone who fails to conform to accepted norms of "rightness." Some members of stigmatized categories accept the general society's definition of themselves and strive to become "normal" and thus acceptable. They straighten their hair or their noses or shorten their names and attempt to "pass," to remake themselves in society's image. For a deaf person this requires, Ben Schowe writes, the "skills of a tightrope walker and the accident hazards are also comparable."[1] Others, however, either cannot or will not conform. They accept, perhaps embrace, the fate of Lowman's bitterweed: life in a constantly hostile environment where they struggle to find shelter and to resist. Traditionally, and for many peoples, the solution has been to turn the majority culture's own weapon against it: to construct a different version of reality and to shelter inside. The outsider thus becomes insider.

Variant definitions of reality are hard for one or a few people to maintain, though; a genuinely personal and markedly original reality is often taken as a mark of mental illness. But if a substantial number of people who carry the same stigma can join together they might be able to construct a social life based on their version of how life ought to be. They will have to deal with the general culture in some areas of life, but they can keep inviolate much that is important and nurturing. Thus, black people, deaf people, Jews, and other historic rejects from the mainstream have constructed communal lives that glorify and explain, and thus fortify their members against, their particular bitter experience. Of groups of this type the deaf community arose fairly recently, having begun in earnest only with the widespread establishment of asylum schools. The theory of political nationalism explains why this is so. Cultural groups develop strong feelings of internal solidarity and identification, the theory holds, when they come together in sufficient numbers and in conditions that emphasize both their similarities to one another and their differences from surrounding powerful others. Urbanization did this for many nationalities of Central and Eastern Europe, colonialism did it in the Third World, immigration did it for American "ethnics," and residential schools did it for the deaf.

The life of such reject groups generally goes on outside the notice of the general population; in the general estimation, it may even be beneath notice. A writer preparing an article on the deaf actor Bernard Bragg was cautioned by an editor not to slight the "isolation" that Bragg and other deaf people feel. "What isolation?" came the astonished question. What isolation would such a famous, active, and admired man feel? "In his world Bragg is an important man. He's in demand, not isolated." The editor considered a moment. He had grown up with a deaf schoolmate, an intensely committed but not wholly successful oralist who had no social life with the deaf and very little with the hearing. The hearing man had always assumed that all deaf people lived that way; the idea that deaf people could have an active and satisfying life among themselves came as something quite new.

The general culture's indifference cannot be reciprocated, however. Often small and precariously placed, minority cultures care intensely about the majority's good will, which they value, often quite accurately, as the only safeguard of their fragile well-being. Thus, actions of individuals who can be identified as members become important as reflections for good or ill on the entire group. Among deaf people this anxiety—obvious also in the communal life of Jews, blacks, Italian-Americans, and others—tends to center on the perfidy of deaf peddlers, renegades who practice a very lucrative form of begging disguised as vending little cards displaying the manual alphabet. The deaf community regards these people as an organized criminal conspiracy; indeed, they do appear to work in rings. But the intense resentment of the main-line deaf arises from more than anger over potential damage to their carefully cultivated image as industrious and sober citizens. Deaf peddlers constitute a double insult, observes Paul C. Higgins, a sociologist and son of deaf parents, on the basis of his field study of the deaf community of Chicago. Their very high income mocks the honest toil of the respectable deaf, and it is earned by reinforcing the worst stereotypes among the hearing. If deaf people felt themselves less vulnerable and exposed, this handful of outcasts would make little difference. Indeed, deaf people may well overestimate the peddlers' influence on the hearing, but in the present circumstances the intense feelings against them is a gauge of the deaf community's subordination.

Many groups try to keep their inner lives private, but the deaf culture is particularly opaque to outsiders. Most of it goes on in sign language, and most of the members either cannot or do not care to master the general speech. The difference in modality in itself keeps many intruders away, and diglossia protects the innermost culture from all but the most persistent snoops. ASL is very difficult for hearing people to master; the reason is not linguistic, although there are genuine difficulties on this score. The real reason, as we have seen, is social. Deaf signers simply do not permit most hearing signers to learn ASL. Pidgin sign English buffers the deaf culture's contact with hearing friends who sign. Learning ASL depends not so much on mastery of grammatical constructions as on admission to the inner realms of intimacy. This can cause very real problems for deafened adults who wish to join the deaf culture.

It is not even clear that all full-fledged members of the community must be fluent ASL signers. The literature on the sociolinguistics of deafness is still small, but already large enough to have spawned its own academic debates. Woodward, Markowicz, and other scholars associated with Stokoe's sign language laboratory at Gallaudet believe that ASL is a *sine qua non* for full membership in the deaf community. Higgins, on the other hand, argues that communication styles cover a wider spectrum and that attitudes rather than a limited range of particular skills define membership. Furfey and Harte do not explicitly discuss this question, but they imply a certain variability in communication skills with a strong emphasis on sign language.

No one denies, however, that communication style has very strong social overtones for deaf people. How a signer learned to sign, and the kind of sign he uses, disclose both his personal history and his social relationship with the deaf community. True "native" signing very close to ASL means a long-standing and very intimate association, usually an early onset of deafness, and a youth in a residential school. Sexual signs, for example, both "off color" and clinical, were, until Woodward published a book on the subject, very closely held within the deaf community. Even some relatively skilled interpreters have stated that such a vocabulary did not exist, because someone outside the community hardly ever had a chance to learn it. Knowledge of these signs, Woodward believes, defined the circle of adult sexuality within the deaf community. Only people likely to take a deaf spouse got to know them, not even the hearing children of deaf parents. New instructors at Gallaudet have traditionally gotten a special introduction to student obscenity as a matter of self-defense, as students may playfully teach unsuspecting novices to use vulgar signs. Students taught one high-ranking newcomer the sign for "whore" in place of that for "experience." He didn't get the joke until he returned from a trip to report to stunned colleagues that he had "had many interesting experiences." So the summer before they start to lecture, new faculty have solemnly filled their notebooks with signs supplied by students alternating among giggles, blushes, and high-minded brazenness.

Now that Woodward has let the cat out of the bag, in the interest of better sex education, medical diagnosis, and legal clarity, it will be interesting to see if new "secret" sexual signs evolve to restore privacy. Woodward's own theory of the social function of ASL implies that his dictionary may shortly be outdated.

Native signing close to ASL is, paradoxically, both a high- and a low-prestige form, depending on context, and the same is true of forms close to pidgin English. The latter imply a certain aura of sophistication and worldly success, such as a middle-aged black person with graduate degrees might cultivate. The former, however, implies a genuineness, a claimed cultural purity and integrity, a closeness to the "people," such as a young black nationalist might espouse. To some extent, though not exactly, it is the difference that once existed between the dashiki and the three-piece suit. To the dismay of speech advocates, being as "deaf" as possible has a certain cachet, especially among those young people for whom it represents a conscious choice. In some student circles, interest in speech and hearing aids brands one a "hearie"—an "Uncle Tom." Campus cliques and adult friendships generally follow communication style and often reflect common educational history. Gallaudet enrolls students from every sort of communications background, and the cafeteria tells the story. Every style of signing can be found among the bright visual chatter at the tables, and students usually find their seats—and their friends—among others who communicate as they do. For most deaf people, of course, communication style doesn't reflect free choice any more than regional accent does among the hearing.

Attitude rather than specific practice forms the acid test of membership in the deaf community. People who belong "accept their deafness," as the saying goes. What this phrase—something between a cliché and a creed—exactly means is not easy to pin down. It has to do with assimilating the fact of deafness—differentness, really—into one's self-image, with abandoning the hope of ever being "normal," with seeing the whole of one's being and saying that it is good. It has to do with not seriously wishing or wanting to be other than one is. A well-adjusted black person recognizes that in some circumstances it might be more convenient to be white, but gives the matter no serious thought. He locates the source of injustice in society rather than in the self. A deaf person who "accepts his deafness" probably wouldn't mind being able to hear for certain specific purposes, but has no serious desire to build his life on any foundation other than deafness. To him deafness is not a "handicap" but a "human difference."

But it's a human difference of a very special kind. We have thus far discussed how the deaf community resembles ordinary minority groups. In some ways, however, how it differs from them is more important. Unlike black people or Hispanics or Lithuanian-Americans, the deaf community stands apart because of people's adaptation to particular physical limitations. Black people possess the same intellectual, physical, and spiritual endowments as white people; anything a member of one race can learn a member of the other can, if properly taught, learn too. The social disabilities of blacks result entirely from the social meaning given to their skin color. Remove that meaning and the need for social separation disappears. So, to simplify the matter a good deal, integrating black people fully into white society requires little more than a firm desire to do so. Nothing physical, intellectual, or spiritual stands in the way of a black and a white baby being raised to be identical in everything but appearance.

The difference between a deaf child and a hearing one, however, often goes much deeper and reflects physical necessity rather than social preference. Only a small proportion of deaf children learn to communicate fluently in the manner of the general community and even these miss many levels of social interaction based on sound. The deaf child's basic knowledge, attitudes, and assumptions probably differ profoundly from the hearing child's. Hearing loss is a deprivation so devastating that hearing people can hardly imagine what a deaf child's world

must look (and sound) like. As Thomas and James Spradley concluded, after their family's long and painful bout with strictly
oral education for a young deaf daughter: "A deaf child's idea of
normal cannot possibly coincide with a hearing parent's idea of
normal."[2] They do not mean that a deaf child cannot act normally or is abnormal in some other way than auditorily, but that
the very basis of cognition in a world without meaningful sound
is—has to be—different. And the ways appropriate for coping
with that cognition must be different too.

To put the matter plainly, deaf people cannot do everything
that hearing people can, and society has made some of those
things overridingly important. The special social status thus
derives in part from real rather than invented differences.

But only in part. Prejudice against the deaf has a long and
sorry history and has often excluded people from benefits and
opportunities that should rightfully have been theirs. "Deaf and
dumb"—that ancient, thoughtless epithet as odious to the deaf as
"nigger," "kike," and "spic" are to others—still pops up everywhere. People today at least know when they're insulting someone about ancestry; many don't realize when they drop as bad
an insult about disability. "Deaf and dumb" as a categorical
phrase is false in two senses: not all deaf people are mute (sense
1 of "dumb") and no more than the usual proportion of them are
stupid (sense 2). Two old lines of etymology come together in
this single word, to the everlasting chagrin of the deaf. The present depressed economic state of the deaf community, as con-
trasted with their parity with the hearing a century ago, resulted
from powerlessness and neglect rather than from lack of ability.
Outside society's normal channels of news and information and
poorly educated besides, deaf people have traditionally found it
hard to organize for political action. Only very recently have
they begun concerted efforts to assert their needs and make their
political presence felt. And powerlessness, of course, means a
smaller piece of the pie.

Socially, too, the roots of prejudice run deep into the defenses
of the hearing. For those unfamiliar with deafness, meeting a
deaf person can be profoundly awkward. Nothing in ordinary
life prepares one for the encounter and its particular demands.
As a general rule, contact between members of different groups

tends to reduce stereotypes; blacks and whites working together, for example, quickly learn to regard one another as individuals as much as representatives of "them." But this doesn't always hold between the hearing and the deaf; an ill-prepared meeting may actually make things worse. The hearing person's usual ways of handling an awkward situation don't work. Ignoring the differences, glossing over them, skating around them, do not help establish contact. The hearing person becomes frustrated, rattled, embarrassed, when nothing gets across. He may even come to resent the deaf person for "causing" the situation. The sociologists Simpson and Yinger comment that although stereotypes tend to break down when communication goes easily, "incidental, involuntary, tension-laden contact is likely to increase prejudice."[3] The hearing person may well remember that the odd voice or mannerisms or apparent muteness made him intensely uncomfortable, not that the other person was a person much like himself.

Prejudice lies at the root of many of the problems deaf people face in this society, but not of all, and that is a very crucial difference between them and other ethnic groups. True integration of the bulk of the deaf community would mean changes so profound as to overturn habits thousands of generations old, habits that go to the core of human social life and may well antedate *Homo sapiens*. So far as is known, humankind has always used vocal language as its major communication medium. Our nervous systems and our societies are built around that fact; no quantity of good intentions can overcome it. To live a fully human life, deaf people, like all people, need emotional ease and closeness, a sense of recognition, a place, as the saying goes, to be somebody. Ordinary society cannot provide that for most of those with early profound hearing losses. To claim otherwise deludes the complacent and punishes the innocent. Only very specially designed environments let them be fully themselves; fortunately, they have had the wit and the stamina to construct much of what they need. Much more than prejudice keeps them apart from the hearing world: the very nature of their loss.

A basis in disability rather than heredity means that the deaf community differs from other minority subcultures in a far profounder way. As we have seen, only one deaf child in ten has deaf parents; or, in other words, nine out of ten learn to be deaf people outside the home and often in opposition to the family. This has deep consequences for both relationships and identity. All young people find their selfhood by separating themselves, with greater or lesser travail, from their parents. Most expect, even hope, however, to grow into adults not unlike those their ancestors have been. Not so of most deaf children of hearing families, who could not, no matter how hard they tried, grow up to resemble their parents in that most tantalizing of traits, the ability to hear. They must find a practical and satisfying way of being deaf, and if the home will not provide it, then someone else must.

For generations in America that someone has been the state residential school, which traditionally received all the hardest cases, the kids with the poorest hearing and the least chance of oral success. More precisely, that someone has been the other children in the school. The authorities—until recently, hearing adults at least officially committed to oralism—have stood *in loco parentis* both legally and psychologically, encouraging speech and suppressing sign.

The children, rather than the adult authorities, traditionally administer the rite of passage to newcomers and welcome them into the community of their own kind. Most adults who were deaf as children can describe the same experience—the frustration, anger, and loneliness of home; arrival at school; the sudden dawning of community and relationship. Of all adult cultures in the world, this is one of the very few handed down, generation after generation, from child to child. Few suppressed bands of believers have invented, preserved, or handed on a heritage in the face of greater opposition or with more ingenuity and determination than the deaf children who taught one another sign language in secret. Most state schools eventually acquiesced, of course; by junior high school age the slower students traditionally began to take their classes in sign. But until the late 1960s, no school in this country actually taught sign language. They first tried to prevent kids from learning it, then accepted it as a *fait accompli*.

Parents' attitudes mirror the pivotal position of the state school in deaf culture. Hearing families often view sending their children away as institutionalizing them, consigning them to a feared and unsavory necessity. And the children, often completely ignorant of the meaning of the abrupt separation—for their precarious communication with their parents may not bear so weighty a message—often view it as rejection. For the deaf parent, however, the only pain is the separation felt by any parent of a child at boarding school. The child is attending the parent's own alma mater, or an institution much like it. He has been prepared for the experience for months, perhaps since babyhood. It is no more an abandonment than an upper-class family's sending a son to Exeter or a daughter to Miss Porter's.

Ethnic identity—the recognition of oneself as a member of a particular group—costs most deaf more dearly than other people. They form it young and in opposition—indeed, even more than other minority identities, it makes sense only in opposition. To be deaf is to be not hearing; it is to be one of us and not one of them.

The cost shows in the anger undergirding the dichotomy. It is anger not about being deaf—for most people eventually accept the unalterable facts about themselves or go mad—but about what was done to the child one used to be by hearing people and in the name of making one like them. Accidents of birth, faulty heredity, freak illnesses, accidents, even botched medical care are understandable, at least emotionally if not cosmically. Unrelenting malice and cruelty to children—or actions perceived as such by a terrified child—are not. Talk with even very worldly deaf people educated in the old way, and in more cases than not you will find, surprisingly close to the surface, and barely hidden by education, good manners, humor, or experience, the running sores of anguish and resentment, the gaping, unstanchable wounds of wrongs done decades before; a bottomless fury; an identical litany of slapped hands, tied wrists, punishments, scoldings, tedium, humiliation.

The schools, as one of their graduates said, were "father and mother" to the children, who used to go away at four or five or six for most of the year, visiting home—and "visiting" is the right word—in summer and at Christmas. The school became home because it was where the heart was, and vacations were interruptions to be dreaded, even resisted. Yerker Andersson, who served as dormitory counselor in several institutions, remembers small boys and girls crying because they had to go home, where no one understood them.

For those who don't join the deaf community either by birth into a deaf family or through a childhood at a deaf school, the third important chance is high school graduation, when the ingredients of an adult identity must be assembled. Some go to Gallaudet and other programs for the deaf from mainstream programs in regular schools or from hearing colleges that proved academically or socially too demanding. Before post-secondary educational opportunities became as broad as they are today, some young oralists used to drift into the orbit of a local deaf community and there find companionship, friendship, perhaps even romance. Marriage seems a fairly crucial step in the formation of identity for those wavering about association with the deaf community. A spouse who falls definitely inside of it will exert a strong centripetal pull; unions of two deaf, one a signer and the other a non-signer, usually move the oralist partner in the direction of sign. But a spouse who falls definitely outside—either hard-of-hearing or normally hearing—often has the opposite effect. A hearing husband rarely lets his deaf wife draw him into a deaf social orbit, and hearing wives report resistance, even hostility to their attempts to mix socially with deaf women.

Thus, belonging to the deaf community is a social rather than an auditory fact—it is an act of will. Surveying Baltimore, Furfey and Harte found some "deaf" people whose audiograms made them hard-of-hearing at most and some "hard-of-hearing" people with very profound losses. People born before hearing aids became generally available often ended up in state schools despite what today would be relatively minor physical disabilities; there they learned to be deaf. A modern aid might restore their hearing but would destroy their social world at the same time. Some oral successes, furthermore, find life among the hearing too frustrating or superficial. Cicourel and Boese theorize that oral skills generally make poor vehicles for true intimacy, and oral deaf people often do have trouble forming deep relationships. The hearing may be too impatient and the deaf too hard to understand. "Even the deaf who are rated 'excellent' in communication with the hearing are far from normal in communication skills," Furfey and Harte found.[4]

Belonging to the deaf community implies more than theoretical identification; it means active involvement with local deaf people and their institutions. "While the deaf are the most cohesive minority group in the United States—with their own language, clubs, churches, and even Olympic games—" remarks Rosenthal, a bit wistfully, "the hard of hearing are rarely fraternal. For all our numbers, there are no hard of hearing clubs that I know of except for those under the aegis of institutions. Hard of hearing people do not socialize or form groups to meet each other and discuss mutual problems, as do other people with a common difficulty."[5] Indeed, the hearing-impaired who decline to associate themselves with the deaf community in a sense define its outer limits.

The community views people as insiders or outsiders, but those inside by virtue of their active, public commitment cover quite a wide range of attitude and behavior. The Chicagoans Higgins studied included a fair-sized contingent of people who depend primarily on oral skills. They don't totally reject signing, however, and many use it, if imperfectly. Only hard-line oralists fall totally beyond the pale, Higgins concludes. And if random observations around Washington mean anything, some younger, more pragmatic ODAS members (many of whom sign a bit) might even sneak in. Despite internal differences, however, the deaf community closes ranks when dealing with the outside. Higgins reports, for example, that "a [deaf] Jewish synagogue donated items to a bazaar run by a deaf Lutheran church and not to a synagogue run for hearing Jews."[6]

The range of styles—from very "deaf" to "almost hearing"—is a subtle amalgam of necessity and opportunity. Some have no choice except that place on the communication and social spectrum where they find themselves. Any other adaptation is simply beyond their physical abilities or their resources of time, money, or stamina. But others face a range of tantalizing possibilities and thus of real choices. They could, if they wanted to, " 'pass for white' among the hearing,"[7] or at least try. A true double life appears possible, with all its allure and all its moral ambiguity.

Those with real options stand on the razor's edge of decision and they feel the double pulls that are the essence of choice. Thus, deaf community, identity, and interaction with the hearing tangle into an unyielding knot. None of these considerations makes sense without the others. Desire to pass among hearing people means trying to be like them; rejection of their standards means the opposite. "Membership in the community," Higgins observes, "seems to lessen the desire to improve one's speech and lipreading abilities. Members of the community have little desire to pass as hearing. Therefore, communication with the hearing is more inhibited than if the deaf were more committed to becoming as much like the hearing as possible."[8] But things are not really that simple, he tacitly admits, except for those without a real alternative. Many members of the community can and do lipread, some quite well. "Signers see [deaf] speakers as not as fully committed to the deaf world as they should be."[9]

Does that feeling merely mask envy and resentment? One "oral success" who has spent her life among the hearing, but who has tried and failed several times to connect with the deaf, believes it does. "I envy them their ease," she says, but they seem to envy her her options, her worldliness. She learned to sign in one of the English-based versions, but that didn't seem to help. She felt no common ground except hearing loss, and although they expected her to feel an affinity based on that alone, she did not. The cultural gap—the gap in experience and understanding—was simply too large. They seemed, in some indefinable way, innocent and immature, "curiously old-fashioned." And indeed, hearing people often make this same observation. Members of the deaf community, even relatively educated and sophisticated people, frequently strike one as decent, "square" in both senses, and in a way that goes far beyond dress, unfashionable. They seem "out of it" in a way that members of certain strict Protestant sects often do. But instead of organdy prayer caps, sober colors, and sensible shoes, they wear an invisible but palpable aura of unworldliness. "They try to keep up to date, but they can't," our oralist says. She herself takes pride in knowing the general society's news of politics, fashion, and culture. She doesn't follow the news of the deaf world and has no interest in it. Indeed, she has lost patience with the whole vexed controversy. "I'm a hearing person who can't hear," she says. Deafness is to her a physical fact and no more.

The social meaning of her life, and indeed of the people she rejects and who reject her in turn, comes down to the awful opposition of the hearing and the deaf. But what if the dichotomy were not so sharp? Suppose children could grow up without having it seared into their souls that they must be one or the other? This possibility—indeed, this likelihood—David Denton believes, is one of the very best arguments for early manual communication by hearing parents. He sees a profound and heartening difference between the children raised under his school's new policy and those he knew early in his career. The TC youngsters seem to grow up seeing the world not as two irremediably hostile camps, but as a continuum of people, some more, some less like oneself. In the first months of the Maryland school's sign classes for parents, a five-year-old boy made "one of the most powerful statements" Denton had ever heard. His parents had learned sign language; "Mom and Dad are deaf now," the little boy said and signed.

Mom and Dad and the child and his school all belonged to that special class of people who were "deaf," that is, like the child's image of himself. No longer would children need to draw solace from the scanty resources of their own youth; no longer would the people closest to them remain implacably apart. "Daddy has improved [in being] deaf," another little child signed; as Daddy practiced his signs and got better at them, he became more like his son and each of them more like the other. A third little boy signed one day that he wanted himself, Mommy, and Daddy all to go to heaven together. The parents probed; it turned out that the boy feared going first because he thought no one there could sign. The distinction between those like the child and those unlike him persists, but it need no longer arise in the pain of rejecting and being rejected by those he ought to love most. Maybe for these children the distinction will not bear its terrible traditional weight of anguish.

The greatest effect of TC on the campus, Denton says, "is the growth of trust between hearing and deaf." Children now can believe their teachers more willingly that auditory and speech training may do some good. Much of the old bitterness is gone, and oral skills may not be treason if hearing people can be "deaf." No one will know the long-range effects of these changes until these children are adults; by then the deaf community may have a somewhat different emotional base. Certainly, Denton believes, it may well be more hospitable to friendly hearing people, just as certain neighborhoods of the hearing world will be more open to the deaf.

Even if these changes come about, however, the deaf community will retain many of its basic features. Most larger population centers have substantial numbers of deaf people who gather for a variety of social, religious, athletic, and cultural activities. Washington, D.C., even boasts a "caucus" of deaf homosexuals. Closed off from the general community, the deaf world is a small town within the bigger city, with all that that entails in warmth and friendliness and in gossip and factionalism. A deaf grapevine runs from coast to coast, bound together by school friendships, family ties, mutual acquaintances; active community members thus live in a continental small town with many local branches. News spreads quickly and widely, and reputation precedes any move to a new home. The memory of small incidents can persist for decades. The late Frederick Schreiber, executive director of the NAD, had a name sign said to refer to a beard he tried to grow in college.

A bad name must be lived down; it cannot be outrun, and secrets rarely stay put. If deaf community members tend toward conservative family and sexual relationships, distrust of psychiatric care and concepts, and a generally very conventional social style, the reason may lie not only in low education or working-class status or isolation from general cultural trends, but partly in simple fear of wagging fingers and tongues and clacking TTYs. Ostracism from the deaf community means an isolation greater than a hearing person can know; there is no new town in which to make a fresh start.

Within the community, however, there is a range of acceptable styles and a corresponding range of cliques and factions. Speaking versus signing is the greatest social divide. Next, geographic ties appear far from negligible, although deaf people from small places strongly tend to move to larger ones. ASL has regional variants, often but not always coinciding with state lines, the enrollment boundaries of the state residential schools. Sign language also shows fissures along generational, racial, and educational lines. They, along with sex and the quality Higgins calls "sophistication," are the major determinants of personal relationships and public status. Class position as defined by the outside world—occupation, income, style of life—carries much less weight than among the hearing. First, except in a very few localities, the deaf class structure is incomplete; the handful in upper-middle-class occupations are too few to form a true class. Secondly, underemployment and prejudice mean that occupation reflects ability, background, and interests much less truly among the deaf than among the hearing.

Those with reputations for worldly success do occupy a special, if sometimes ambiguous, status. Hearing society views them as "leaders," although their true ability to influence action and opinion may be largely illusory. More exactly, those who communicate well with the hearing and can move among them fairly easily often act as mediators, spokesmen, and general facilitators for those with troubles beyond the resources of the deaf community to handle. The educated act as figureheads or advocates or what black people used to call "credits to the race." People come to them for advice and inside (actually, outside) information. But whether the community holds these benefactors in a high level of generalized esteem is another question. Advanced education is a magnet with a double pull, attracting both admiration and resentment. Like other newcomers to social mobility, the deaf community sets great store by titles and advanced degrees, even honorary ones. *Deaf American* and other magazines, like other minority publications, assiduously chronicle achievements that strike outsiders as quite ordinary: modest business successes, graduate degrees from universities of less than the first rank, jobs in the lower and middle reaches of professional fields. These things obviously have a meaning to readers or editors would not include them. They represent attainment in the face of heavy odds and deserve recognition. But turn the sign for "university" upside down and, as we have seen, it means "intellectual snob" or "stuck up about college."

Reputation has great import for another reason. This is a face-to-face culture. When Rosenthal said that the deaf are gregarious, he meant in part that they get together a lot, often markedly more than hearing people. They *have* to get together; there's no other way of satisfying the basic human craving for sociability. They generally can't kibbitz on the job or pass the time of day with the neighbors or chat with shopkeepers or drop in at the corner tavern. Typing into a TTY has none of the warmth of chatting on the phone. Everywhere outside the deaf club or the houses of community members, in fact, is foreign territory—not exactly hostile, perhaps, but with none of the psychic comforts of home. So deaf people, though scattered almost randomly through metropolitan areas, reconstitute their portable neighborhood weekend after weekend, at formal and informal gatherings, in large and small groups.

They are gregarious in another sense too. Like all Americans, they support as many associations as they have special interests. Groups of all kinds, religious, social, cultural, athletic, honeycomb this relatively small community. Indeed, supporting all these institutions is a considerable strain, as the members are far from wealthy. Many sizable towns support a deaf club or community center, which holds weekly or monthly socials in its own meeting room. Many denominations hold religious services, either as offshoots of hearing churches or synagogues or as freestanding congregations. In addition, some hearing churches interpret their regular services for the deaf. The Lutherans and Roman Catholics have done especially effective outreach to deaf co-religionists.

Athletics plays an important part in deaf social life. *Deaf American* devotes considerable space to school and adult teams, leagues, and meets, and a special pictorial magazine covers nothing else. Achievement culminates in the world games of the Fédération des Sports Silencieux, the so-called deaf Olympics, which draws athletes from many countries to quadrennial meets in most major winter and summer sports. Local softball, volleyball, or bowling teams structure the social life of many weekend duffers. Cultural activity seems less prominent than among the hearing, perhaps because music is largely out of bounds, but amateur theater exists in a number of places and a national literary society encourages aspiring writers. Dancing, both social and artistic, is not only possible but popular with many. And craft activities—carpentry, needlework, photography, graphic arts, and the like—appeal both because of their low verbal demands and because they use the skills many people learned in vocational training at state schools. In early 1980, furthermore, the great wasteland of commercial television opened to the deaf. Supported by the federal government, two commercial networks and public television began supplying a total of fifteen hours of prime-time programming a week for "closed" or "hidden" captioning. With this process the captions appear only on specially adapted sets, only on sets, in other words, of people who want to see them. Thus no unwelcome caption line bothers hearing viewers, and deaf viewers can follow shows with understanding at the same time the general public sees them. Whether this will greatly affect the cultural interests or news awareness of the deaf community is not clear, but it may well, like the TTY, have the side effect of encouraging increased literacy.

Typing on the telephone is only a partial solution to the greatest problem technology—in the ironic person of Alexander Graham Bell—has imposed on the hearing-impaired. By pervading every cranny of society, by altering mores and etiquette, by outmoding visits and letters as the media of much business and social intercourse, the telephone has more effectively barred the hearing-impaired from the life of the general community than any other single factor. The core of the TTY system, the acoustic coupler, was invented by the deaf physicist Robert Weitbrecht. It transforms impulses from a teletype machine or similar device into sounds that can be transmitted by an ordinary phone, then picked up and changed back to electricity at the other end and used to activate a second teletype machine. Built around outmoded and thus easily obtainable equipment—a crucial factor in commercial feasibility—the network was developed by a deaf-organized and deaf-run company, Teletypecommunications for the Deaf, Inc., which distributed machines to homes and businesses. The early equipment was cumbersome—although recently several portable models have appeared on the market—and can only contact another, compatible device. Most of the world's millions of telephones remain out of reach, but the several thousand available TTYs do present a larger, if still closed, circle of possibilities. (Some people favor the term TDD, telecommunications device for the deaf, because the newer versions use electronic visual displays rather than teletype machines.) Typing takes considerably more time than talking, so TDD calls cost more than comparable voice calls, and this inequity has yet to sway the authorities who set telephone rates. The TDD also requires a good command of written English. Thus, some who might benefit from the device find their poor writing too great an embarrassment.

Besides encouraging a higher standard of written English, the TDD has had another unforeseen but striking social effect. It showed hearing-impaired people of all ideological persuasions and social situations the basic and overriding commonality of their political interests. Everyone afflicted by serious hearing loss needs access to a TDD, needs the skills to use it, and needs fair treatment by the rate-setting authorities. No one, regardless of customary communication method or level of culture, can "pass" in the hearing world over the phone. (The sole exception involves the extension phones used by some people with good speech. An interpreter listens in and gives a simultaneous translation, and the impaired person speaks for himself. But this system requires special equipment and a hearing helper.) The movement to put equipment into the hands of as many as possible brought elements of the manual and oral camps together in their first common effort. Whether the new political militancy stirring among the deaf and the growth of pragmatic coalitions that disregard the old debate in fact owe much to working together for TDD is difficult to determine, but the effort couldn't have been bad practice.

Deaf people and their hearing friends have invented some clever uses of TDD to open new windows. Signals decipherable by the acoustic coupler can be broadcast by radio as well as sent by wire; thus TDDs in some parts of the country translate special news broadcasts and weather reports. The "beeps" can also be recorded on tape for future reference or for mailing. The wonder is not that so many uses have been found for this ingenious device, but just the opposite—that so few have been thought of in the most technologically inventive of societies, and that deaf people have had to wait so long for those that do exist.

But, in a sense, this equivocal relationship of deaf people to one of the society's central implements stands for the deaf community's relationship to the society at large. Beyond the periphery of our notice—for in America, anyone who can't be reached by telephone in a certain sense does not exist—hemmed in by the terms of other people's convenience, the deaf community gets by with a cumbersome and limited imitation of the genuine article. The society does not so much tolerate or ignore them, for both of those imply a recognition of one's existence, but largely fails to notice that they are even there.

CHAPTER 12

Mainstreaming

Few important institutions in American life credit their origins to little children. In the golden haze of historical legend, though, two small deaf girls, Alice Cogswell and Mable Hubbard, look like pivotal figures. "Were it not for Alice," the manualists intone; "were it not for Mable," the oralists echo, everything would have been different. But for these children, the central establishments of deaf education would not exist. Well, perhaps. But like many comforting historical explanations, this one hides a somewhat less palatable truth. The American School owes its existence not to Alice, nor even to Thomas Gallaudet and Laurent Clerc, but to Mason Fitch Cogswell. And Clarke came into being not through Mable's struggles, or John Clarke's, but through Gardiner Greene Hubbard's. Two enterprising, relentless, and well-connected fathers are the truly pivotal figures. Even though deaf people have long been politically and economically quite powerless, their parents have not.

Many years later Mable Hubbard Bell described the success of her father's efforts as "the triumph of love." Alice Cogswell probably saw her father's work in the same light. Leaving their doubtlessly very genuine paternal emotions aside, the institutions these two men founded represented the triumph of something else quite as important. They embodied the triumph of the fathers' images of what their daughters' lives should be.

This is an important point to keep in mind as we consider the present and future effects on deaf people of another group of pivotal children. Thirteen mentally retarded Pennsylvania youngsters, suing in state court, overturned the arrangements that have traditionally governed "special" education in this country and made a revolution every bit as important as those associated with the Hubbards or the Cogswells. Because of them, and a series of subsequent court decisions and congressional acts, the whole unwieldy vessel of education for the handicapped took a sudden 180-degree turn from its traditional practice of segregating "exceptional" children in special schools and classes and is now steaming ponderously but at full speed into the uncharted waters of integration. Encouraging the handicapped to attend ordinary schools to the greatest extent possible has become the new national course.

That these waters harbor hidden reefs, shoals, and even submerged wrecks ought to surprise no one, but that the navigators (Congress and the courts) were largely unaware of these dangers when they set the new course probably should. Various cartographers offered as many conflicting charts of the relevant tides, currents, and channels, but a group very familiar with some of the lurking perils, the manual deaf community and its friends, failed, largely through its own neglect, even to make their fears known until the voyage was well underway.

Large-scale mainstreaming may well be our third great experiment in deaf education. It will affect the lives of children with many kinds of handicaps, but because of the special nature of deafness and the central role of schooling in the lives of the American deaf, it may have a particular impact on them. Some—primarily in the oralist camp—have hailed it as a new birth of freedom for children; others—mainly among the manualists—darkly fear serious problems for many. Like every significant event in American educational history, this development has intensified the methods debate, raised it to a new pitch of desperation, jacked up the financial ante, and nourished black suspicions about the motives of opponents. And the stakes here are very large; not only the course of thousands of individual childhoods rides on the outcome, but the fate of bureaucracies, budgets, and institutions.

At the core of the new philosophy are two ideas: first, that the public school systems owe free education to all children as a matter of right; second, that this education should take place in the "least restrictive environment" compatible with the child's handicap. This phrase appears only once in the legislation, but it bids fair to rank with the most decisive writings on handicap in decades. It is one of those figures of legal speech—"all deliberate speed" and "maximum feasible participation" are others—that seem to embody certainty but in fact disguise possibly insoluble conflict. What speed is speedy enough? How much participation is the most feasible? Who decides what is restrictive to whom? Years of litigation could not solve the first two questions, and will probably prove no more fruitful in settling the third.

The Congress, however, gives some guidance. The more an educational environment resembles a normal public school classroom, the less restrictive it is thought to be. The burden of proof now lies with those who would educate a child in other than a normal class, for that by definition imposes the least restrictions. The reasons run all the way back to *Brown* v. *Board of Education*. Separate cannot be equal; segregation creates invidious comparisons and consequent stigma; maximum opportunity for personal and social development lies in the freest possible associations. This may well be true for many disabilities.

In this case as in everything else, though, deafness is the wild card. Does a public school classroom truly restrict a deaf child less than a special class or school where he might communicate more easily and freely in sign? Some people—it is not hard to guess who—say yes, and others—their identity is no more obscure —say no. But now, the new law states, it is largely up to the parent to decide. Two centuries of expert opinion have totally failed to reach any resolution, and the Congress, in the innocence of its benevolence, has brought the war home. Rigid school policies about categories of disability may no longer govern children's futures; instead, a committee consisting of parents, teachers, administrators, and experts in disability is to construct an individual educational plan (IEP) for each handicapped child. The parents must understand and approve, or at least acquiesce in it. Those who disagree have several levels of appeal.

The new civil rights, therefore, inhere not in the person most directly affected, the child, who is often completely unable to judge, but in the parent, who exercises them in his behalf. (Children able to participate in the decision may be included on the committee.) This appears a reasonable procedure, perhaps the only reasonable procedure possible, except for one hidden flaw. It assumes that the parents' interests are identical to the child's. As we have seen, though, they often diverge, and when interests diverge the holder of political power gets to put his into practice. Thus the conflict at the core of mainstreaming as a predominant government policy of deaf education.

A deaf mother of deaf children explains. "I thought of myself as a cold woman, like my mother and her mother before her. We knew that when we had children and they were deaf, that when they were six or seven years old we would have to send them away . . . to the state school. . . . I know that 'mainstreaming' isolates my kids, denies them many of the important things they need—but I have a need too, to be a real mother. I kept them home and mainstreamed them."[1]

This woman sees the situation more clearly than many parents because she sees it from both sides. She knows her motives for what they are. Ironically, though, her position carries greater poignance than that of parents who feel the full emotional force of only their own side of the argument. Unlike her, they may not realize that they *can* deprive their children of anything valuable by keeping them from the deaf community in their early years, or that the need to be a "normal" parent of a "normal" child exists much more strongly in the parent than in the child. The deaf mother might comfort herself that she and her husband, through their own deep involvement in the deaf community, can pass on the skills the children will need to take their places in it when the time comes. What she guiltily sees as her own selfishness need not do permanent damage either to the children or to her relationship with them. But many parents of mainstreamed children may not even suspect the possibility of such dangers. They may learn of them, to their sorrow, when it is too late.

Part of the problem is that a national policy favoring the mainstreaming of deaf children is an afterthought, a by-product of a wholly different struggle. In 1972 the thirteen retarded children, along with the Pennsylvania Association for Retarded Children. (PARC), sued the state for failing to provide them the free public education their tax dollars supposedly entitled them to. Later that same year, in *Mills* v. *Board of Education of the District of Columbia,* the parents of seven other retarded children excluded from public schools because of their handicaps brought suit in the national capital. In both cases the courts overturned the exclusionary rules, establishing the principle that all children may demand, and all school systems must provide, a free education at public expense as a matter of right. Until that time many school systems had summarily excluded many children they defined as handicapped—deaf, many hard-of-hearing, blind, retarded, orthopedically and neurologically disabled, emotionally disturbed, even "learning-disabled"—from the regular classroom. Some districts provided some instruction to some children with some disabilities, but many did not. They left families to seek help elsewhere, often at their own expense, or to do without; for many this meant sending children to residential institutions, either public or private.

The court decisions did not imply, however, that the public schools were the proper educational milieu for most or even many handicapped children. They merely required that the public school *systems* acknowledge their responsibility to the handicapped children who lived within their boundaries and to consider the local public schools as a possibility in meeting their needs. The intention was to expand, rather than to constrict, the available options. Then, in 1975, Congress passed Public Law 94-142, the Education for All Handicapped Children Act, which applied the principles of access and local responsibility to the whole nation. This law required the states to seek out all unserved handicapped children and to develop, for them and all other handicapped children, suitable plans for education. Local school districts must then carry the plans out.

Considering what else was going on in deaf education at the time, this sudden swing to the regular public schools seems a bit bizarre, but the deaf and hearing-impaired were essentially irrelevant to this developing body of statute and precedent. In the context of mental retardation the emphasis on the public schools makes very good sense.

By the early 1970s, a generation after *Brown* v. *Board of Education* and a decade after the black civil rights movement, the racial and cultural bias masquerading as scientifically verifiable retardation remained a national disgrace. Some children suffer from genuine, physiologically based retardation, of course, but for others the diagnosis is less clear-cut. Like the ability to hear, intellectual endowment is distributed on a continuum. Some children are a lot smarter than others, and some are so slow that they constitute a considerable nuisance in the classroom. IQ tests gave educators the tools for quantifying and categorizing what appeared to be intelligence, and the concept of mental retardation as a special condition appeared. At first a child had to score below 70 to count as retarded, but in the 1920s and 1930s the borderline crept up to 80 or 85. Because 80 falls just one standard deviation away from the mean (an IQ of 100), this new definition led to the discovery of many more retarded children and to a big jump in enrollment. Between the early 1950s and the late 1960s the number in programs for the retarded grew by a factor of six. Many of the judgments stigmatizing young children were arbitrary—who is "borderline retarded" depends as much on the location of the border as on the characteristics of the child—and a shocking number—up to a quarter by some estimates—were incorrect. The tests showed a dismaying lack of sensitivity to cultural factors; children from outside the dominant middle-class culture generally did badly. The successive white immigrant groups thus showed a truly miraculous increase in "intelligence" over the years. Preposterous as it now seems, turn-of-the-century educators bemoaned the extraordinary rates of retardation among the children of Jewish, Irish, Polish, Italian, and other immigrants, all traces of which "blight" had vanished within a generation. That the 1950s and 1960s saw massive migrations of rural southern blacks to the unfamiliar culture of the northern cities cannot have been unrelated to the high rates of "retardation" their children displayed.

For many of these children, who suffer from a disability invented and then misdiagnosed by educational statisticians, exclusion from the public schools was nothing short of cultural discrimination and admission to regular classes was often an obvious and complete "cure." Even for children afflicted with real, organically based mental slowness, a more stimulating life among normal children can bring real benefits. Under the new law the schools can no longer slough off the hard cases, but have to give serious thought to their needs and produce sound, positive reasons for excluding them from regular instruction.

A further factor favoring the new policy, if not so much its passage by Congress, then certainly its adoption by local school authorities, is its apparent thriftiness. If the regular schools could absorb children now in special institutions, then certainly, it must seem to legislators, superintendents, and budget officers, those very costly establishments could close down, or at least stop gobbling up so large a share of the educational dollar, and the federal government's per capita contribution toward expenses would make a good fiscal deal even better. The combined weight of parental ambition, bureaucratic parsimony, and legislative righteousness proved irresistible. And the public schools, never particularly gifted at educating even bright, normal kids with no problems, became the new hope of the nation's disabled children.

Throughout this legislative drama, the world of deaf education could be found occupying its customary educational, intellectual, and political backwater. If the oralist forces failed utterly to spot total communication in time to "nip it in the bud," as one prominent oralist moaned, then the manualist establishment matched their performance on mainstreaming. Part of the problem, of course, is the general public's ignorance of the politics of deafness. Having received the warm and vocal support of certified experts, most congressmen quite understandably failed to realize the existence of another opinion, held with a passion as intense, supported by evidence no flimsier, and advocated by experts just as erudite. In the event, therefore, deaf and hard-of-hearing children were included with all the others, and the Congress went on record as supporting their integration into the regular schools as a matter of national policy. Indeed, few lawmakers seemed even to guess the importance of the few phrases mandating integration; the bill was viewed largely as a financial package to help the states meet their new financial responsibilities.

Reaction within the deaf world, naturally, split utterly along ideological lines. Latham Breunig and Gary Nix of the Bell Association, for example, hailed PL 94-142 as an advance toward social justice equal to the great civil rights act of 1964. At least as early as the 1890s, Clarke and others began encouraging students to enter regular schools, which most people on that side of the argument view as the best possible educational, psychological, social, and even audiological outcome. For manualists, however, the reaction was first shock and then grave and deepening concern. At stake were not only the futures of individual children, but the futures of the institutions that had taken decades to build and that were finally coming round to total communication. The oralists emphasize exploiting the new freedom to wrest children who can succeed among the hearing from arbitrary assignment to schools and programs for the deaf. The manualists underline the importance of not stampeding children into situations where they can't cope. The difference shows clearly in the titles of two booklets intended to inform parents of the new law's ramifications. The Bell Association calls its publication *The Rights of Hearing-Impaired Children*. Gallaudet College, as a federally funded institution unable openly to criticize the law, but in its heart of hearts fearful, chose *PL 94-142 and the Deaf Child*.

Despite the misgivings of their rivals, joy on the oralist side was unrestrained. Not only did the law bring invaluable help, but it came at a crucial time; the spread of total communication in the schools and day programs for the deaf might not be stoppable, but at least more children could be placed beyond its reach. With the burden of proof on those who would remove the child from the local school system rather than on those who would keep him there, many more children would be able to remain if their parents insisted. The Bell Association undertook the Children's Rights Program, backed by a network of Federal and Local Action Group (FLAG) coordinators, to inform parents of their rights of due process and appeal under the law and to encourage them to follow through. As former president Latham Breunig stated, "Under the program parents are given the awareness of the right of their children to whatever educational form they choose. If they want their child to have an oral education, such is their right."[2]

In fact, however, Breunig somewhat overstates the case. The law does not precisely say that the parent can insist on the type of education he chooses. It says, rather, that he and the education authorities and sometimes even the child must agree on a written statement of the child's educational goals and the means proposed to attain them. The parents do have the right to appeal to an impartial examiner and to obtain an evaluation by an educational expert of their own choosing. The ultimate decision, however, does not rest solely with them. The law states, in the only passage where the phrase occurs, that the child must receive his education in "the least restrictive environment commensurate with his needs." The blithe assumption that this judgment involves a mere factual determination invites, indeed guarantees, endless litigation. One need only think of Freddy Howard's mother.

Reasonable oralists, however, do not favor fanaticism. They merely argue that many children with hearing impairments have been able to keep up, even excel, in public schools and that many more could probably do so in the future if properly guided and prepared. Furthermore, they believe, the child gains important benefits from living at home and among the cultural majority rather than in a small minority. The choice they see is not between the state school on the one hand and cold-turkey public schooling on the other. The law has encouraged expansion of the whole range of options. At one end, normal treatment in the ordinary classroom—"complete mainstreaming"—can work for some. Others can keep up in the public schools if they get some special help, services such as speech therapy and private tutoring, in addition to their regular class work. For those who need greater support but can still get by in some regular classes or activities, a so-called resource room in the regular school can provide special equipment, specially trained teachers, and such special classes as are required. Sometimes a self-contained special class in a regular school permits the child to remain in contact with normally hearing agemates while getting the special instruction he needs. Freestanding day schools allow a child to have the services of a special school without leaving home. And residential schools, of course, still necessarily provide the solution for some children.

"The majority of hearing-impaired children," the Lings and Pflaster write, "can learn enough speech to attend regular school at least part of the time."[3] The majority of hearing-impaired children, of course, are not severely or profoundly deaf. As in much else, the degree of hearing loss appears to govern a child's potential for mainstreaming. Gary Nix provides a useful checklist of traits to look for. Basically, the mainstreaming candidate Nix envisions is a bright child whose understanding, speaking, and reading skills fall close to those of his future classmates. He is independent, cooperative, aggressive, and resilient, not too sensitive, and socially as adept as others his age. He has good self-control, an understandable speaking voice, a decent handwriting, adequate vocabulary and syntax, and a stable family both committed to the project and able to accept his handicap well enough to help him over the rough spots. He is, in effect, an "oral success" and a capable, well-adjusted child.

Geniuses aside, such a child probably has no worse than a moderate hearing loss, although some people with severe and even profound pure-tone losses have attended and completed regular schools and even colleges without special help. In some situations an interpreter can help an otherwise qualified person through particularly difficult situations. But even for children whose linguistic or social skills do not come up to the mark, the oralists argue that any bias ought to favor integration. This means, in part, that the special support that children might require, should they become suitable for even partial mainstreaming, ought to be readily available within the public school system. It also means that oral-aural education ought to be freely available to those who want it or whose parents want it. In her 1978 presidential message to the Bell Association, Winifred Northcott called for a parallel oral track in any public school system that maintains a total communication track.

The manualists do not dispute that quite a few children *can* attend and complete regular schools; they wonder whether they ought to. As usual, the two camps refuse to discuss the same issues; on this matter too the arguments sail past one another. The manualist objections come down to two essential doubts: whether public school systems can provide decent supportive services to small numbers of deaf children and whether the public school is in any worthwhile sense the "least restrictive environment" for a deaf child.

To take the simpler point first: They argue that deafness occurs rarely among children. No more than one in a thousand is born deaf; no more than two in a thousand are deaf before they come to school. Only very large school systems will have more than a handful of deaf children in any particular grade. Many grade schools and even high schools might go for years without encountering a single one. Only a metropolitan area is likely to produce enough deaf children to fill a school. This, after all, is the original reason for the residential schools: Bringing together enough deaf children to justify a special plant and faculty meant that most of them had to travel some distance from home. Even this did not generally create a large enough student body to justify a really first-rate establishment. By some estimates a good public comprehensive high school cannot be run economically for fewer than 1,000 students. Most residential schools for the deaf have a fraction of that figure, spread over a dozen or more grades. The Model Secondary School for the Deaf, designed for about 400 academically select students, must draw from well beyond the District of Columbia and the five surrounding states that were to provide its enrollment.

If a school system is doing right by its deaf students, this argument goes, it will spend at least as much per pupil as the state residential school does. And the school district, possibly quite new to the task, will have to produce from somewhere the expert knowledge, the special equipment and materials, and the experience required to deal with deafness. And with blindness, retardation, cerebral palsy, orthopedic disabilities, and all the other special demands of serving people with different handicaps. Classroom teachers will have to learn to cope with new and subtle difficulties along with the day-to-day task of teaching their normal students. Nor is this fear fanciful. Already some classroom teachers have received half a dozen or more children with as many different handicaps in one room already full of normal children.

The temptation to scrimp will be very strong, and even if conscious stinginess were not to blame, ignorance might be. More than one school system has turned down parents' requests for state school placement, or even for an interpreter in a mainstream class, on the ground that these special considerations would tend to "restrict" the child. They would, of course, restrict the budget even more.

At this level the argument is not against mainstreaming per se, but for programs well funded and large enough to provide the services and materials that deaf children need. Most educators now acknowledge that the extreme segregation of the past harmed deaf children by alienating them from their familes, fostering dependence, and keeping them ignorant of the general society's mores. Many residential schools now require frequent weekends at home.

The fact that a regular school takes on a deaf student, however, does not mean that it can, or even intends to try to, do right by him. The law states that expense cannot be considered in developing the placement most suitable for each child; but it provides little guidance in how a possibly hard-pressed school system is to finance a number of these ideal, but possibly very costly, individual programs. Parents must therefore vigilantly guard against chiseling at their child's expense. Competently staffed and organized mainstreaming may be very expensive, but shoddy mainstreaming can be very tempting to administrators because it is also very cheap.

But the more basic question has to do with the very concept of restriction. "Deaf adolescents who successfully attend mainstreamed schools are successful academically," writes Oscar Cohen of Lexington, "but [except] for the rare exceptions, are lonely, lack involvement in the social milieu of the school, and lack the avenues of energy release and identity experiences so crucial at this stage. Deaf teenagers need peers with whom they feel comfortable. In most cases these peers, too, will be deaf."[4] Betty Broecker, director of the New Jersey Division of the Deaf, spoke of her plans to return to her home town for the thirtieth reunion of the Vineland High School class of 1949, where she finished in the top third. But this time she's taking an interpreter. Deaf since age eight, she says, "I am looking forward to engaging in conversation with my former school friends, and for the first time I will be able to understand what they are saying to me."[5]

For children and especially adolescents, these critics believe, the "other" curriculum of friendships, camaraderie, sports, and activities is at least as important as school work. Is a child truly in his "least restrictive environment" unless he can take full part in everything his classmates are up to, unless he can date, hold office, try out for the team, edit the paper, go to parties, hang around, be one of a "crowd"? Can a child at a severe communicative disadvantage even begin to experience a normal, nurturing childhood among hearing youngsters? In what sense except age and physical proximity are they his "peers"?

Any program that would offer students the advantages of integrated education must not, advocates of this position argue, deprive them of the advantages they derive from a segregated one. Experience with deaf students on college campuses primarily designed for the hearing seems to indicate that deaf students do best in a mainstream setting if they are present in a "critical mass"—a group large enough to justify the expense of high-quality support services and to constitute a social universe where the young person's individuality, not his disability, defines his relationships. How many people constitute such a critical mass probably depends on the characteristics of both the school and the students, but it must be reasonably substantial, and thus probably too large for many smaller school districts to gather in one place.

Despite the deaf schools' often quite genuine academic inferiority, therefore, some reputable educators still argue for them. Deaf children will have to live among the hearing, these critics concede, but they will also have to live among themselves. Muriel Horton, a deaf woman mainstreamed through her whole education, writes of those who attended schools for the deaf, "They have been given the tools with which to utilize the raw knowledge available in any school system. They have experience and skill in questioning, participating, leading, and coping with the world. They have the true sense of self-identification and community that comes from competition, information sharing, and interaction with other children and adults with whom they could fully and freely communicate. And as adults these are the things that contribute to successful employment and full, balanced lifestyles. Some of these things do not and never will exist in 'mainstreamed' and 'integrated' programs."[6]

Physical proximity has no social meaning without communication. Otherwise, in Mervyn Garretson's phrase, the deaf child is "an island in the mainstream." Roslyn Rosen, a deaf staff member at MSSD says, "I'm mainstreaming myself in a doctoral program at Catholic University. I go with an interpreter. Even so, my degree of participation there isn't nearly what it is here on this campus. When discussion bounces around the room I lose contact. Who is saying what? I don't even know when there's a pause. I wait and wait and when I do speak I'm interrupting. I feel silly, and here I am, a person with all the skills and capabilities for mainstreaming. I don't interact with other students. Maybe it's not necessary, but it's lonely. What about kids at a young age? It's hard for them even to express that feeling."[7]

This is not to say that no deaf children have the skill and stamina to feel more at ease than Rosen does; but the damage from isolation can be real and long-lasting. Horton tells of a deaf woman in her twenties who, after a lifetime of mainstreaming, entered group therapy to find out: "How do you meet people? How do you start a conversation? What do people talk about with each other?"[8]

These critics also resent the law's implicit preference for the company and the mores of the "normal." If being a normal person equals success, they say, then being among the handicapped must mean failure. For the many deaf children who could not succeed in a regular school, no matter how hard they tried, success must be defined in some realistically attainable terms. The residential schools stand in increased danger of stigma, at the same time that the country believes itself becoming more open to the handicapped.

And indeed, the future of the residential schools has become a serious concern. As PL 94-142 has drained off the easier, "cleaner" cases, multiple-handicapped children account for an increasing proportion of the enrollment. Much harder to educate than the traditional student, an otherwise normal child who is "only" deaf, these other children have forced some states to reorient their programs and alter their standards. Many educators believe the current situation an aberration, however. "After they've sacrificed half a generation to mainstreaming," more than one has said, "parents and schools will realize what they've done. There will be a backlash." Thus, they work to keep the schools' budgets up and their doors open so that, when the hoped-for return happens, the schools will be waiting.

Whom do the integrated programs in fact serve? According to a 1977 study by the Office of Demographic Studies, they draw from a "group of hearing impaired children who are very different on many critical dimensions from those who attend other types of special education programs."[9] The mainstreamed children in this study have milder and later losses than those in special schools and classes. Over 70 percent of children with mild hearing losses attend regular schools, as opposed to only 8 percent of those with profound losses. Conversely, over 60 percent of residential school students had profound losses as opposed to 1 percent whose losses were mild. Integrated programs enrolled over twice as many post-lingually deaf children as residential schools, day schools, or self-contained classes. Although these data do not reflect the full impact of PL 94-142, it is obvious that hearing loss type and level do appear to influence placement decisions very strongly.

But perhaps not entirely. Nearly half the students over fifteen attended residential schools. Some other factor is obviously at work here, perhaps the social demands of adolescence. And, as we have seen before, socioeconomic background exerts a far from negligible influence. Children in integrated programs come, on the average, from more prosperous families. Only 10 percent of residential school children had parents earning over $20,000 in 1977, as opposed to 16 percent of those in the mainstream. For incomes over $5,000, the respective figures were 78 percent and 89 percent. Thus, one residential school child in five came from a home earning less than $5,000 in 1977, as opposed to one mainstreamed child in ten. The complete meaning of these figures is not clear, but they do support the oral bias we have already noticed in upper-income families.

In this, as in the deaf child's whole life, his parents' hopes, fears, and values do much to govern his fate. And now the government has given parents a whole new range of options and the moral and legal responsibility to exercise them, a whole new set of opportunities, as both sides say, to "sell a whole generation down the river." Parents must take up part of the burden of judgment and decision that professional educators have failed to carry. Even more than in the past their understanding of their children's needs and prospects will find expression in concrete curricula. Each child has a unique array of strengths and weaknesses and a special set of requirements. More than ever before, children's happiness depends on parents exercising power in the cause of clarity and good sense.

CHAPTER 13

We and They

Waiting out World War I on his Pacific island, Bronislaw Malinowski had a lot of time to think about canoes. He used it wisely, on detailed, inventive studies that eventually led him to a profound insight into the nature of culture. Start anywhere, he believed, even, as he did, with something as prosaic as a canoe, and if you ask enough questions about it (Whom does it belong to? How did he come to own it? What does he use it for?), if you're persistent and penetrating enough, you can lay a culture's inner secrets bare. You can find out what people believe and why they believe it and why they do what they do. Everything, he thought, is more than a thing in itself; it is a phenomenon in a social universe.

If shoelaces and table manners lead to the very heart of culture, then so rich a paradox as hearing impairment must be a superhighway to social insight. And, indeed, we who hear normally can learn a good deal about ourselves by asking even a few questions about how we feel about those who don't. We don't often ask those questions, however, perhaps because we shrewdly suspect that we won't like the answers, perhaps because we find abnormality distasteful, and perhaps, simply, because we are afraid.

Fear is not an unintelligent first reaction to disability. Among

the things that immediately strike a normal person who goes
among the disabled with an open mind is that there is no reason
for their disability. There are causes, of course, physiological for-
mulations that explain what makes this or that person's auditory
mechanism work defectively, in much the same way that a medical textbook might explain how a bullet kills. But there are no
existentially satisfying *reasons* why this or that person should
have suffered such a fate. Why, the question comes, unbidden
and ultimately terrifying, why this person and not me? Why
should George, in the prime of his young manhood, react so adversely to streptomycin? Why should Sally's mother have con-
tracted rubella while pregnant? Why should Tom, between the
ages of five and seven, just gradually stop hearing? They did no
more to deserve it than I ever have; if it could happen to blame-
less them, then it could have, it might, indeed it can happen
to me. They are myself in other circumstances. And that, for
most people, is a fearsome thought.

"Those who are not outsiders," Paul Higgins observed in his
study of deaf Chicagoans, "find it frightening to think of themselves as outsiders."[1] Those who are not outsiders find it difficult
to imagine how they could live other than they do, how real life
is even possible under other circumstances. Social scientists call
this attitude ethnocentrism; it is the psychic assertion of the superiority of one's own way of life and the concomitant rejection
of ways of life that differ from it. It is a nearly universal and
socially very useful feeling; it allows people to live voluntarily in
the way that, in the final analysis, is mandatory anyway. It keeps
societies cohesive and allows them to transmit their values to the
rising generations. It can foster loyalty, solidarity, honor, and
sacrifice.

But it has its costs. It supports the structure of human societies, but often at the expense of the human spirit. At bottom, ethnocentrism is the tendency to regard a different kind of person
as less human than oneself; it is the simple refusal to put oneself
in his place and grant him the same feelings, the same dignity,
the same ability to experience. It is to deny that his truth is as
true as my own. We fear to be the outsider because we do not
know, cannot bring ourselves to know, how he can live a de-
cently human life and be so unlike ourselves.

Ethnocentrism has governed our society's treatment of all kinds of "others"—we recognize it now in a rogue's gallery of forbidden "isms"—racism, sexism, agism. But perhaps even more profoundly it has governed our treatment of the handicapped. We would rather not think about what living with their losses would mean to us; it's easiest, then, not to enter their experience at all. And this ethnocentrism is all the more pernicious because it is all the more unconscious. We can, if we wish, force ourselves to think of other races or the other sex as our equal. But a disabled person? He is someone we are supposed to help, to make allowances for, to pity. If he has the same right to anger, to independent experience, to wholeness within the context of his loss, then he is fully myself in other circumstances, and I cannot treat him except as I would wish to be treated myself.

But the fear persists, fed by the ignorance that spawned it. If I do not accept his wholeness, then I will not enter his experience, and I can never learn how it is that he can make a life very different from mine and yet equally real. The only way past fear is through it; the only way to know something of another's life is to try to live it.

No normally hearing person, of course, can ever experience the whole reality of deafness. To suggest otherwise is to insult daily, silent fortitude. A normally hearing person cannot ever know the awesome psychic permanence of deafness, but he can understand hearing loss on a superficial level, as a manner of physical being. All it takes is a few hours and a pair of hearing aids set to produce white noise (a general, featureless background). It's almost impossible to simulate profound deafness in a person with good hearing; the human audition is so maddeningly acute that enough noise to block out everything we hear would be positively harmful. But enough noise to muffle normal speech and drown out most ambient noise presents no real danger.

So, with two noisy hearing aids in place, we could set out on our way. We might walk, for example, down a familiar street. It looks the same, but in some way it yields less of itself. We are, in a sense, more alone, more closely inside ourself and cut off from our surroundings, although we watch closely and devour every visual detail with our eyes. There is no sound to tell us anything, not even that of our own steps or the rustle of our own clothing. No car noises. No birds. No airplanes overhead. No shaking leaves or barking dogs or human voices to populate the world around us with living things. A pair of pedestrians, deep in conversation, overtake and pass us. This is startling; we had no idea they were approaching, and we react clumsily. Not knowing their direction or speed, we can't tell which way to step to let them by. We grasp nothing of what they say. It's like being in a foreign country, but not really. There we would at least have heard them approach.

But now we turn into a street we don't know, looking for a certain address. The first approaching person is a woman with a baby carriage; she probably lives in the neighborhood and would be a good person to ask. We phrase the question and ask it, but it sounds funny. In fact, it doesn't sound like much at all, just a small hoarse whisper beyond the rim of the pervading racket. It doesn't sound right to her either, because she throws an uncertain look, just a fleeting puzzlement, then considers her answer. Maybe she didn't understand, we think, maybe we asked too softly. We ask again, this time straining to hear ourself. But she starts; something is wrong, and she's beginning to become uneasy. Then we remember. If we can hear our voice even slightly over the noise in our ears, then it's much louder than it ought to be. Any speech that we can hear is close to shouting.

She gives an answer. We watch her closely, listen intently, but hardly anything comes through. She points and motions and asks with her face if we understand. She shifts uneasily and glances at the child. We nod yes and continue on what appears to be our way. It takes some time to reach our destination; the third person we accosted for directions had the sense to write them down. Next time we'd study a map before setting out.

Four friends are waiting for a lunch date at a restaurant. When we arrive at the table they're already deep in conversation. They nod and smile and someone tells us the topic. We don't catch it, but they plunge on ahead. The person on our right isn't talking at the moment, so we remark casually on the weather. The general conversation stops and everyone turns suddenly to us. Shouting again. Someone makes a joke—at least we surmise that from the fact that they all laugh—and the conversation starts up again. The person to our right asks, we think, whether it was hard to get here. We give an answer appropriate to the question we understood. It must not be quite right, because doubt flickers for a second in her eyes and she says something more slowly. We get even less of that, but nod and turn to take a roll. The conversation continues around us. If we could discover the topic, we decide, it would be easier to speechread some of what's being said. We watch intently, futilely, for almost an hour. Without a solid clue to what they're talking about, we could be, indeed we become, a piece of the scenery. Speaking directly to the person on either side, and watching and listening intently, we exchange some very simple ideas—the sandwich is good, the coffee is cold. But at last comes psychic withdrawal from the general conversation, the giving up of the pretense of following.

Watching people's faces told very little. More came through when we seemed to hear something, when a voice slipped, like early rays of the rising sun, above the horizon of the noise. Then we could try to guess what had been said, so in that sense we had an advantage over those who had never heard speech. But the intensity of concentration stripped conversation of all subtlety. Understanding even simple thoughts took such effort that anything beyond charades seemed impossible.

Then, at last, the time is up, the ear molds come out, and sound floods back into consciousness. Footfalls, slamming doors, running water, snatches of nearby conversation draw a vivid map of the surroundings. One's own voice comes back under control, becomes again a well-honed tool instead of a blunt instrument. Others' voices become vehicles for ideas instead of obstacles to them.

This is one person's experience. Others report more or less difficulty. Practice and instruction could doubtless make lipreading somewhat more useful. The temptation to communicate manually might well increase. But these are, in a sense, mechanical details. What of the core? What have we learned in human terms?

The first clue is the unexpected sense of elation that accompanies the strangeness. It seems not the giddiness of fear, but the exhilaration of adventure. It salutes every small success; it seems to proclaim that this, too, can be overcome, that one is no less human for having fewer means of attaining human goals. Deafness emerges from the experience at once more and less forbidding. The struggle to participate in society seems more stark and formidable than ever one could have imagined. Difficulties lie on every hand, two and three thick. Pleasures and opportunities melt away. One draws closely in for comfort.

Yet the abhorrence has gone; it is possible to live humanly even in these straits. If one could copy the courage of those who have already navigated this sea of troubles, then safe passage is possible. If they are myself in other circumstances, then in their circumstances I could be they.

Our experiment might strike those truly deaf as insolent, arrogant, an exercise in psychic slumming, but there is no other way for a normally hearing person to understand except to try. The normal cannot overcome their fear and their unease unless they perceive the handicapped as humans like themselves, struggling in much-straitened circumstances. They cannot begin even to glimpse their ethnocentrism, much less overcome it, unless they understand that there exist points of view greatly distant from their own, and yet as deeply true. English does not distinguish two senses of knowing, as the Romance languages do: the knowing of intellect that influences only ideas, and the knowing of experience that changes attitudes.

But what attitudes, and how do they affect our relations with the deaf? This country has suffered from two different kinds of bad conscience in all these dealings. More than any other nation we have pursued two opposing but simultaneous policies.

For more than a hundred years we have both attempted to suppress the deaf subculture and permitted it to endure. All other countries of the Western world (the only ones that have had genuine policies, rather than merely customs, for dealing with the deaf) have adopted a single one at a time and enforced it at the national level, if not with complete success, then at least with a whole heart. But our contrariness seems to arise from a profound ambivalence to minorities and minority cultures. There is at once something un-American about them and something equally un-American about suppressing them.

The country was constructed out of many different cultural

groups, and perhaps for that reason feels uncomfortable when they endure. Too strong a loyalty to ethnicity must compete with the national loyalty, which has no profound social basis—no fealty to king, no state church, no uniform "racial" memory—to hold it together. In some areas of the world, such as the Middle East and parts of Europe, cultural and religious groups—organic tribes—were the building blocks of society. In the Middle East, for example, the Arabs, Armenians, Maronites, Jews, and others persisted for centuries within a single empire as identifiable blocs, each with their own language, religious practice, legal code, economic function, and social customs. The government, a cosmopolitan imperial power, neither asked nor expected these groups to surrender their habits or their identities to a national whole. Indeed, the groups themselves had independent standing as instruments of the state.

In the United States, however, a minority culture has been a stage in the passage to Americanness. Even the black people, kept apart for the economic and social convenience of whites, had to surrender their indigenous cultures when they reached these shores. The recent nostalgia for ethnic roots and rites arises among the descendants of immigrants, not among immigrants themselves, precisely because the most obtrusive aspects of ethnicity—the immigrant language and social distinctiveness—are largely gone. The residue of foods, names, and holiday customs adds color without subtracting from the ability to blend seamlessly into American life. We have no deep tradition of long-lasting differences in superficial behavior. To be an American is to speak English without an accent, to partake of the national culture and the national cuisine, which is the real melting pot. Pizza, bagels, tacos, frankfurters have largely lost their original national associations and become different versions of the true American national dish, finger food eaten on the run.

The immigrants' desire to become American, to master the way of life and especially the language, persists in their descendants' disdain for bilingualism. Americans are notoriously bad linguists. Nationals of other countries routinely learn several languages—any college-educated Swiss, for example, speaks English, French, and German fluently—but Americans can receive doctorates without demonstrating even rudimentary knowledge of a single foreign tongue. Until recently educators regarded bilingualism as an educational problem rather than an intellectual opportunity. The evidence is clear that bilingualism harms a child only when the language of emotional loyalty is socially devalued. Speaking two languages from babyhood limits the size of the child's vocabulary in each during the early years (although the total vocabulary is of normal size) and may slightly retard mastery of peripheral grammatical constructions, but it has no significant effect on reading or other skills and offers the tremendous and irreplaceable advantage of dual native fluency. But still Americans distrust it; only if the child speaks a flawless English is he fully American.

"The majority culture expects to be addressed in its own language," wrote the great linguist Uriel Weinreich.[2] This is especially true in a country where majority membership is theoretically open to nearly everyone—certainly to everyone white and native-born. In more traditional societies, on the other hand, cultural identity is a permanent family trait and the minority cultural group can be the matrix of social life generation after generation. In the traditional Middle East, for example, the cultural "majority," the ruling Turks, were a numerical minority in most of their domains. Multilingualism reflected both the structure of society and the nature of social identity. Here, however, multilingualism goes against much of our history, experience, and aspiration.

But this deep distrust of native foreignness collides with another profound legacy of the immigrant past. Our ancestors came to this country not only to be Americans, so the legend goes, but to be free. They came to worship God or seek their fortunes or speak their minds as they saw fit; they came to live after their own fashions. As long as they hurt no one else by their eccentricity, we have a bad conscience about preventing them. Americans backhandedly but profoundly respect the obstinately eccentric, provided they also pay their taxes and stay off the welfare rolls. The Amish, doggedly preserving eighteenth-century work and life in the shadow of the nuclear generators; the Hassidic Jews, meticulously reconstructing pre-World War II Poland in Brooklyn—such peoples win our admiration, even our envy, with their rectitude, their energy, their sureness of purpose.

They are strange and aloof, but they do no harm, they maintain their property, and, after all, it's a free country.

And likewise, the manual deaf have worked doggedly to keep what they see as theirs. And likewise, they have done us no harm by their differentness, nor are they bad neighbors or poor workers or public nuisances. Once they arrive at the age when a man stops living in his father's house and establishes his own castle, we feel we have no choice but to let them be. We have no more right, we believe, to prevent law-abiding adults from pursuing their own interests among those they perceive as their own kind than we do to forbid people to become Jehovah's Witnesses or vegetarians. And American education, as David Wright points out, ultimately values pragmatism over ideology. We would rather keep a person off the dole than assure his theoretical purity. Thus, state schools might have disapproved of sign language, but they tolerated it because the legislatures paying the bills wanted taxpaying artisans rather than pure oral successes.

The difference between the manual deaf and the Amish, of course, is that Amish adults had Amish parents. Few judges and fewer legislators willingly interfere with a parent's right to indoctrinate his own child. Thus, minority cultures can pass uninterrupted from adults legally and morally free to exercise their preferences, to children legally and morally under their control. If clusters of families choose to live apart from the general community for generations on end, this poses no real psychic threat to their neighbors in the mainstream. One cannot imagine himself suddenly Amish as he might see himself suddenly deaf. An Amishman is a product of a long and careful socialization; he did not result from a sudden, inexplicable microbial or physical event. He is not, in the sense that a handicapped person is, myself in other circumstances.

This is not to say that training and socialization play no part in the deaf person's development. Like everyone else, deaf people carry the indelible marks of what they have felt, learned, and been taught. But a special socialization did not cause their differentness; rather, their differentness required a special socialization.

But even that socialization differed radically from those of other cultural minorities in at least one sense. Most cultural minorities endure because they control the education of their children; adult members of the group systematically teach the special values and world view to the rising generation. Children learn to be adult members by imitating people who already are. But not so the present and immediately past generations of culturally deaf adults. Since the late nineteenth century hearing people have held almost exclusive control of schools for the deaf. Only since the rise of total communication have deaf educators once again attained positions of prestige and influence. Outsiders have traditionally overseen the indoctrination of the young, and the deaf culture's values passed from generation to generation as opposition to adult models rather than as affirmation of them.

This peculiar structure has had another pernicious effect. Hearing people, even those who associated with deaf people most closely, rarely met deaf adults as colleagues or equals. They remained, for the psychic protection of the normally hearing, what they had been at school: spiritual minors, defective children needing our guidance and protection. If they remain in our minds imperfect replicas of ourselves, who must perpetually seek but never attain our own effortless flawlessness, then we needn't encounter them as fully adult and human beings hampered in attaining their fully adult and human desires.

This tendency appears even more openly in dealings with the orthopedically handicapped. It has been called the "Chatterley syndrome": the exclusion of the person in the wheelchair from full membership in the human race, a denial sometimes of the possibility of adult sexuality. Frank Bowe, a deaf expert on the condition of the handicapped, reports on experiments at Dartmouth College that concluded that able-bodied people usually "express neutral to positive feelings toward disabled individuals,"[3] but "physiological readings," a truer test of inner feelings, tell another story. Eye movements, perspiration, and other involuntary indicators show "high anxiety, avoidance of the disabled person's eyes, and rejection of his or her presence." The able-bodied also tend not to contradict the disabled; "a falseness may pervade interactions between disabled and nondisabled people," Bowe observes.[4] The able-bodied, in short, refuse to encounter the disabled on grounds of full humanness.

"A handicap," Bowe writes, in a profound philosophical obser-

vation masquerading as a bit of jargon, "is an interaction between a disability and a given environment."⁵ A disability is a
physical fact; only a particular situation gives it social meaning.
A deaf person is handicapped, not in his human essence, but because we insist on speaking in his presence. We insist on speaking to him for reasons that have little to do with him and much
to do with ourselves. But what if conditions changed? Who is
handicapped then? Joanne Greenberg writes of a deaf printer's
sympathy for the "noise-tormented hearing," the "normal" men
unable to work or even think in the clamor of the pressroom.
Donald Peterson, a chemistry professor who lost his hearing and
sense of balance to childhood meningitis, has often acted as a
subject in government studies of dizziness and motion sickness.
He recalls one particularly stormy winter day on a boat in the
North Atlantic. Most of the seasoned officers and crew gave way
to uncontrollable nausea, while the deaf experimental subjects,
landlubbers all, contentedly played cards in the wildly lurching
wardroom.

Society, however, sees the disabled in terms of its own needs,
and this is the profoundest ethnocentrism of all. Society used to
consider the deaf subhuman because many of them couldn't
speak, Hans Furth observes. Later, when it learned that some of
them could master speech, this became the key to their acceptance. "While this feat was not considered possible in the past,"
he writes, "today it is thought to be the normal and predominant
situation among the deaf."⁶

If people cannot be made to fit society's mold, if they cannot
easily serve its purposes, it can deal with them in one of two
basic ways. It can accept their possibly bothersome presence or
it can attempt to make them disappear. In his intriguing and inventive study of agencies serving the blind, Robert Scott has isolated two basic rehabilitation philosophies leading to two
distinct outcomes for blind people. What he calls the accommodative approach keeps the blind together under the aegis
of organizations that provide them employment and social life.
From the standpoint of society at large it makes them disappear. The restorative approach, on the other hand, seeks to equip
the individual to resume his normal life and employment, to live
among the sighted, and to sever his dependence on the agency.

In essence, it makes the blind and blindness more obtrusively present in the general society. Most agencies, Scott writes, have favored the accommodative approach, not for the good of blind clients, but for the good of the agencies and the donors who support them. "Basic assertions made about the blind by advocates of the accommodative approach—that most blind people are incapable of true independence, or that most of them prefer their own company, or that the blind need to perform certain kinds of work because of their disability—are an ideological justification for an agency's treatment of blind clients in a manner more compatible with the needs of the larger community than with those of blind people. The needs of the blind are not determined from scientific studies of the impact of blindness on the functioning of the human organism; they are invented in order to justify the creation of programs and institutional arrangements required to palliate community reactions and fears about blindness."[7]

Accommodative agencies, Scott writes, both salve the community's conscience and serve its prejudices by keeping the blind out of sight. In so doing they also teach blinded persons to be socially "blind"—dependent and incompetent. Restorative agencies, which, he states, have more trouble raising funds, send obviously blind people back into the community regardless of the community's sensibilities. They produce a different kind of individual—more aggressive and competent and often highly successful at returning to former friendships and occupations. And here, also, the government's desire to get disabled people off the dole and onto the tax rolls has been influential; probably the most successful restorative agency, Scott reports, is the Veterans Administration, which has an excellent record of returning blinded veterans to independence.

As Helen Keller observed, blindness separates people from things; deafness separates them from people. Blindness has been called a disorder of mobility; deafness, a disorder of communication. Blind people are inconvenient because they need special help to carry out certain tasks; deaf people are inconvenient because they need special help to live a full social life. Keeping blind people together tends to decrease their independence and the richness of their lives because they cannot easily fulfill for each other the special needs their disability imposes.

Blind people speak and communicate normally; their disability requires no special culture or communication. (Braille is merely tactile English.) Keeping deaf people apart, on the other hand, tends to decrease their independence and the richness of their lives because they can most easily fulfill for each other the special requirements their disability imposes. They can move about as freely as any other sighted person, but many of them need their own special culture and means of communication. If permitted to select their own associates freely, many blind people would probably choose to be among "normals" more often than would many deaf people. Among the blind, communication ability is a negligible factor in choosing friends. For many deaf, it may well predominate.

Pure oralism is a weird inversion of Scott's accommodative approach. It attempts, by opposite means, to achieve the same result: making the social effects of the handicap disappear. If deaf people can blend inconspicuously into hearing society, then hearing people need not confront the unpalatable reality of deafness. (The hearing-aid industry's emphasis on invisibility seeks the same result and encourages the same values.) When successful, of course, oralism does amply serve the needs of society; it produces an individual able to pass among his fellow citizens with neither special help nor special notice, a person willing and even eager to make all the accommodations himself. When it fails, however, as it usually has in the past, it produces an idividual ill-prepared to make his own way in the world unless he can pick up some of the skills of manualism. Graduates of pure oral programs who lack *any* effective means of communication are far from rare, as Conrad's study and many anecdotal reports show. Weighting the odds in favor of society's convenience can exact a fearful price from individuals.

Manualism, on the other hand, when combined with speech training, uses means opposite to those of the restorative approach to achieve similar ends: an individual who can make his own sometimes difficult way regardless of society's unease or consternation. He cannot do everything that the normally endowed can do, yet he refuses to disappear. He goes among them as what he is, a person irremediably different. Joanne Greenberg and Glenn Doolittle quote a blind teacher: "On the surface they

want you to think, 'We want you blind and deaf people to be
part of us. We're accepting you—including you.' But it is non-ac-
ceptance, it's really saying, 'We want you to be *like* us. We cannot accept your blindness.'"[8]

The analogy between Scott's dichotomy and the two great
categories of deaf communication is far from perfect, of
course. The argument against pure oralism rests as much on
practical failure as on philosophical objections. Were most deaf
people truly able to communicate fully through oral methods,
the discussion would have to begin on an entirely new basis; indeed, were that true, it probably would never have begun. And a
true "restorative" approach to deafness must needs include competent training in oral skills; real independence in this society
requires some ability to communicate with the vast majority of
one's fellow citizens. No one has ever taken Scott's advice and
asked the deaf what they themselves prefer, but they have taken
a kind of straw poll among themselves. The National Association
of the Deaf, which encourages sign language, claims nearly
20,000 members; the Oral Deaf Adults Section of the Bell Association, which opposes it, nearly 200. The desire to hide a painful
fact, to make it disappear for the convenience of parents, friends,
society at large, necessarily expands the woe of those required to
do the hiding and shrinks the opportunity and eventually the capacity of individuals to encounter one another in their full humanness.

Acknowledging the full humanness of another person means
admitting that his behavior, however bizarre or misguided it
seems to me, might make perfect sense to him. "The fact that
the deaf live in a hearing world means that their activities become defined from the point of view of hearing, not of deaf persons," write Cicourel and Boese.[9] By hearing definitions some of
the things they do are strange, ineffective, limiting to advancement and opportunity, misguided, and bizarre. The ethnocentrism of the hearing is so profound that it has long hampered the
research we need to understand the ramifications of deafness. It
is a condition so foreign to general experience that we do not
have terms to encompass it or know what questions to ask about
it. But as much as the Amish, deaf people of every persuasion

have the right to be what they wish to be. Indeed, they have as much right as I do myself.

And if I experience another as fully human, then he can experience me in the same way. Parents who accept their child's deafness for what it truly means to the child and not to their image of the child need not "lose" him to a foreign culture. They can follow him as far as their abilities allow into his world, and he can follow them in the same way into theirs. A society that respects the rights of its citizens to be their true selves need not lose its strength; it can gain their richness. A fully human person is one from whom I can learn as well as one whom I can teach. We hearing may have much to teach the deaf about sentence structure, about breath control, about articulation. But they have much to teach us about perseverance, integrity, and good cheer.

NOTES

CHAPTER 1

1. p. 30.
2. p. 250.

CHAPTER 2

1. *The Deaf Population of the United States.*
2. *Deafness and Learning,* p. 2.
3. Washington *Post,* February 26, 1978, p. 61.

CHAPTER 3

1. Whetnall and Fry, p. 49.

CHAPTER 4

1. p. 255.
2. *Youth in a Soundless World,* p. 8.
3. *Deafness and Learning,* p. 21.
4. p. 11.
5. p. 58.
6. p. 5.
7. p. 5.
8. "Social and Psychological Development," p. 74.
9. *Educating the Deaf,* p. 100.
10. p. 51.
11. Quoted in Meadow, "Sociolinguistics, Sign Language, and the Deaf Subculture," p. 25.
12. p. 268.
13. Loc. cit.
14. Loc. cit.
15. p. 86.
16. "Deafness and Mental Health," p. 9.
17. p. 130.
18. "Deafness and Mental Health," p. 12.
19. *Deafness and Learning,* p. 79.

CHAPTER 5

1. p. 20.
2. Loc. cit.
3. *Deafness and Learning,* p. 107.
4. *Thinking Without Language,* p. 209.
5. "Profound Deafness as a Psycholinguistic Problem," p. 154.
6. Loc. cit.
7. Ibid., p. 150.
8. Loc. cit.
9. p. 170.
10. p. 66.
11. "Prerequisites for Language Acquisition by the Deaf," p. 34.
12. Ibid., p. 35.
13. *Biological Foundations of Language,* pp. 308–9.
14. "Prerequisites for Language Acquisition by the Deaf," p. 37.
15. Loc. cit.
16. p. 90.
17. p. 8.
18. p. 9.
19. Quoted in Wright, p. 151.
20. p. 208.

CHAPTER 6

1. p. 36.
2. p. 3.
3. p. 111.
4. p. 113.
5. p. 437.
6. p. 37.
7. Loc. cit.

CHAPTER 7

1. Quoted in Wright, p. 136.
2. Quoted in Lane, "Notes for a Psycho-History of American Sign Language," p. 4.
3. Quoted loc. cit.
4. Quoted ibid., p. 5.
5. p. 167.
6. Quoted ibid., p. 177.
7. p. 15.
8. *The Wild Boy of Aveyron,* p. 253.

9. Loc. cit.
10. p. 22.
11. Quoted in Wright, p. 173.

CHAPTER 8

1. p. 205.
2. *Educating the Deaf,* p. 197.
3. "Psychological Contributions," p. 31.
4. p. 5.
5. p. 397.
6. p. 13.
7. "Toward a Definition of Oral Success," p. 9.
8. p. 60.
9. *Thinking Without Language,* p. 210.
10. p. 40.
11. Streng, Kretschmer and Kretschmer, p. 90.
12. p. 120.
13. Loc. cit.
14. p. 193.
15. "Facts and Fantasies About the Verbal Abilities of Deaf School Leavers," p. 146.
16. p. v.
17. p. 25.
18. p. vi.
19. Moores, *Educating the Deaf,* p. 56.
20. p. 40.
21. p. 41.
22. p. 43.

CHAPTER 9

1. Wright, p. 5.
2. p. 90.
3. "Effects of Cued Speech upon Speechreading," p. 216.
4. p. 20.
5. p. 6.
6. Quoted in Woodward, "Historical Bases of American Sign Language," p. 4.
7. Ibid., p. 20.
8. "Ameslan: The Communication System of Choice," p. 209.

CHAPTER 10

1. p. 23.
2. p. 158.

3. p. 157.
4. p. 137.
5. p. 109.
6. p. 113.
7. *Educating the Deaf*, p. 224.
8. Loc. cit.
9. p. 151.
10. p. 159.

CHAPTER 11

1. p. 50.
2. p. 249.
3. Quoted in Higgins, p. 141.
4. p. vi.
5. p. 198.
6. p. 37.
7. p. 103.
8. p. 161.
9. Loc. cit.

CHAPTER 12

1. Quoted in Greenberg and Doolittle, p. 50.
2. p. 14.
3. p. 203.
4. p. 273.
5. Quoted in Lamendola.
6. p. 9.
7. Quoted in Thomson, p. 13.
8. p. 7.
9. Karchmer and Trybus, p. 3.

CHAPTER 13

1. p. 85.
2. Quoted in Markowicz and Woodward, p. 4.
3. p. 22.
4. Loc. cit.
5. p. 155.
6. *Thinking Without Language*, p. 602.
7. p. 93.
8. p. 100.
9. p. 32.

SOURCES

Altshuler, Kenneth Z. "Sexual Patterns and Family Relationships," pp. 92–112 in John D. Rainer et al. (eds.), *Family and Mental Health Problems in a Deaf Population*. New York: State Psychiatric Institute, 1963.

——. "The Social and Psychological Development of the Deaf Child," pp. 55–86 in Peter J. Fine (ed.), *Deafness in Infancy and Early Childhood*. New York: Medcom Press, 1974.

Andersson, Yerker. "The Deaf as a Subculture," pp. 21–26 in *An Orientation to Deafness for Social Workers: Papers from the Conference (March 18–20, 1975)*. Washington: Gallaudet College Public Service Programs, n.d.

Auerbach, Leon. "The National Association of the Deaf Then and Now," *Deaf American*, September 1978, pp. 15–16.

Ballantyne, John. *Deafness*. 3rd ed.; Edinburgh: Churchill, Livingstone, 1977.

Battison, Robin; Markowicz, Harry; and Woodward, James. "A Good Rule of Thumb: Phonology in American Sign Language," in A. Fasold and Roger Shuy, *Analyzing Variation in Language*. Washington: Georgetown University Press, 1975.

Bellefleur, Philip A. "TTY Communication: Its History and Future," pp. 107–13 in Robert Frisina (ed.), *A Bicentennial Monograph on Hearing Impairment: Trends in the USA*. Washington: Alexander Graham Bell Association for the Deaf, 1976.

Bellugi, Ursula. "Studies in Sign Language," pp. 68–84 in Terrence J. O'Rourke (ed.), *Psycholinguistics and Total Communication: The State of the Art*. Washington: American Annals of the Deaf, 1972.

Bender, Ruth. *The Conquest of Deafness: A History of the Long Struggle to Make Possible Normal Living to Those Handicapped by Lack of Normal Hearing*. Cleveland: Case Western Reserve University Press, 1970.

Benderly, Beryl Lieff. "The Gift," *Washingtonian*, October 1978, pp. 179–83.

Berman, Eugene. "Autonomous and Unique Features of American Sign Language," *American Annals of the Deaf*, February 1972, pp. 20–24.

Bernhardt, Bill. *Just Writing*. New York: Teachers and Writers, 1977.

Blanton, Richard; and Brooks, Penelope H. "Some Psycholinguistic Aspects of Sign Language," pp. 243–70 in I. M. Schlesinger and Lila Namir (eds.), *Sign Language of the Deaf: Psychological, Linguistic, and Sociological Perspectives*. New York: Academic Press, 1978.

Bornstein, Harry. *Systems of Sign*. Washington: Gallaudet College, n.d. (mimeo).

Borrild, K. "Cued Speech and the Hand-Mouth Method: A Contribution to the Discussion," pp. 231–39 in Gunnar Fant (ed.), *International Symposium on Speech Communication Ability and Profound Deafness*. Washington: Alexander Graham Bell Association for the Deaf, 1972.

Bowe, Frank. *Handicapping America: Barriers to Disabled People*. New York: Harper & Row, 1978.

Bragg, Bernard. "Ameslish—Our American Heritage: A Testimony," *American Annals of the Deaf*, December 1973.

Breunig, H. Latham. *Bell Revisited*. Northampton, Mass.: Clarke School for the Deaf, 1977.

—— and Nix, Gary W. "Historical and Educational Perspectives," *Volta Review* (special issue: *The Rights of Hearing-Impaired Children*), September 1977.

Brill, Richard D. "The Superior IQs of Deaf Children of Deaf Parents," pp. 151–61 in Peter J. Fine (ed.), *Deafness in Infancy and Early Childhood*. New York: Medcom Press, 1974.

——. "Total Communication as a Basis of Educating Deaf Children," pp. 132–50 in Peter J. Fine (ed.), *Deafness in Infancy and Early Childhood*. New York: Medcom Press, 1974.

Calvert, Donald R. "Communication Practices: Aural/Oral and Visual/Oral," pp. 76–81 in Robert Frisina (ed.), *A Bicentennial Monograph on Hearing Impairment: Trends in the USA*. Washington: Alexander Graham Bell Association for the Deaf, 1976.

—— and Silverman, S. Richard. *Speech and Deafness: A Text for Learning and Teaching*. Washington: Alexander Graham Bell Association for the Deaf, 1975.

The Changing Role of School Programs for Deaf Children. Washington: Conference of Executives of American Schools for the Deaf, 1977.

Cicourel, Aaron V. "Sociolinguistic Aspects of the Use of Sign Language," pp. 271–314 in I. M. Schlesinger and Lila Namir (eds.), *Sign Language of the Deaf: Psychological, Linguistic, and Sociological Perspectives*. New York: Academic Press, 1978.

—— and Boese, Robert J. "Sign Language Acquisition and the Teaching of Deaf Children," in Dell Hymes, Courtney Cazden, and Vera John (eds.), *The Functions of Language in the Classroom*. New York: Teachers College Press, 1971.

Cohen, Oscar P. "The Deaf Adolescent: Who Am I?" *Volta Review*, September 1978, pp. 265–74.

Conrad, R. "Facts and Fantasies About the Verbal Abilities of Deaf School Leavers," *The British Deaf News*, October 1977, pp. 145–47.

——. "Matters Arising," pp. 146–55 in *Methods of Communication Currently Used in the Education of Deaf Children*. London: Royal National Institute for the Deaf, 1976.

——. "Profound Deafness as a Psycholinguistic Problem," pp. 145–55 in Gunnar Fant (ed.), *International Symposium on Speech Communication Ability and Profound Deafness*. Washington: Alexander Graham Bell Association for the Deaf, 1972.

——. "Short-Term Memory in the Deaf: A Test for Speech Coding," pp. 247–53 in David M. Boswell and Janet M. Wingrove (eds.), *The Handicapped Person in the Community*. London: Tavistock Publications, 1972.

——. "Toward a Definition of Oral Success," *Gallaudet Today*, Spring 1977, pp. 6–9.

Cornett, R. Orin. "Effects of Cued Speech upon Speechreading," pp. 223–30 in Gunnar Fant (ed.), *International Symposium on Speech Communication Ability and Profound Deafness*. Washington: Alexander Graham Bell Association for the Deaf, 1972.

——. "Cued Speech," pp. 213–22 in Gunnar Fant (ed.), *International Symposium on Speech Communication Ability and Profound Deafness*. Washington: Alexander Graham Bell Association for the Deaf, 1972.

Crandall, Kathleen. "Reading and Writing Skills and the Deaf Adolescent," *Volta Review*, September 1978.

Croneberg, Carl G. "The Linguistic Community," pp. 297–311 in William C. Stokoe, Jr., Dorothy C. Casterline, and Carl G. Croneberg (eds.), *A Dictionary of American Sign Language on Linguistic Principles*. Washington: Gallaudet College Press, 1965.

Crystal, David; and Craig, Elma. "Contrived Sign Language," pp. 141–68 in I. M. Schlesinger and Lila Namir (eds.), *Sign Lan-*

guage of the Deaf: Psychological, Linguistic, and Sociological Perspectives. New York: Academic Press, 1978.

Davis, Hallowell. "Acoustics and Psychoacoustics," pp. 9–46 in Hallowell Davis and S. Richard Silverman (eds.), Hearing and Deafness. New York: Holt, Rinehart and Winston, 1970.

Denmark, John. "The Education of Deaf Children," pp. 234–43 in David M. Boswell and Janet M. Wingrove (eds.), The Handicapped Person in the Community. London: Tavistock Publications, 1974.

——. "Methods of Communication in the Education of Deaf People," pp. 73–79 in Methods of Communication Currently Used in the Education of Deaf Children. London: Royal National Institute for the Deaf, 1976.

Denton, David M.; Brill, Richard G.; and Swaiko, Nancy M. "Schools for Deaf Children," pp. 103–31 in Peter J. Fine (ed.), Deafness in Infancy and Early Childhood. New York: Medcom Press, 1974.

DiCarlo, Louis M. The Deaf. Englewood Cliffs, N.J.: Prentice-Hall, 1964.

Erting, Carold; and Woodward, James. Sign Language and the Deaf Community: A Sociolinguistic Profile. Washington: Gallaudet College Linguistic Research Laboratory, n.d. (mimeo).

Ewing, Irene A.; and Ewing, A. W. G. Speech and the Deaf Child. Washington: The Volta Bureau, 1954.

Falberg, Roger. A Psycholinguistic View of the Evolution, Nature, and Value of the Sign Language of the Deaf. M.A. thesis, Wichita State University, 1964.

Fant, Louie J., Jr. Ameslan: An Introduction to American Sign Language. Northridge, Calif.: Joyce Motion Picture Co., 1972.

——. "Ameslan: The Communication System of Choice," pp. 205–16 in Peter J. Fine (ed.), Deafness in Infancy and Early Childhood. New York: Medcom Press, 1974.

——. "ASL and Siglish: The Various Forms of Sign Language," pp. 189–204 in Peter J. Fine (ed.), Deafness in Infancy and Early Childhood. New York: Medcom Press, 1974.

Freeman, Roger D. "Some Psychiatric Reflections on the Controversy over Methods of Communication in the Life of the Deaf," pp. 110–18 in Methods of Communication Currently Used in Education of Deaf Children. London: Royal National Institute for the Deaf, 1976.

Furfey, Paul Hanley; and Harte, Thomas J. Interaction of Deaf and Hearing in Baltimore City, Maryland (Studies from the Bureau of Social Research, No. 4). Washington: Catholic University of America Press, 1968.

Furth, Hans G. *Deafness and Learning: A Psychosocial Approach.* Belmont, Calif.: Wadsworth Publishing Company, 1973.

——. *Thinking Without Language: Psychological Implications of Deafness.* New York: The Free Press, 1966.

The Gallaudet Almanac. Washington: Gallaudet College Alumni Association, 1974.

Galloway, Victor H. "Mental Health: What It Means to the Typical Deaf Person," pp. 51–62 in Kenneth Z. Altshuler and John D. Rainer (eds.), *Mental Health and the Deaf: Approaches and Prospects.* Washington: Department of Health, Education, and Welfare, 1969.

Garretson, Mervin. "Concept of the Least Restrictive Environment," *Gallaudet Alumni Newsletter* (special issue: *PL 94-142 and Deaf Children*), June 1977.

——. "Total Communication," pp. 88–95 in Robert Frisina (ed.), *A Bicentennial Monograph on Hearing Impairment: Trends in the USA.* Washington: Alexander Graham Bell Association for the Deaf, 1976.

Goffman, Erving. "Stigma and Social Identity," pp. 79–92 in David M. Boswell and Janet M. Wingrove (eds.), *The Handicapped Person in the Community.* London: Tavistock Publications, 1974.

Greenberg, Bernard. *Measuring College Potential of Language Handicapped Students.* Paper presented at American Association of College Registrars and Admissions Officers, St. Louis, April 1971.

Greenberg, Joanne. *In This Sign.* New York: Holt, Rinehart and Winston, 1970.

—— and Doolittle, Glenn. "Can Schools Speak the Language of the Deaf?" *The New York Times Magazine,* December 11, 1977.

Gregory, Susan. *The Deaf Child and His Family.* London: George Allen and Unwin, 1976.

Healey, William C. "Integrated Education," pp. 68–75 in Robert Frisina (ed.), *A Bicentennial Monograph on Hearing Impairment: Trends in the USA.* Washington: Alexander Graham Bell Association of the Deaf, 1976.

Higgins, Paul Cole. *The Deaf Community: Identity and Interaction in a Hearing World.* Ph.D. dissertation, Northwestern University, 1977.

Hoemann, Harry W. *The American Sign Language.* Silver Spring, Maryland: National Association of the Deaf, 1975.

—— et al. "The Spelling Proficiency of Deaf Children," *American Annals of the Deaf,* October 1976, pp. 489–93.

Horton, Muriel. "Mainstreaming for Deaf Children: A Step Forward?" *Disabled USA*, January 1977.

Jacobs, Leo. *A Deaf Adult Speaks Out*. Washington: Gallaudet College Press, 1974.

Jarvik, Lissy Feingold; Salzberger, Rose M.; and Falek, Arthur. "Deaf Persons of Outstanding Achievement," pp. 131–40 in John D. Rainer et al. (eds.), *Family and Mental Health Problems in a Deaf Population*. New York: State Psychiatric Institute, 1963.

Jensema, Carl. *The Relationship Between Academic Achievement and the Demographic Characteristics of Hearing Impaired Children and Youth* (Series R, No. 2). Washington: Office of Demographic Studies, Gallaudet College, 1975.

—— and Trybus, Raymond. *Communication Patterns and Educational Achievement of Hearing Impaired Students* (Series T, No. 2). Washington, D.C.: Office of Demographic Studies, Gallaudet College, 1978.

Kallman, Franz J. "Main Findings and Some Projections," pp. 234–48 in John D. Rainer et al. (eds.), *Family and Mental Health Problems in a Deaf Population*. New York: State Psychiatric Institute, 1963.

Karchmer, Michael A.; and Trybus, Raymond J. *Who Are the Deaf Children in Mainstream Programs?* (Series R, No. 4). Washington: Office of Demographic Studies, Gallaudet College, 1977.

Keller, Helen. *The Story of My Life*. New York: Airmont Publishing Company, 1965.

Kidd, Judith. "Parents and Public Law 94-142," *Volta Review* (special issue: *The Rights of Hearing Impaired Children*), September 1977.

Koestler, Frances. *The Unseen Minority: A Social History of Blindness in America*. New York: David McKay, 1976.

Kretschmer, Richard R. "Language Acquisition," pp. 60–67 in Robert Frisina (ed.), *A Bicentennial Monograph on Hearing Impairment: Trends in the USA*. Washington: Alexander Graham Bell Association for the Deaf, 1976.

Lamendola, Linda. "Working to Bridge Communication Gap with the Deaf," *The Sunday Star-Ledger*, May 27, 1979.

Lane, Harlan. "Notes for a Psycho-History of American Sign Language," *Deaf American*, September 1977.

——. *The Wild Boy of Aveyron*. Cambridge: Harvard University Press, 1976.

Lane, Helen S. "Developing Capacity for Independent Living," *Volta Review*, September 1978.

Lenneberg, Eric H. *Biological Foundations of Language*. New York: John Wiley & Sons, 1967.

——. "Prerequisites for Language Acquisition by the Deaf," pp. 34–52 in Terrence J. O'Rourke (ed.), *Psycholinguistics and Total Communication: The State of the Art*. Washington: American Annals of the Deaf, 1972.

Levine, Edna S. "Psychological Contributions," pp. 23–34 in Robert Frisina (ed.), *A Bicentennial Monograph on Hearing Impairment: Trends in the USA*. Washington: Alexander Graham Bell Association for the Deaf, 1976.

——. *Youth in a Soundless World: A Search for Personality*. New York: New York University Press, 1956.

Lieth, Lars von der. "Social-Psychological Aspects of the Use of Sign Language," pp. 315–32 in I. M. Schlesinger and Lila Namir (eds.), *Sign Language of the Deaf: Psychological, Linguistic, and Sociological Perspectives*. New York: Academic Press, 1978.

Ling, Daniel. *Speech and the Hearing-Impaired Child: Theory and Practice*. Washington: Alexander Graham Bell Association for the Deaf, 1976.

—— and Ling, Agnes. *Aural Habilitation: The Foundations of Verbal Learning in Hearing-Impaired Children*. Washington: Alexander Graham Bell Association for the Deaf, 1978.

——; ——; and Pflaster, Gail. "Individualized Educational Programming for Hearing-Impaired Children," *Volta Review*, May 1977.

Lloyd, Lyle L.; and Dahle, Arthur J. "Detection and Diagnosis of a Hearing Impairment in the Child," pp. 12–23 in Robert Frisina (ed.), *A Bicentennial Monograph on Hearing Impairment: Trends in the USA*. Washington: Alexander Graham Bell Association for the Deaf, 1976.

Lowell, Edgar L. Pp. 30–33 in *Methods of Communication Currently Used in the Education of Deaf Children*. London: Royal National Institute for the Deaf, 1977.

Lybarger, Samuel F. "Personal Hearing Aids," pp. 113–20 in Robert Frisina (ed.), *A Bicentennial Monograph on Hearing Impairment: Trends in the USA*. Washington: Alexander Graham Bell Association for the Deaf, 1976.

Markowicz, Harry; and Woodward, James. *Language and the Maintenance of Ethnic Boundaries in the Deaf Community*. Paper presented at the Conference on Culture and Communication, Philadelphia, 1975.

Meadow, Kathryn P. "A Developmental Perspective on the Use of Manual Communication with Deaf Children," pp. 87–98 in

Methods of Communication Currently Used in the Education of Deaf Children. London: Royal National Institute for the Deaf, 1976.

——. "Sociolinguistics, Sign Language, and the Deaf Subculture," pp. 19–33 in Terrence J. O'Rourke (ed.), *Psycholinguistics and Total Communication: The State of the Art.* Washington: American Annals of the Deaf, 1972.

Meisegeier, Richard W. "Deafness and the Socialization Process," pp. 15–20 in *An Orientation to Deafness for Social Workers: Papers from the Workshop.* Washington: Gallaudet College Public Service Programs, 1975.

Merrill, Edward C., Jr. "Providing an Appropriate Educational Environment," *Gallaudet Alumni Newsletter* (special issue: *PL 94-142 and Deaf Children*), June 1977.

Mindel, Eugene D.; and Vernon, McCay. *They Grow in Silence: The Deaf Child and His Family.* Silver Spring, Md.: National Association of the Deaf, 1971.

Moores, Donald F. "Communication: Some Unanswered Questions and Some Unquestioned Answers," pp. 1–10 in Terrence J. O'Rourke (ed.), *Psycholinguistics and Total Communication: The State of the Art.* Washington: American Annals of the Deaf, 1972.

——. *Educating the Deaf: Psychology, Principles, and Practices.* Boston: Houghton Mifflin Company, 1978.

Mulholland, Ann M.; and Hourihan, John P. "Parents and Due Process in Education of the Handicapped: A Case History," *Volta Review,* September 1977.

Mulrooney, Jean. "The Newly-Deafened Adult," pp. 35–38 in *An Orientation to Deafness for Social Workers: Papers from the Workshop.* Washington: Gallaudet College Public Service Programs, 1975.

Newman, Lawrence. "Two Children: A Study in Contrasts," pp. 162–86 in Peter J. Fine (ed.), *Deafness in Infancy and Early Childhood.* New York: Medcom Press, 1974.

Nix, Gary W. "The Least Restrictive Environment," *Volta Review,* September 1977.

——. "Mainstream Placement Question/Checklist," *Volta Review,* September 1977.

Northcott, Winifred. "President's Message," *Volta Review,* October 1978.

Oyer, Herbert J. *Communication for the Hearing Handicapped: An*

International Perspective. Baltimore: University Park Press, 1976.

Powers, Helen. *Signs of Silence: Bernard Bragg and the National Theatre of the Deaf.* New York: Dodd, Mead, 1972.

Provonost, Wilbert L. "Communicating with the World-at-Large," *Volta Review,* September 1978.

Rainer, John D. "Crucial Aspects of Mental Health and Mental Disorder in the Deaf," pp. 11–14 in Kenneth Z. Altshuler and John D. Rainer (eds.), *Mental Health and the Deaf: Approaches and Prospects.* Washington: Department of Health, Education, and Welfare, 1969.

Ramsdell, D. A. "The Psychology of Hard-of-Hearing and the Deafened Adult," pp. 435-48 in Hallowell Davis and S. Richard Silverman (eds.), *Hearing and Deafness.* New York: Holt, Rinehart and Winston, 1970.

Rawlings, Brenda; and Jensema, Carl J. *Two Studies of the Families of Hearing Impaired Children* (Series R, No. 5). Washington: Office of Demographic Studies, Gallaudet College, 1977.

Rimmer, Gill. "The Hard of Hearing in Britain: Are Their Needs Being Met?" pp. 254–64 in David M. Boswell and Janet M. Wingrove (eds.), *The Handicapped Person in the Community.* London: Tavistock Publications, 1972.

Risberg, A.; and Martony, J. "Cued Speech: A Comment," pp. 241–43 in Gunnar Fant (ed.), *International Symposium on Speech Communication Ability and Profound Deafness.* Washington: Alexander Graham Bell Association for the Deaf, 1972.

Rosen, Roslyn. "Deafness and Implications for Mainstreaming," *Gallaudet Alumni Newsletter* (special issue: *PL 94-142 and Deaf Children*), June 1977.

———; Skinski, Edmund; and Pimentel, Al. "PL 94-142: An Analysis of Its Evolution, Features, and Implications," *Gallaudet Alumni Newsletter* (special issue: *PL 94-142 and Deaf Children*), June 1977.

Rosenthal, Richard. *The Hearing Loss Handbook.* New York: Schocken Books, 1978.

Schein, Jerome D.; and Delk, Marcus T. *The Deaf Population of the United States.* Silver Spring, Md.: National Association of the Deaf, 1974.

Schlesinger, Hilde S. "The Acquisition of Bimodal Language," pp. 57–96 in I. M. Schlesinger and Lila Namir (eds.), *Sign Language of the Deaf: Psychological, Linguistic, and Sociological Perspectives.* New York: Academic Press, 1978.

———. "Mental Health and Deafness," *Gallaudet Today,* Fall 1978.

—— and Meadow, Kathryn P. *Sound and Sign: Childhood Deafness and Mental Health*. Berkeley: University of California Press, 1972.

Schlesinger, I. M.; and Namir, Lila. "Introduction," pp. 1–11 in I. M. Schlesinger and Lila Namir (eds.), *Sign Language of the Deaf: Psychological, Linguistic, and Sociological Perspectives*. New York: Academic Press, 1978.

Schowe, B. M. *Identity Crisis in Deafness: A Humanistic Perspective*. Tempe, Ariz.: The Scholars Press, 1979.

Scott, Robert A. *The Making of Blind Men: A Study in Adult Socialization*. New York: Russell Sage Foundation, 1969.

Sheavyn, E. M. Pp. 119–22 in *Methods of Communication Currently Used in the Education of Deaf Children*. London: Royal National Institute for the Deaf, 1976.

Silverman, S. Richard. "From Aristotle to Bell—and Beyond," pp. 375–83 in Hallowell Davis and S. Richard Silverman (eds.), *Hearing and Deafness*. New York: Holt, Rinehart and Winston, 1970.

Spradley, Thomas S.; and Spradley, James P. *Deaf Like Me*. New York: Random House, 1978.

Stokoe, William C., Jr.; Casterline, Dorothy C.; and Croneberg, Carl G. *A Dictionary of American Sign Language on Linguistic Principles*. Washington: Gallaudet College Press, 1965.

Streng, Alice H.; Kretschmer, Richard R., Jr.; and Kretschmer, Laura W. *Language, Learning, and Deafness*. New York: Grune & Stratton, 1978.

Stuckless, E. Ross. "An Interpretive Review of Research on Manual Communication in the Education of Deaf Children: Language Development and Information Transfer," pp. 139–45 in *Methods of Communication Currently Used in the Education of Deaf Children*. London: Royal National Institute for the Deaf, 1976.

——. "Manual and Graphic Communication," in Robert Frisina (ed.), *A Bicentennial Monograph on Hearing Impairment: Trends in the USA*. Washington: Alexander Graham Bell Association for the Deaf, 1976.

Switzer, Mary E.; and Williams, Boyce R. "Life Problems of Deaf People, Prevention and Treatment," *Archives of Environmental Health*, August 1967.

Tervoort, Bernard T. *Developmental Features of Visual Communication: A Psycholinguistic Analysis of Deaf Children's Growth in Communicative Competence*. (North Holland Linguistic Series). New York: American Elsevier Publishing Company, 1975.

Thomson, Peggy. "Good Signs from MSSD," *American Education*, May 1978.

Vernon, McCay. "Deafness and Mental Health: Some Theoretical Views," *Gallaudet Today*, Fall 1978.

——. "Non-Linguistic Aspects of Sign Language, Human Feelings and Thought Processes," pp. 11–19 in Terrence J. O'Rourke (ed.), *Psycholinguistics and Total Communication: The State of the Art*. Washington: American Annals of the Deaf, 1972.

——. "Psychological Aspects in Diagnosing Deafness in a Child," pp. 87–100 in Peter J. Fine (ed.), *Deafness in Infancy and Early Childhood*. New York: Medcom Press, 1974.

Whetnall, Edith; and Fry, D. B. *The Deaf Child*. Springfield, Ill.: Charles C Thomas, 1964.

Woodward, James. *How You Gonna Get to Heaven If You Can't Talk with Jesus? The Educational Establishment vs. the Deaf Community*. Paper presented at the Annual Meeting, Society for Applied Anthropology, Amsterdam, March 1975.

——. "Historical Bases of American Sign Language," pp. 333–48 in Patricia Siple (ed.), *Understanding Language Through Sign Language*. New York: Academic Press, 1978.

——. "Manual English: A Problem in Standardization and Planning," pp. 1–13 in *Recent Developments in Manual English: Papers Presented at a Special Institute*. Washington: Department of Education, Gallaudet College, 1973.

——. "Sex Is Definitely a Problem: Interpreters' Knowledge of Signs for Sexual Behavior," *Sign Language Studies*, Fall 1977.

——. "Signs of Change: Historical Variation in American Sign Language," *Sign Language Studies*, Spring 1976.

——. *We Can't Ignore the Signs Any Longer*. Paper presented at the Verbal Ape Symposium, Ohio State University, March 1977.

—— and DeSantis, Susan. "Negative Incorporation in French and American Sign Language," *Language in Society*, Fall 1977.

Wright, David. *Deafness*. New York: Stein & Day, 1969.

APPENDIX

Recommended Further Reading

Advice

Rosenthal, Richard. *The Hearing Loss Handbook*. New York: Schocken Books, 1978. A gold mine, especially for the newly deafened and hard-of-hearing. Sound, reasoned advice in many practical areas. The material on hearing aids is absolutely first-rate.

Personal Accounts

Greenberg, Joanne. *In This Sign*. New York: Holt, Rinehart and Winston, 1970. This stunning novel does the impossible—it puts the hearing reader inside the hearts and heads of "low verbal" deaf people. Must reading.

Jacobs, Leo. *A Deaf Adult Speaks Out*. Washington: Gallaudet College Press, 1974. American society as seen by a prominent —and congenitally deaf—TC educator.

Schowe, B. M. *Identity Crisis in Deafness: A Humanistic Perspective*. Tempe, Ariz.: The Scholars Press, 1979. (Distributed by the National Association of the Deaf.) Reflections and research drawn from a long and thoughtful—and deaf—life. Manual orientation.

Spradley, Thomas S.; and Spradley, James P. *Deaf Like Me*. New York: Random House, 1978. A family's struggles with strict oral education, their joy and relief at discovering sign. Immediate and engrossing.

Wright, David. *Deafness*. New York: Stein & Day, 1969. The British poet's fascinating, elegantly written account of his early years fill Part I of this book. An oral view.

Psychological Aspects

Furth, Hans G. *Deafness and Learning: A Psychosocial Approach.* Belmont, Calif.: Wadsworth Publishing Company, 1973. A brief, clear summary of the intellectual effects of early deafness. Favors manual communication.

Mindel, Eugene D.; and Vernon, McCay. *They Grow in Silence: The Deaf Child and His Family.* Silver Spring, Md.; National Association of the Deaf, 1971. An impassioned but well-documented plea for early manual communication as an essential for preventing emotional problems. A seminal work.

History

Bender, Ruth. *The Conquest of Deafness.* Cleveland: Case Western Reserve University Press, 1970. An opinionated and somewhat dry—but still very useful—oral view of history.

Wright, David. *Deafness.* New York: Stein & Day, 1969. Part II contains fine writing, sound research, from a British oralist's standpoint.

Oral Training

Calvert, Donald R.; and Silverman, S. Richard. *Speech and Deafness: A Textbook for Learning and Teaching.* Washington: Alexander Graham Bell Association for the Deaf, 1975. A college text—but a readable one—outlining the major oral techniques.

Ling, Daniel; and Ling, Agnes H. *Aural Habilitation: The Foundation of Verbal Learning in Hearing-Impaired Children.* Washington: Alexander Graham Bell Association for the Deaf, 1978. A clear exposition of Ling's position.

Demography

Schein, Jerome D.; and Delk, Marcus T. *The Deaf Population of the United States.* Silver Spring, Md.: National Association of the Deaf, 1974. Everything you always wanted to know about the pre-vocationally deaf, based on a national survey.

Medicine

Ballantyne, John. *Deafness.* 3rd ed.; Edinburgh: Churchill, Livingstone, 1977. A technical but clear outline of the medical aspects.

Periodicals of Interest

Deaf American. The monthly magazine of the National Association
of the Deaf. Popular in style, covering news, sports, personali-
ties. Carries ads for many useful products.
American Annals of the Deaf
    Gallaudet University
    Washington, DC 20002
    The scholarly journal of the manualist camp.
Volta Review. The publication of the Bell Association. A scholarly
    journal published seven times a year.
The Broadcaster
    814 Thayer Avenue
    Silver Spring, MD 20910
    A newspaper.
Silent News
    P.O. Box 23330
    Rochester, NY 14692
    A newspaper.
Many local groups, schools, hearing centers, and organizations also
publish magazines and newsletters.

Educational Resources

The annual Directory Issue of the *American Annals of the Deaf* lists
many schools, camps, and other programs of interest to the families of
deaf children. Can be purchased separately.
    The John Tracy Clinic
        806 West Adams Boulevard
        Los Angeles, CA 90007
        Offers free oral correspondence course for preschool children.

ORGANIZATIONS

Oralist

    Alexander Graham Bell Association for the Deaf. The leading advo-
        cate of oral education and communication.
        3417 Volta Place NW
        Washington DC 20007

Constituent sections of the Bell Association (all at the same address):

American Organization for the Education of the Hearing Impaired. "Comprised of qualified educators who are concerned with improving auditory-oral teaching of all hearing impaired students."

International Parents' Organization. "Comprised of thousands of parents of hearing impaired children who are working singly and in local groups to expand the educational, social and vocational options for their children."

Oral Deaf Adults Section. Composed of "hearing impaired adults who use speech, speechreading, and residual hearing regularly in their social and business contacts." Has several hundred members nationally.

Manualist

National Association of the Deaf. The main organization of deaf Americans. Has about 20,000 members nationally.
814 Thayer Avenue
Silver Spring, MD 20910
American Society for Deaf Children
814 Thayer Avenue
Silver Spring, MD 20910

Insurance Society

National Fraternal Society of the Deaf
1300 W. Northwest Highway
Mt. Prospect, IL 60056
Both an insurance company and a social organization.

Social and Special Interest Groups

Most good-sized population centers have one or more clubs for deaf people. A number of Christian denominations maintain churches or missions to the deaf or provide interpreted services. *Deaf American* publishes directories of clubs and religious groups each month. Religious activities for deaf Jews are a bit harder to find outside of one or two main centers. National Congress of Jewish Deaf can help. Write to 250 Jay Street, #M-210, Brooklyn, NY 11201.

Communications Resources

Sign Language Programs
    Gallaudet University
    Washington, DC 20002
    Can direct you to sign language instruction in your local area.
National Cued Speech Association
    P.O. Box 31345
    Raleigh, NC 27622
    Can provide information on instruction in cued speech.
Telecommunications for the Deaf, Inc.
    814 Thayer Avenue
    Silver Spring, MD 20910
    Can provide information on obtaining a TTY for the home.
National Captioning Institute
    5203 Leesburg Pike
    Suite 1500
    Falls Church, VA 22041
    Can provide information on television captioning devices.
Registry of Interpreters for the Deaf, Inc.
    51 Monroe Street, Suite 1107
    Rockville, MD 20850
    Can provide lists of qualified, professional oral and sign language interpreters and schedules of suggested fees.
Hearing centers in many localities can provide speechreading instruction.

INDEX

Other books of related interest:

A Deaf Adult Speaks Out, by Leo M. Jacobs. This personal narrative bitingly describes the issues of mainstreaming deaf children, total communication versus oralism, employment opportunities and public policy toward deaf people, by a member of the Deaf community. 200-page softcover, ISBN 0-930323-61-0.

A Place of Their Own, *Creating the Deaf Community in America*, by John Van Cleve, Ph.D., and Barry A. Crouch, Ph.D. This book unveils the development of the Deaf community and the importance of schools for the deaf as the setting for the growth of American Sign Language. 224-page softcover, ISBN 0-930323-49-1.

At Home Among Strangers, *Exploring the Deaf Community in the United States*, by Jerome D. Schein, Ph.D. This engrossing study examines American Sign Language, Deaf culture, theater and literature, family life, and economics. It also offers a theory of the future of the Deaf community. 264-page clothbound, ISBN 0-930323-51-3.

The Other Side of Silence, *Sign Language and the Deaf Community*, by Arden Neisser. This classic first raised public awareness about deafness through interviews with deaf people, cynical teachers, linguists disputing theories about sign language, and others. A new foreword sparks fresh insights on the Deaf community's progress. 306-page softcover, ISBN 0-930323-64-5.

The Week the World Heard Gallaudet, by Jack R. Gannon. The "Deaf President Now" Revolution by Gallaudet University electrified the nation. In this book, more than 200 photographs, many in color, and interviews with the central figures bring this historical occasion to life again. 176-page clothbound, ISBN 0-930323-54-8; softcover, ISBN 0-930323-50-5.

For more information on these and other books, write for a free catalog:

Gallaudet University Press
800 Florida Avenue, NE
Washington, DC 20002-3695

To order, call toll-free 1-800-451-1073.